IN
SHAKESPEARE'S
DAY

Other Titles in the Fawcett Premier

LITERATURE AND IDEAS SERIES

IRVING HOWE, General Editor

IN
SHAKESPEARE'S
DAY

Edited by J. V. Cunningham

A FAWCETT PREMIER BOOK
Fawcett Publications, Inc., Greenwich, Conn.
Member of American Book Publishers Council, Inc.

CONTENTS

PART IV

Literary-Dramatic Criticism: The Tradition

PART V

The Literary-Dramatic Situation

PART VI

Show Business

PART VII
Sources

PART VIII
Shakespeare's Works in His Lifetime

PART IX
Shakespeare's Works in Aftertimes

PART X
On Interpretation

IN
SHAKESPEARE'S
DAY

INTRODUCTION

There is Shakespeare experienced and Shakespeare explained. I remember as a boy reading the plays without introduction or notes in individual volumes bound in an imitation leather that smelled awful. It was an almost uncued experience, and I think I can remember something of the freshness and distance of that reading. Now, if the purpose of dramatic art, in Shakespeare's day and in ours, is "to hold the mirror up to nature," there must be a communicable constant, open to boy and scholar; else it would not be the mirror and it would not be nature. But if what is shown there—and there are other mirrors—are the features of virtue and images of scorn, these vary throughout our own world; they have changed in my own society in my lifetime. And if they are shown implicated in "the age and body of the time," abstracted in brief chronicle, some sense of the time must be intuited or acquired. Otherwise, the given is not given, and the "form" the poet impresses on the time, as a seal on wax, is for us impressed on water.

Much of the given—mirror, nature, the time—is given in the text if we will believe it, including the theory of drama just abstracted from *Hamlet*. If we will believe it. But we departmentalize art, especially canonized art, confine it to aesthetic patterns, and process the experience. We are told why the family warns Ophelia not to get involved with Hamlet, but we take the warnings as characterizing the warners and not as the facts of high political life at the time. We read as *character* what Aristotle calls *thought*. But to be told is one thing, to perceive is another, for that involves the persuasion of actuality. And so one needs not only the text but some such book as this, a book to browse in, thumb through, perhaps to read. A book of evidence, not of conclusions. A book of implicit answers looking for questions.

If it is not quite clear what to look for, it is partly because looking is thwarted by premature clarity. Begin, first, with

simple, unfocused curiosity, and then with absorption there
will come an ambience, an unreferred feel for the time,
acquaintance seeking familiarity. Go with a German tourist
to the Court of Queen Elizabeth and observe government by
ceremony and magnificence, then cross the Thames by water
taxi and see *Julius Caesar* at the Globe. Soon you will find
that your experience of a play, of *Hamlet*, is invaded by a
certain literalness. There were traveling players who turned
up at provincial courts, pirates were not story-book, and the
"same strict and most observant watch" of the first scene was
an experience of 1599. On the other hand, the ghost does not
wear the "ghost suit" and "ghost bodice" listed in another
company's theatrical inventory of 1598, but appears in "complete steel" and in his dressing gown, "in his habit as he
lived." And so the texture of your experience of the play
little by little becomes dense.

So far small detail, now for the large. The next step is
crossreference, and first on disguise. We regard it as a story
element, something that happens in fiction, as in the source
for *Measure for Measure*. For, if the best kind of plot, as
Aristotle says, involves "discovery," "a change from unknown
to known, happening between those characters whose happiness or unhappiness forms the catastrophe of the drama,"
then disguise and mistaken identity are obvious means. It is
the disguise of Viola that ties the knot of *Twelfth Night*, and
the revelation of her identity and sex that unlooses it. But
disguise also happened in real life. There is Moll Cutpurse, "a
notorious baggage that used to go in men's apparel and
challenged the field of divers gallants," and there is the
disguise of make-believe in the game of courtly sex, as with
the French king and his bride.

Again, at the end of *King Lear* Regan is murdered, Goneril commits suicide, Cordelia is executed, Edmund killed in
trial by combat, Gloucester's death is reported, and Lear
himself "is gone indeed." But in the sources for the story,
France and Cordelia are victorious, Lear is restored to the
throne, and all the principals, except Albany and Cornwall,
are alive. The change deeply distressed Dr. Johnson. Yet "the
movement of events in tragedy," according to Diomedes, "is
almost always from happy circumstances to bitter deaths,
accompanied at the end with the perception that the fortunes
of the house involved have gone to ruin." The House of Lear
is destroyed, as was the House of Hamlet, and succeeded by

the House of Gloucester. The story is seen in a "tragic glass." Nevertheless, *The Tragedy of Cymbeline* has a happy ending.

This suggests the need for negative capabilities, for a parsimony with generalizations and with value judgments, both useful and necessary but not idly to be employed. To start a sentence "Tragedy is" or "The Elizabethans thought" is to preclude the claims of variety and the hesitations of ignorance. The Elizabethans thought many, and sometimes contradictory, things, though it is true they did not think some things we do. However, Marlowe was thought to be an atheist, "daring God out of heaven with that atheist Tamburlaine." We read both "Bloodshed by bloodshed still is nourished" and "for empire and greatness it importeth most that a nation do profess arms as their principal honor, study, and occupation." The first points to Macbeth, the second to Henry V and, perhaps, Fortinbras. Plays were divided into five acts on Horace's authority, and Gloucester is blinded on stage despite Horace. So also with value judgments. To compare the Shakespearean passage with Plutarch's description of Cleopatra and ascribe the differences to Shakespeare's genius is to bet on a race after it is official, and to miss the race.

Finally, each of us has his own interests, his own competencies, and one or other of these may be relevant to Shakespeare. I am an old hand with the iambic pentameter and the perception of style, and am interested also in realizing the literary situation as it was when Shakespeare entered it. So I look at the testimony. The first reference to him in that connection is as a player turned poet, one of "those antics garnished in our colors," that is, in our livery (players are the poet's servants), but also in our colors of rhetoric, our figures of speech, our new style. And this jack-of-all-trades "supposes he is as well able to bombast out a blank verse as the best of" the new poets. Perhaps by writing bombast, but that meaning is a little later and derived from such passages as this. The metaphor here is new. Bombast was the foam rubber of the time with which you padded out the fashionable parts of the body. Now the obvious way to stuff out a blank verse line is with disyllabic possessives and adjectives, epithets that adorn, with the accent on the first syllable: "O tiger's heart wrapped in a woman's hide!" (*1 Henry VI*, 1. 4. 137), or "From jigging veins of rhyming mother wits" (Prologue to *1 Tamburlaine*). It is to write "a bombast circumstance/Horribly stuffed with epithets of war" (*Othello*,

1. 1. 13–14). This yields you what Nashe calls "the spacious volubility of a drumming decasyllabon."

Enough. These are instances. Let not "my anticipation prevent your discovery."

J. V. CUNNINGHAM

PART I

Elizabeth I and England

QUEEN ELIZABETH AT GREENWICH (1598)

Elizabeth, the reigning Queen of England, was born at the Royal Palace of Greenwich, and here she generally resides, particularly in summer, for the delightfulness of its situation. We were admitted by an order, which Mr. Rogers (Daniel Rogerius) had procured from the Lord Chamberlain, into the Presence Chamber hung with rich tapestry, and the floor, after the English fashion, strewed with hay, through which the Queen commonly passes in her way to chapel. At the door stood a gentleman dressed in velvet, with a gold chain, whose office was to introduce to the Queen any person of distinction that comes to wait on her. It was Sunday [Sept. 6, New Style], when there is usually the greatest attendance of nobility. In the same hall were the Archbishop of Canterbury, the Bishop of London, a great number of counselors of State, officers of the Crown, and gentlemen, who waited the Queen's coming out, which she did from her own apartment when it was time to go to prayers, attended in the following manner:

First went gentlemen, barons, earls, knights of the Garter, all richly dressed and bareheaded; next came the Lord High Chancellor of England, bearing the seals in a red silk purse, between two, one of whom carried the royal scepter, the other the sword of state in a red scabbard, studded with golden fleur-de-lis, the point upwards; next came the Queen, in the 65th year of her age (as we were told), very majestic; her face oblong, fair but wrinkled; her eyes small, yet black and pleasant; her nose a little hooked, her lips narrow, and her teeth black, (a defect the English seem subject to, from their too great use of sugar); she had in her ears two pearls with very rich drops; her hair was of an auburn color, but false (*crinem fulvum, sed factitium*); upon her head she had a small crown, reported to be made of some of the gold of the celebrated Luneburg table; her bosom was uncovered, as all the English ladies have it till they marry; and she had a necklace of exceeding fine jewels; her hands were slender, her fingers rather long, and her stature neither tall nor low; her air was stately, her manner of speaking mild and obliging.

That day she was dressed in white silk, bordered with pearls of the size of beans, and over it a mantle of black silk shot with silver threads; her train was very long, the end of it borne by a marchioness; instead of a chain, she had an oblong collar of gold and jewels. As she went along in all this state and magnificence, she spoke very graciously, first to one, then to another (whether foreign ministers, or those who attend for different reasons), in English, French, and Italian; for besides being well skilled in Greek, Latin, and the languages I have mentioned, she is mistress of Spanish, Scotch, and Dutch (*Belgicum*). Whoever speaks to her, it is kneeling; now and then she raises some with her hand. While we were there, William Slawata, a Bohemian baron, had letters to present to her; and she, after pulling off her glove, gave him her right hand to kiss, sparkling with rings and jewels—a mark of particular favor. Wherever she turned her face as she was going along, everybody fell down on their knees. The ladies of the court followed next to her, very handsome and well-shaped, and for the most part dressed in white. She was guarded on each side by the gentlemen pensioners, fifty in number, with gilt halberds. In the antechapel, next the hall where we were, petitions were presented to her, and she received them most graciously, which occasioned the acclamation of *God save the Quene Elizabeth*! She answered it with *I thancke you myn good peupel*. In the chapel was excellent music; as soon as it and the service were over, which scarcely exceeded half an hour, the Queen returned in the same state and order, and prepared to go to dinner. But while she was still at prayers, we saw her table set out with the following solemnity.

A gentleman entered the room bearing a rod, and along with him another who had a tablecloth, which after they had both knelt three times, with the utmost veneration, he spread upon the table, and after kneeling again, they both retired. Then came two others, one with the rod again, the other with a saltcellar, a plate and bread; when they had knelt as the others had done, and placed what was brought upon the table, they too retired with the same ceremonies performed by the first. At last came an unmarried lady of extraordinary beauty (we were told that she was a countess) and along with her a married one, bearing a tasting-knife; the former was dressed in white silk, who, when she had prostrated herself three times, in the most graceful manner approached the table and rubbed the plates with bread and salt with as much awe as if the Queen had been present. When they had waited there a little while, the yeomen of the guard entered, bareheaded, clothed in scarlet, with a golden rose upon their backs, bringing in at each turn a course of twenty-four dishes, served in silver, most of it gilt; these dishes were received by a gentleman in the same order as they were brought and placed upon the table, while the lady-taster gave to each of the guard a mouthful to eat of the particular dish he had brought, for fear of any poison. During the time that this guard, which consists of the tallest and stoutest men that can be found in all England, one hundred in number, being carefully selected for this service, were bringing dinner, twelve trumpets and two kettle-drums made the hall ring for half an hour together. At the end of all this ceremonial a number of unmarried ladies appeared, who with particular solemnity lifted the meat off the table, and conveyed it into the Queen's inner and more private chamber, where after she had chosen for herself the rest goes to the ladies of the Court. The Queen dines and sups alone with very few attendants; and it is very seldom that anybody, foreigner or native, is admitted at that time, and then only at the intercession of some distinguished personage.

—Paul Hentzner, *Travels in England*, trans. by Richard Bentley (1757), in *England as Seen by Foreigners in the Days of Elizabeth and James the First*, ed. by William Brenchley Rye (London, 1865), pp. 103-107.

DESCRIPTION OF ENGLAND:
MANNERS AND CUSTOMS (1598)

The soil is fruitful and abounds with cattle [live stock],
which inclines the inhabitants rather to feeding than ploughing, so that near a third part of the land is left uncultivated
for grazing. The climate is most temperate at all times, and
the air never heavy, consequently maladies are scarcer, and
less physic is used there than anywhere else. There are but
few rivers. Though the soil is productive, it bears no wine;
but that want is supplied from abroad by the best kinds, as of
Orleans, Gascon, Rhenish, and Spanish. The general drink is
ale, which is prepared from barley, and is excellently well
tasted but strong and intoxicating. . . . There are many hills
without one tree or any spring, which produce a very short
and tender grass and supply plenty of food to sheep; upon
these wander numerous flocks extremely white, and whether
from the temperature of the air or goodness of the earth,
bearing softer and finer fleeces than those of any other
country. This is the true Golden Fleece, in which consist the
chief riches of the inhabitants, great sums of money being
brought into the island by merchants, chiefly for that article
of trade. The dogs here are particularly good. It has mines of
gold, silver, and tin (of which all manner of table utensils are
made, in brightness equal to silver, and used all over Europe), of lead, and of iron, but not much of the latter. The
horses are small but swift. Glass-houses are in plenty here.

The English are grave like the Germans, lovers of show;
followed wherever they go by whole troops of servants, who
wear their masters' arms in silver fastened to their left arms,
and are not undeservedly ridiculed for wearing tails hanging
down their backs. They excel in dancing and music, for they
are active and lively, though of a thicker make than the
French; they cut their hair close on the middle of the head,
letting it grow on either side; they are good sailors and better
pirates, cunning, treacherous, and thievish; above three hundred are said to be hanged annually at London; beheading
with them is less infamous than hanging; they give the wall as

the place of honor; hawking is the common sport with the gentry. They are more polite in eating than the French, consuming less bread but more meat, which they roast in perfection; they put a great deal of sugar in their drink; their beds are covered with tapestry, even those of farmers; they are often molested with the scurvy, said to have first crept into England with the Norman Conquest; their houses are commonly of two stories, except in London, where they are of three and four, though but seldom of four; they are built of wood, those of the richer sort with bricks, their roofs are low, and where the owner has money, covered with lead. They are powerful in the field, successful against their enemies, impatient of anything like slavery; vastly fond of great noises that fill the ear, such as the firing of cannon, drums, and the ringing of bells, so that in London it is common for a number of them that have got a glass in their heads ... to go up into some belfry, and ring the bells for hours together, for the sake of exercise. If they see a foreigner very well made or particularly handsome, they will say, "It is a pity he is not an Englishman."

—Paul Hentzner, *Travels in England,* trans. by Richard Bentley (1757), in *England as Seen by Foreigners in the Days of Elizabeth and James the First,* ed. by William Brenchley Rye (London, 1865), pp. 109-111.

LONDON (1599)

London is the capital of England and so superior to other
English towns that London is not said to be in England, but
rather England to be in London, for England's most resplendent objects may be seen in and around London; so that he
who sightsees London and the royal courts in its immediate
vicinity may assert without impertinence that he is properly
acquainted with England. The town is called in Latin Lon-
dinum, in French Londres, by the ancients Trinovantum, and
is situated on the river Thames (Tamesis) sixty Italian miles
or sixty thousand paces from the sea, which ebbs and flows as
far as London and yet further, as may be observed every six
hours from the banks and from the bridge. For which reason
ocean craft are accustomed to run in here in great numbers
as into a safe harbor, and I myself beheld one large galley
next the other the whole city's length from St. Catherine's
suburb to the bridge, some hundred vessels in all, nor did I
ever behold so many large ships in one port in all my life.

This river, the foremost in all England because of the city
of London, does not swell or gain in size, no matter how
long it may rain, which is a remarkable thing; and in all parts
of this river swans in great numbers may be seen at all times,
and it is forbidden to catch them, since they serve as down
stuffing to her Majesty.

And while a very fine long bridge is built across this
stream, it is more customary to cross the water or travel up
and down the town as at Lyons and elsewhere by attractive
pleasure craft, for a number of tiny streets lead to the
Thames from both ends of the town; the boatmen wait
there in great crowds, each one eager to be first to catch
one, for all are free to choose the ship they find most
attractive and pleasing, while every boatman has the privilege

22

on arrival of placing his ship to best advantage for people to step into.

The wherries are charmingly upholstered and embroidered cushions laid across the seats, very comfortable to sit on or lean against, and generally speaking the benches only seat two people next to one another; many of them are covered in, particularly in rainy weather or fierce sunshine. They are extremely pleasant to travel in and carry one or a couple of boatmen. I took a ferry across the river to a boathouse where the Thames runs in, and there I saw the Queen's barge, quite closed up and very prettily designed with gangways, and beside it in this same boathouse there stood another ship in which the oarsmen had to sit to steer the Queen's barge in and out, and so that it might glide more smoothly it was lashed on to this steerage boat, for none was allowed to row in it.

Much salmon and sturgeon are caught with lines in this river.

The bridge across the river is of squared stone, very long and with twenty arches, and on it are built very splendid, finely constructed dwelling houses of prosperous merchants, [which] makes the appearance of a very fine street.

At the top of one tower almost in the center of the bridge, were stuck on tall stakes more than thirty skulls of noblemen who had been executed and beheaded for treason and for other reasons. And their descendants are accustomed to boast of this, themselves even pointing out to one their ancestors' heads on this same bridge, believing that they will be esteemed the more because their antecedents were of such high descent that they could even covet the crown, but being too weak to attain it were executed for rebels; thus they make an honor for themselves of what was set up to be a disgrace and an example.

Just as only recently here in Basle the young earl of Suffolk, grandson to the duke of Norfolk, in order to raise the honor of his family, showed that he was so well connected that his forefathers' heads too were on the tower of London Bridge for having coveted the English crown, and so were executed. On this same bridge are, as aforesaid, many tall handsome merchant dwellings and expensive shops, where all manner of wares are for sale, resembling a long street.

The water tower ... in which is a water conduit, is likewise on this bridge, which is only open to the river in three places; otherwise one walks between the houses as a street.

Below the bridge the river falls away so that when it is at its lowest and the tide is out, it is extremely dangerous to pass through; if, however, due to the incoming tide, the river has risen, one may still feel a drop in the level, but now without danger, as I myself made the experiment. The bridge is not in the center of the town but right away near the citadel.

This city of London is so large and splendidly built, so populous and excellent in crafts and merchant citizens, and so prosperous that it is not only the first in the whole realm of England but is esteemed one of the most famous in all Christendom; especially since the wars in the Netherlands and France it has increased by many thousands of families ... who have settled in this city for religion's sake, and these have been very kindly received, and special places of worship allotted them in which to hear sermons in their own tongue— I myself went to the French church the day after my arrival on September 19, and heard a French service there.

Most of the inhabitants are employed in commerce; they buy, sell, and trade in all the corners of the globe, for which purpose the water serves them well, since ships from France, the Netherlands, Germany, and other countries land in this city, bringing goods with them and loading others in exchange for exportation. For which reason they allow some ten percent interest, because through shipping much may be effected and attained with money.

There are also many wealthy merchants and money changers ... in this city, some of whom sell costly wares while others only deal in money or wholesale transactions.

In one very long street called Cheapside dwell almost only goldsmiths and money changers on either hand, so that inexpressibly great treasures and vast amount of money may be seen here.

The Exchange is a great square place like the one in Antwerp, ... a little smaller though, and with only two entrances and only one passage running through it, where all kinds of fine goods are on show; and since the city is very large and extensive, merchants having to deal with one another agree to meet together in this palace, where several hundred may be found assembled twice daily, before lunch at eleven, and again after their meal at six o'clock, buying, selling, bearing news, and doing business generally.

The city is governed almost like a republic ... by the burghers themselves without the King's councilors, because of the many services they have rendered to the King, and they are masters of much of the city revenue. Their chief ... is called the first lord or burgomaster and is elected annually from amongst the burghers, and he must have an income of at least a hundred thousand English pounds, every pound (sterling) having the value of 20 sh. or 10 franks. And this is in order that he may comport himself with more magnificence, likewise his descendants who are all ennobled on his account, while in addition he himself is knighted so as better to uphold his status. As soon as anyone is elected mayor ... he may demand a gift of some thousand pounds from the city, not more than ten thousand pounds however, and the smaller the demand made, the greater the honor. Moreover he must daily hold an open board to which inhabitants and strangers, men or women, may go even unbidden. And since the mayor ... understood that we, although unknown to him, desired to eat with him, he sent us—Jakob Stüber, Herrn Julius, and myself—an invitation by one of the city retainers to come to lunch on October 13, whither we then betook ourselves. As it drew near to lunch time, two men of distinction came to our lodging from the mayor, ... to advise us that the gentlemen were foregathered. On arrival the sword-bearer, ... who frequently proceeds before the mayor, received us and led us through the house to a handsome apartment, where the gentlemen bade us a warm welcome, and the women received us with a kiss. Then we were handed scented water, perfumed with musk, and costly preparations to wash our hands; and when we and our interpreter were seated at table in our cloaks, he called upon his son to say grace.

Straightway all manner of lavish dishes were served most decorously. And there were two servers or carvers who removed one plate after another from the table to another covered table nearby, and they did nothing else but carve and serve. They laid the food in small pewter bowls, placing these before each person upon plates, one course after another, all most perfectly and richly prepared and served with delightful sauces, while diverse other dishes to stimulate the appetite surrounded one.

The drinks consisted of the best beer and all manner of heavy and light wines to follow, as for instance, Greek, Spanish, Malmsey, Lanquedoc, French, and German, for in

England all kinds of wine can be had for comparatively little money because of the low freightage by sea.

After two helpings of roasts, stews, and other things, dessert was served, consisting only of sweetmeats, tarts, and pastries, not to be compared for delicacy with the entrees. Finally he gave us thanks for the honor we did him in lunching with him, and he asked us to accept his hospitality, and Mr. Button thanked him in the English tongue on our behalf, for he had spoken for us often while the meal lasted, since we understood nothing of what they said to us, either in Latin, French, or Spanish. And this banquet continued until towards evening, when once again we were accompanied home.

On the morning of October 6, I and my party visited the castle [the Tower] situated in London not far from the Thames, and very magnificent and well fortified.

—Thomas Platter, *Travels in England 1599,* trans. by Clare Williams (London, 1937), pp. 153-159.

JULIUS CAESAR AT THE GLOBE (1599)

On September 21 after lunch, about two o'clock, I and my party crossed the water, and there in the house with the thatched roof witnessed an excellent performance of the tragedy of the first emperor Julius Caesar with a cast of some fifteen people; when the play was over, they danced very marvelously and gracefully together as is their wont, two dressed as men and two as women.

On another occasion not far from our inn, in the suburb at Bishopsgate, if I remember, also after lunch, I beheld a play in which they presented diverse nations and an Englishman struggling together for a maiden; he overcame them all except the German who won the girl in a tussle and then sat down by her side, when he and his servant drank themselves tipsy, so that they were both fuddled and the servant proceeded to hurl his shoe at his master's head, whereupon they both fell asleep; meanwhile the Englishman stole into the tent and absconded with the German's prize, thus in his turn outwitting the German; in conclusion they danced very charmingly in English and Irish fashion. Thus daily at two in the afternoon, London has two, sometimes three, plays running in different places, competing with each other, and those which play best obtain most spectators. The playhouses are so constructed that they play on a raised platform, so that everyone has a good view. There are different galleries and places, however, where the seating is better and more comfortable and therefore more expensive. For whoever cares to stand below only pays one English penny, but if he wishes to sit he enters by another door and pays another penny, while if he desires to sit in the most comfortable seats which are cushioned, where he not only sees everything well but can also be seen, then he pays yet another English penny at another door. And during the performance food and drink are carried round the audience so that for what one cares to pay one may also have refreshment. The actors are most expensively and elaborately costumed; for it is the English usage for eminent lords or knights at their decease to bequeath and leave almost the best of their clothes to their serving men, which it is unseemly for the latter to wear, so that they offer them then for sale for a small sum to the actors.

How much time, then, they may merrily spend daily at the play everyone knows who has ever seen them play or act.

There is also in the city of London not far from the horse market, which occupies a large site, a house where cockfights are held annually throughout three quarters of the year (for in the remaining quarter they told me it was impossible since the feathers are full of blood) and I saw the place which is built like a theater. ... In the center on the floor stands a circular table covered with straw and with ledges round it, where the cocks are teased and incited to fly at one another, while those with wagers as to which cock will win sit closest around the circular disk, but the spectators who are merely present on their entrance penny sit around higher up, watching with eager pleasure the fierce and angry fight between the cocks, as these wound each other to death with spurs and beaks. And the party whose cock surrenders or dies loses the wager; I am told that stakes on a cock often amount to many thousand of crowns, especially if they have reared the cock themselves and brought their own along. For the master who inhabits the house has many cocks besides, which he feeds in separate cages and keeps for this sport, as he showed us. He also had several cocks, none of which he would sell for less than twenty crowns; they are very large but just the same kind as we have in our country. He also told us that if one discovered that the cocks' beaks had been coated with garlic, one was fully entitled to kill them at once. He added, too, that it was nothing to give them brandy before they began to fight, adding what wonderful pleasure there was in watching them.

Every Sunday and Wednesday in London there are bear-baitings on the other side of the water, and I ferried across on Sunday the 18th of September with the earl of Benthem [?] and my party, and saw the bear and bullbaiting. The theater is circular, with galleries round the top for the spectators, the ground space down below, beneath the clear sky, is unoccupied. In the middle of this place a large bear on a long rope was bound to a stake, then a number of great English mastiffs were brought in and shown first to the bear, which they afterwards baited one after another; now the excellence and fine temper of such mastiffs was evinced, for although they were much struck and mauled by the bear, they did not give in but had to be pulled off by sheer force, and their muzzles forced open with long sticks to which a broad ironpiece was attached at the top. The bears' teeth were not sharp so they could not injure the dogs; they have them broken short. When the first mastiffs tired, fresh ones were brought in to bait the bear.

When the first bear was weary, another was supplied and fresh dogs to bait him, first one at a time, then more and more as it lasted, till they had overpowered the bear, then only did they come to its aid. This second bear was very big and old, and kept the dogs at bay so artfully with his paws that they could not score a point off him until there were more of them. When this bear was tired, a large white powerful bull was brought in, and likewise bound in the center of the theater, and one dog only was set on him at a time, which he speared with his horns and tossed in such masterly fashion that they could not get the better of him, and as the dogs fell to the floor again, several men held the sticks under them to break their fall so that they would not be killed. Afterwards more dogs were set on him but could not down him. Then another powerful bear was fetched and baited by six or seven dogs at a time, which attacked him bravely on all sides but could not get the better of him because of his thick pelt.

Lastly they brought in an old blind bear which the boys hit with canes and sticks; but he knew how to untie his leash and he ran back to his stall.

On leaving, we descended the steps and went behind the theater, saw the English mastiffs, of which there were one hundred and twenty together in one enclosure, each chained up to his own separate kennel, however. And the place was evil-smelling because of the lights and meat on which the butchers feed the said dogs.

In a stall adjoining were some twelve large bears, and several bulls in another, all of them kept there merely for the sport described above.

With these and many more amusements the English pass their time, learning at the play what is happening abroad;

indeed men and womenfolk visit such places without scruple, since the English for the most part do not travel much but prefer to learn foreign matters and take their pleasures at home.

—Thomas Platter, *Travels in England 1599*, trans. by Clare Williams (London, 1937), pp. 166-170.

ENGLISH CUSTOMS AND AMUSEMENTS (1617?)

Again, it is a singularity in the nature of the English that they are strangely addicted to all kinds of pleasure above all other nations. This of old was justly attributed to idleness when the multitude of monasteries and the great trains and large housekeepings of lords and gentlemen were nurseries of thieves and idle persons, so as we were served for the most part by strangers [foreigners] in all manual trades. But since the putting down of monasteries and of these great trains and large housekeepings, howsoever I cannot deny that out of this natural addiction to pleasure (or idleness if you will so call it) and out of natural boldness less to fear death than want, more persons are executed in England for stealing and robberies by the highway than in many vast kingdoms abroad. Yet do not these offenses so much abound as in those former times, and for manual trades we are now almost altogether served by natives, who for necessity to eat their own bread are in good measure grown industrious artisans.

But for the point of pleasures the English, from the lords to the very husbandmen, have generally more fair and more large gardens and orchards than any other nation. All cities, towns, and villages swarm with companies of musicians and fiddlers, which are rare in other kingdoms. The city of London alone hath four or five companies of players with their peculiar theaters capable of many thousands, wherein they all play every day in the week but Sunday with most strange concourse of people, besides many strange toys and fancies exposed by signs to be seen in private houses, to which and to many musterings and frequent spectacles the people flock in great numbers, being naturally more newfangled than the Athenians to hear news and gaze upon every toy.

As there be in my opinion more plays in London than in all the parts of the world I have seen, so do these players or comedians excel all other in the world. Whereof I have seen some straggling broken companies that passed into Netherland and Germany followed by the people from one town to another though they understood not their words, only to see their action; yea, merchants at fairs bragged more to have seen them than of the good markets they made. Not to speak of frequent spectacles in London exhibited to the people by fencers, by walkers on ropes and like men of activity, nor of frequent companies of archers shooting in all the fields; nor of saints' days, which the people not keeping (at least most of them or with any devotion) for church service yet keep for recreation of walking and gaming.

What shall I say of dancing with curious and rural music frequently used by the better sort and upon all holydays by country people dancing about the Maypoles with bagpipes or other fiddlers, besides the jollities of certain seasons of the year of setting up Maypoles, dancing the morris with hobby-horses, bringing home the lady of the harvest and like plebeian sports, in all which vanities no nation cometh anything near the English. What shall I say of playing at cards and dice frequently used by all sorts rather as a trade than as recreation, for which all strangers much blame us. As the English are by nature amorous, so do they above other nations assert and follow the pleasant study of poetry and therein have in good measure attained excellency.

To conclude with hawking and hunting, no nation so frequently useth these sports as the English. No nation of greater compass alloweth such great proportions of lands for parks to impale fallow and red deer. And as England has plenty of red deer, so I will boldly say that it, perhaps one shire of it, hath more fallow deer than all the continent of the world that I have seen. And for the parks of fallow deer lately planted in Denmark, Brabant, and Holland, they have been stored in our age out of England by the late Queen's favor.

No nation followeth these pastimes and exercises on horseback and on foot so frequently and painfully in any measure of comparison. England yields excellent sparrow hawks, and Ireland hawks of divers kinds but especially excellent goshawks, and gentlemen with great charge procure plenty of the best hawks from foreign parts. Not only gentlemen but yeomen frequently hunt the hare not only with greyhounds but hounds, in keeping whereof for that purpose divers yeomen join together, for England wants not Actaeons eaten up by their own dogs. And for all these sports and other uses England hath without comparison greater number and better dogs than any other nation, as mastiffs for keeping the house, rough water dogs for the duck, greyhounds for the hare, divers kinds of hounds for all huntings, and spaniels for hawking, and bloodhounds to track stolen deer or other things, and little dogs for women's pleasure, and all those beautiful and good and some most rare, as the said bloodhounds, and tumblers for coneys [rabbits], and setting dogs to catch partridges by the net (which sport notwithstanding is unlawful).

Again, the nature of the English is very singular above other nations in liberality and bounty of presents, gifts, and rewards, if it be not rather prodigality or folly, as when gentlemen and great men will pay more than is due in small things because they will not stand to change money, in greater because they will not stand to examine reckonings but rather would seem negligent in spending, and in all voluntary rewards assert bounty above their quality and means, as I could show by many instances. The universities of England are most famous, wherein no kingdom can compare with it by many degrees, as I have showed in the discourse of the universities in Germany and also in France.

London hath four singularities above all other cities, as the monuments of Westminster, the goldsmiths' row in Cheapside, the Exchange for merchants' meeting, and the bridge over Thames. And generally no kingdom may compare with England for churches, especially the sumptuous and large building and the number of cathedral churches. Not to speak of famous antiquities throughout all England excellently described by our famous antiquary Mr. Camden.

England hath great magnificence in the feasts and ceremonies of the King's coronation but is singular above all other kingdoms or cities in the yearly Feast of St. George and the particular feasts of installing each knight of the Garter, and in the yearly triumphs and pageants of the city of London when the new mayor takes his oath, and especially in the tables of the mayor and especially sheriffs of London, all the year open to entertain all men of quality, natives and strangers, who may freely resort to them.

England hath the best barbers and the most commodious inns of all the world besides.

The English language is very copious of words and expressions of anything to be spoken, and being mixed is therefore more and not less to be esteemed as I have showed in the former discourse of the Italian tongue. . . .

England excels all other countries in the goodness and number of ambling nags and geldings, and no other nation hath so many and easy pads to ride upon, nor in any measure chairs and stools so frequently bombasted and richly adorned. But strangers, seeing most of our gentlemen ride upon hard northern saddles, wonder they should use them abroad who desire to set so soft at home. The custom for each parish to keep a register of all children christened, whereby any man may prove his age (being a thing important for many cases of law and otherwise), was first begun in England in the time of King Henry VIII, and the Romans, having borrowed it of us, call it the custom of England, but I know no other country that useth it. England hath three very old and very laudable customs used in no other kingdom that I know. First, for children at morning and evening to ask their parents' blessing and extraordinarily their godfathers, when they meet them. Secondly, that all malefactors are followed from village to village by public officers with hue and cry. Thirdly, that when any man is at the point of death, a great bell is tolled to warn all men to pray for him while he yet liveth, and when the party is dead, by a number of several strokes at the bell, notice is given whether the party dead be a man, woman, or child, and then the bell is rung out. As likewise at the burial all the bells of the church for some hours are rung out. Touching bells, England hath many singularities, as in the general greatness of them, some one (as that of Lincoln Minster) requiring the help of many men to toll it and some dozen or twenty men to ring it out. Also in the incredible number of them, so as I may boldly say England hath more bell metal than all the continent of Europe and that part of Asia which I have seen. Besides that, most churches of England have each of them three, five, or seven bells of differing bigness, which men commonly ring out in musical tunes for recreation, which I never observed to be done in any other country.

—Reprinted in Fynes Moryson, *Shakespeare's Europe*, 2d ed. (1967), pp. 475-80.

THE STRUCTURE OF SOCIETY

Classes of the People

OF THE FIRST PART OF GENTLEMEN OF ENGLAND, CALLED "NOBILITAS MAJOR"

... In England no man is created a baron, except he may dispend of yearly revenue one thousand pounds, or one thousand marks at the least. ...

OF THE SECOND SORT OF GENTLEMEN, WHICH MAY BE CALLED *Nobilitas Minor*, AND FIRST OF KNIGHTS

No man is a knight by succession, not the king or prince ... knights therefore be not born but made. ... In England whosoever may dispend of his free lands forty pounds sterling of yearly revenue ... may be by the king compelled to take that order and honor, or to pay a fine. ...

OF ESQUIRES

Esquires (which we commonly call squires) be all those which bear arms (as we call them) or armories ... these be taken for no distinct order of the commonwealth, but do go with the residue of the gentlemen. ...

OF GENTLEMEN

Gentlemen be those whom their blood and race doth make noble and known. ... Ordinarily the king doth only make knights and create barons or higher degrees, for as for gentlemen they be made good cheap in England. For whosoever studieth the laws of the realm, who studieth in the universities, who professeth liberal sciences, and to be short, who can live idly and without manual labor, and will bear the port, charge, and countenance of a gentleman, he shall be called master, ... and shall be taken for a gentleman. ...

OF YEOMEN

Those whom we call yeomen, next unto the nobility, knights, and squires, have the greatest charge and doings in the commonwealth ... I call him a yeoman whom our laws do call *legalem hominem* ... which is a freeman born English, and may dispend of his own free land in yearly revenue to the sum of 40s. sterling ... This sort of people confess themselves to be no gentlemen ... and yet they have a certain preeminence and more estimation than laborers and artificers, and commonly live wealthily.... These be (for the most part) farmers unto gentlemen, ... and by these means do come to such wealth, that they are able and daily do buy the lands of unthrifty gentlemen, and after setting their sons to the school at the universities, to the laws of the realm, or otherwise leaving them sufficient lands whereon they may live without labor, do make their said sons by those means gentlemen. ...

OF THE FOURTH SORT OF MEN WHICH DO NOT RULE

The fourth sort or class amongst us, is of those which the old Romans called *capite censi* ... day laborers, poor husbandmen, yea merchants or retailers which have no free land, copyholders and all artificers. ... These have no voice nor authority in our commonwealth, and no account is made of them, but only to be ruled.

—Sir Thomas Smith, *The Commonwealth of England* (1583), book 1, chapters 17-24.

PART II

Public and Private Events

THE ENGLISH CHRONICLE AND THE EVENTS OF SHAKESPEARE'S LIFE (1558–1616)

1558. Queen Elizabeth I

The 17 of November 1558 came certain news unto the Parliament House of the death of Queen Mary, whereat many rejoiced and many lamented. And forthwith, her death being generally known, they proclaimed the Lady Elizabeth, second daughter to King Henry VIII, Queen of England, France, and Ireland, Defender of the Faith, etc., in London and Westminster. The Queen was then at Bishop's Hatfield, but not proclaimed there until two days after.

1564. April 26. *Christening of William, first surviving child of John and Mary Arden Shakespeare, at Stratford-on-Avon*

1564. Celestial Omens

The 7 of October at night all the north parts of the element seemed to be covered with flames of fire proceeding from the northeast and northwest toward the midst of the firmament, and descended west.

1567. Drought

After a dry summer there followed a sharp winter with such a scarcity of fodder and hay that in divers places the same was sold by the weight for five pence the stone. There followed also a great death of cattle.

1568. Mary Stuart, Queen of Scots

The 16 of May, Mary, Queen of Scots, after her escape made out of Loch Leven, where she had long been imprisoned, arrived at Workington in England, having in her company to the number of sixteen persons, besides four water-men, where she was stayed and conveyed to Carlisle, and from thence to Bolton Castle belonging to Lord Scrope, who with Sir Ralph Sadler, sent down for that purpose, had custody of her till she was committed to the earl of Shrewsbury.

1568. September 4. *John Shakespeare elected bailiff (mayor) of Stratford-on-Avon*

1569.   A Lottery at London

A great lottery of 400,000 lots, each lot 10 shillings, being holden at London in Paul's churchyard at the west door, was begun to be drawn the 11 of January, and continued day and night till the first of May.

1569.   The Northern Rebellion

The 24 of November the Queen's Majesty caused the earls of Northumberland and Westmorland, who rebelled in the North, to be proclaimed traitors, and forthwith prepared an army for their suppression.

1569. The Northern Rebellion

The next night [Dec. 21] the two earls of Northumberland and Westmorland with sundry of the principal gentlemen fled to Hetlaw in Scotland. The other rebels were shortly after taken by the earl of Sussex.

1571.   Trial by Combat

The 18 of June there was a combat appointed to have been fought for a certain manor and demesne lands in the Isle of Harty in Kent. Simon Low and John Ryme, plaintiffs, had brought a writ of right against Thomas Paramour, who offered to defend his right by battle. And the plaintiffs aforesaid accepted to answer his challenge. Hereupon the said Paramour brought before the judges of the Common Pleas at Westminster one George Thorne and the plaintiffs brought Henry Naylor, Master of Defense. Thorne cast down a gauntlet which Naylor took up. Upon the Sunday before the battle should be tried, on the next morrow, the matter was stayed and the parties agreed that Paramour, being in possession, should have the land.

1571.   The Battle of Lepanto

The 9 of November great rejoicing was made at London for the late-come news of a marvelous victory obtained by the Christian army by sea against the Turks the 6 of October last past, wherein was taken and sunk, of the Turks' galleys and brigantines, 230. There were slain of the Turks more than 30,000, besides a great number of prisoners taken, and about 12,000 Christians that had been slaves with the Turks were set at liberty.

1572. A Strange Star

The 18 of November was seen a star northward, very bright and clear, in the constellation of Cassiopeia, which with the three fixed stars of the said constellation made a geometrical figure lozengewise, of the learned men called rhombus. This star in bigness at the first appearing seemed bigger than Jupiter and much less than Venus when she seemed greatest. Also the said star, never changing his place, was carried about with the daily motion of heaven as all fixed stars commonly are, and so continued almost six months. The same star was found to be in place celestial, far above the moon, otherwise than ever any comet hath been seen or naturally can appear. Therefore it is supposed that the significance thereof is directed purposely and specially to some matter not natural but celestial, or rather supercelestial, so strange as from the beginning of the world never was the like.

1576. God's Judgment on a Perjurer

The 11 of February, Anne Averies, widow, forswearing herself for a little money that she should have paid for six pounds of tow [yarn] at a shop in Woodstreet of London fell immediately down speechless, casting up at her mouth the same matter which by nature's course should have been voided downwards till she died. A terrible example of God's judgment upon such as make no conscience of swearing, though it be against their own elder brother.

1578. God's Judgment on a Conjurer

The 17 of January one Simon Pembrooke, dwelling in Southwark, being vehemently suspected to be a conjurer, by commandment of the ordinary judge for those parts appeared in the parish church of Saint Saviour at the court holden there; which Simon busied himself in entertaining a proctor, and having money in his hand, leaned upon the pew wherein the proctor stood; which after he had done a certain space, the proctor began to lift up his head to see what he ailed, and found him departed out of life. And straightway the said Simon fell down, rattling a little in the throat, and never spoke word after. This was done even as the judge came into the church, who said it was the just judgment of God towards those that used sorcery, and a great example to admonish others to fear the justice of God. After his clothes being opened, there were found about him devilish books of conjuration and abominable practices, a picture of a man having three dice in his hand and this writing, "Chance, dice, fortunately," and divers papers of such like matters as he had dealt in for men, such as are mentioned in Leviticus 20:6, "If any soul turn himself after such as work with spirits and after soothsayers to go awhoring, (saith the Lord), I will put my face against that soul, and will cut him off from among my people."

1581. Sir Francis Drake

The 4 of April the Queen dined at Deptford and there after dinner entered the ship wherein Captain Drake had sailed about the world. And being there, a bridge that Her Majesty came over broke, there being upon the same more than two hundred persons, and no hurt was done by the same. And there she knighted Captain Francis Drake in his ship.

1582. November 27. *License, Worcester Episcopal Register, for marriage of William Shakespeare and Ann Hathaway*

1583. Scaffolds Collapsed at Bear Garden

The 23 of January, being Sunday, about 4 o'clock in the afternoon, the old and underpropped scaffolds round about the Bear Garden on the south side of the Thames over against the city of London, overcharged with people fell suddenly down, whereby to the number of eight persons, men and women, were slain and many others sore hurt and bruised. A friendly warning to such as more delight themselves in the cruelty of beasts than in the works of mercy, the fruits of true possessed faith, which ought to be the Sabbath day's exercise.

1583. May 26. *Christening at Stratford-on-Avon of Susanna, first child of William and Ann Shakespeare*

1583. Pirates

In the month of June were sent to the seas a ship called the Bark Talbot and a small bark, both manned with one hundred men under the charge of William Borough, Esquire, clerk of Her Majesty's Navy, for the apprehending of certain outrageous sea rovers, who for that they were many in number and well appointed so boldly behaved themselves as that shortly after it was confidently bruited that they had vanquished in fight the said ship and bark. But within few days after, beyond all expectation, they were by the said W. Borough and his company discomfited and taken to the number of ten sail, whereof three prizes and some of the chief pirates, namely, T. Walton, alias Purser, Clinton, Atkinson. . . . As he went to the gallows, Walton rent his Venetian breeches of crimson taffeta and distributed the same to such his old acquaintance as stood about him. But Atkinson had before given his merry velvet doublet with great gold buttons and his like colored velvet Venetians laid with great gold lace, which he had worn at The Seas of Porbeke, unto such of his friends as pleased him.

1585. February 2.   *Christening of Hamnet and Judith Shakespeare, twins*

1585.   Arundel Towered for Traveling without a License

The 25 of April, Philip Howard, Earl of Arundel, was brought to the Tower of London for attempting to have passed beyond the seas without license of the Queen.

1585.   Executed for Publishing

The 5 of July, T. Awfield, seminary priest, and T. Welby, dyer, were arraigned at London, found guilty, and had judgment to be hanged as felons for publishing of books containing false, seditious, and slanderous matter. These were on the next morrow executed at Tyburn.

1585. July.   Soldiers Sent to the Netherlands

In the month of July soldiers were pressed in the city of London and being furnished for the wars at the charges of the companies, set forth towards the seas on the 13 of August and were transported over into Holland, Zeland, etc., as other the like soldiers out of other parts of the realm before had been.

1586.   Contriving Letters

The 11 of February, Thomas Lovelace was brought prisoner from the Tower of London to the Star Chamber; against whom Her Majesty's Attorney did inform that the same Lovelace upon malice conceived against Leonard Love-lace and Richard Lovelace, his cousins german, had falsely and devilishly contrived and counterfeited a very traitorous letter in the name of Thomas Lovelace (another brother of the said Leonard and Richard, then resident beyond the seas), purporting that the same Thomas should thereby incite and provoke the said Leonard to procure the said Richard to execute Her Highness' destruction, with other circumstances of treason.

This letter he cast in an open highway, pretending thereby that upon the discovery thereof his said kinsmen, Leonard and Richard, should be drawn in question for the treasonable matter against Her Majesty in that bill contained even in the highest degree. For which offense Her Majesty's Attorney prayed that the said Thomas, then prisoner, might receive condign punishment. Whereupon the court adjudged him, that he should be remitted to the Tower from whence he came; that he should be carried on horseback about Westminster Hall with his face to the horse's tail, and a paper on his back wherein to be written: "For counterfeiting of false and treacherous letters against his own kindred, containing most traitorous matters against Her Majesty's person." And from thence to be carried in that manner and set on the pillory in the palace at Westminster, and there to have one of his ears cut off, also to be carried in like manner into London and set on the pillory on market day in Cheape with the like paper; and after that, carried into Kent and at the next assize there to be set on the pillory with the like paper, and his other ear to be cut off. Also to be set on the pillory one market day at Canterbury and another at Rochester in the like manner.

1586. The Babington Plot

In the month of July divers traitorous persons were appre-hended and detected of most wicked conspiracy against Her Majesty, and also of minding to have stirred up a general rebellion throughout the whole realm. For joy of whose apprehension the citizens of London on the fifteenth of the same month at night, and on the next morrow, caused the bells to be rung and bonfires to be made and also banqueted every man according to his ability, some in their houses, some in the streets, with singing of psalms and praising God for preserving of Her Majesty and people of this land. Which doings of the citizens were so well accepted of Her Majesty, as by her letters to them directed may appear.

1587. Mary Stuart, Queen of Scots

The 8 of February, being Wednesday, according to sentence lately given by the nobility, Mary Stuart, Queen of Scots, about two of the clock before noon was executed and suffered death by beheading upon a scaffold set up for that purpose at the great hall of the castle of Fotheringay in the presence of George Talbot, Earl of Shrewsbury; Henry Grey, Earl of Kent; principal Commissioners, and others the gentlemen of the country near adjoining to the number of about three hundred. All her apparel was burned, but her body with the head was royally buried at Peterborough on the first day of August next following.

1588. The Spanish Armada

Great provision was made this year both by land and sea to withstand the invasion by the Spanish Armada against the realm. For, besides the general forces of the realm appointed to be mustered, trained, and put in readiness in the several shires for the defense of the land, there was also a levy made of two several armies. The one to make the body of a camp to reside at Tilbury in Essex to encounter with the enemy if he should attempt to land in any place of that country [county], whereof the earl of Leicester, Lord Steward of Her Majesty's household, was Lieutenant General, as also of the armies levied against foreign invasion. The other, to be employed for the guard of Her Highness's person, under the charge of the Right Honorable the Lord Hunsdon, Lord Chamberlain to Her Majesty. The camp at Tilbury, consisting both of horsemen and footmen raised out of all the shires, were of lancers 253, of light horsemen 769, of footmen 22,000. The army for the guard of Her Majesty's person: lances 481, light horsemen 1,431, footmen 34,500. The navy, set forth and armed to the seas, consisted partly of Her Majesty's ships, partly of the ships of her subjects which were furnished out of the port towns whereunto they belonged. Of this navy the chiefest and greatest part was under the charge of the Lord Charles Howard of Effingham, Lord Admiral of England, and were addressed to encounter with the Spanish fleet. The rest of the ships were assigned to Lord Henry Seymour, Admiral of the Fleet, to guard the narrow seas and to impeach the issuing forth of the ships and vessels prepared by the duke of Parma at Dunkirk.

1588. The Spanish Armada

The 20 of July the Lord Admiral made toward the sea and the same day had sight of the Spanish fleet, in number by estimation 158 sails. The Lord Admiral cast about toward the land to interrupt them from approaching and, having got the wind of them, prosecuted them all that night, and so continually from place to place until the second of August. In which space, having by the power of God wonderfully overcome them, he returned to Margate in Kent. Now the camp being kept at Tilbury in Essex under the charge of the earl of Leicester, the 9 of August Her Majesty repaired thither, where all the whole camp being set in order of battle, she passed through every rank of them to their great rejoicing, and lodged that night and the night following in the house of Mr. Edward Rich, a justice in the parish of Hornedon. On the next morrow Her Majesty returned to the camp, and on the twelfth returned to Saint James, and shortly after the camp was dissolved.

1588. Sailors and Soldiers Hanged

Sir John Norris and Sir Francis Drake being returned, as you have heard, many of their sailors and soldiers shortly after their landing fell sick and died of a stench bred amongst them on shipboard.

Other some of them so rudely behaved themselves about the country and elsewhere that, divers of them being apprehended on August 27, one of them was hanged on the end of a sign at an inn door in Kingston upon Thames for a terror to the rest. And on the 29 of August two more of them were hanged in Smithfield, two at the Tower Hill, two beside Westminster, and one at Tyburn. It was now usual with sailors and others at their return of such voyages to rob, pilfer, and mutiny at their arrival.

1589. Looms

This year, 1589, William Lee, sometime Master of Arts of Saint John's College of Cambridge, devised and perfected the art of knitting or weaving of silk stockings, waistcoats, coverlets, and divers other things by engines or steel looms. Sixteen years after this he went into France and taught it to the French because he was not regarded in England.

1591. William Hacket

The 16 of July, Edmond Copinger and Henry Artington, gentlemen, came into Cheap[side] and there in a car proclaimed news from heaven (as they said), to wit: that one William Hacket, yeoman, represented Christ by partaking His glorified body and by His principal spirit, and that they were two prophets, the one of Mercy, the other of Judgment, called and sent of God to assist him in his great work, etc. These men were afterward apprehended. The 20 of July, Hacket was arraigned and found guilty as to have spoken divers most false and traitorous words against Her Majesty, to have razed and defaced her arms, as also her picture, thrusting an iron instrument into that part that did represent the breast and heart, etc. For the which he had judgment, and on the 28 of July brought from Newgate to a gibbet by the cross in Cheap where, being moved to ask God and the Queen forgiveness, he fell to railing and cursing of the Queen, and began a most blasphemous prayer against the divine Majesty of God. He was there hanged and quartered. His immodest speeches at his arraignment and death utterly disgraced all his former seemed sanctity, wherewith he had shrewdly possessed the common people.

1591.   Earl of Essex Sent to France

In this month of July Robert Devereux, Earl of Essex, was by Her Majesty appointed to have the charge and conduction, as her Lieutenant General, of four thousand footmen and some number of horsemen and pioneers [engineers] sent into France for the assistance of the French king against the confederates of the League. In which expedition he was also honorably accompanied with sundry gentlemen soldiers that voluntarily followed him in his service.

1592.   Almshouses

The Merchant Tailors in London this year founded fair almshouses upon a plot of ground near unto East Smithfield in the parish of St. Botolph without Aldgate. Which plot of ground was given to them by Richard Hilles, sometime master of that company, as also one hundred load of timber by Anthony Ratcliffe, of the same society, alderman. In these almshouses fourteen charitable men, brethren of the said Merchant Tailors yet living, have placed fourteen poor aged sole women, which receive every one of them of their founder sixteen pence or better weekly, besides eight pounds, fifteen shillings yearly, paid for of the common treasury to the said company for fuel.

1592. Burnt for Poisoning
The 4 of September a woman was burnt in Smithfield for poisoning of her husband.

1592. *Shakespeare alluded to in Greene's GROATSWORTH OF WIT (registered Sept. 20) as London actor and playwright*

1593. April 18. *Registration for publication of VENUS AND ADONIS*

1593. Plague
This year was no Bartholomew Fair kept at London, for the avoiding of concourse of people whereby the infection of the pestilence might have increased.

1593. Plague
The whole number this year buried within the city of London, the suburbs, and other places adjoining, as well of the plague as of the other diseases, from the 29 of December 1592 until the 20 of December 1593, was as followeth: within the walls of all diseases, 8,598, whereof the plague, 5,390; without the walls and in the liberties, 9,295, the plague, 5,285; so that within the city and liberties 17,863 of all diseases and 10,675 of plague.

1594. February 6. *Registration of TITUS ANDRONICUS*

1594. May 9. *Registration of THE RAPE OF LUCRECE*

1594. December 28. *"A COMEDY OF ERRORS (like to Plautus' MENECHMUS) was played by the Players"* at Gray's Inn.

1594. Conduits
This year Bevis Bulmar, an ingenious gentleman, made an engine at Broken Wharf, thereby from thence to convey Thames water up into the city, sufficient to serve the whole west part thereof, bring conveyed into men's houses by pipes of lead.

1595. March 15. *Payment "to William Kempe, William Shakespeare, and Richard Burbage, servants to the Lord Chamberlain . . . for two several comedies or interludes showed by them before Her Majesty in Christmas time last past."*

1595. June 29.   Mobs

On the 29 of June, being Sunday, in the afternoon a number of unruly youths on the Tower Hill, being blamed by the Warders of Tower Street Ward to sever themselves and depart from thence, threw at them stones and drove them back into Tower Street, and were heartened thereunto by a late soldier sounding of a trumpet, but the trumpeter and many other of them being taken by the sheriffs of London and committed to prison. About seven o'clock the same night Sir John Spencer, Lord Mayor, rode to the Tower Hill, attended by his officers and others to see the hill cleared of all tumultuous persons, where about the middle of the hill some Warders of the Tower or Lieutenant's men told Sir John that the sword ought not to be borne up there. And two or three catching hold thereof, some bickering was there and the swordbearer hurt. But the Lord Mayor, seeing the hill cleared of all trouble, rode back, the swordbearer bearing up the sword. The 22 of July, in the presence of the earl of Essex and other sent from the Queen, were arraigned in the Guildhall of London five of those unruly youths that were on the Tower Hill apprehended. They were condemned and had judgment to be drawn, hanged, and quartered and were on the 24 of the same month drawn from Newgate to the Tower Hill, and there executed accordingly.

1596. August 11.   *Burial of Hamnet Shakespeare*

1596.   Charity

In the month of August began a new collection for to relieve the poor in this city, so that beside their ordinary pensions in money given to them, they also received weekly two shillings, bread ready baked, every loaf weighing twenty-four or twenty-six ounces the piece. But this charity lasted but a while.

1596. October 20.   *Grant of Arms to John Shakespeare*

1597. May 4.   *Deed conveying New Place, second largest house in Stratford, "one dwelling house, two barns, and two gardens," to William Shakespeare for sixty pounds*

1597. August 29.   *RICHARD II registered*

1597. October 20.   *RICHARD III registered*

1597. *ROMEO AND JULIET published*

1598. February 25. *HENRY IV registered*

1598. Town Burned
On the 3 of April Twiford Town in Devonshire was burnt by casualty of fire. Beginning in a poor cottage, a woman there frying pancakes with straw, the same fired the house, and so to the town about one o'clock in the afternoon. The rage of which fire, lasting one hour and a half, 400 houses burned down, 150,000 pounds consumed in money, plate, merchandise, household stuff, and houses. Fifty persons, men, women, and children, consumed. An almshouse preserved with poor men therein in the midst of the flames. Two thousand pounds weekly was bestowed there in the market on Mondays in Devonshire kerseys [woolen cloths]. Nine thousand people maintained by the clothing of that town in Cornwall and Somersetshire. It was the earl of Devonshire's chief seat where yet stand his castle or court place. Thus much certified to Her Majesty.

1598. *LOVE'S LABOUR'S LOST published*

1598. July 22. *THE MERCHANT OF VENICE registered*

1598. *Francis Meres in PALLADIS TAMIA (registered Sept. 7) names with praise Shakespeare's works so far noticed, and "his sugared sonnets among his private friends," THE TWO GENTLEMEN OF VERONA, A MIDSUMMER NIGHT'S DREAM, and KING JOHN.*

1599. A Tempest Cleans the Streets
The months of March, April, and May cold and dry, but on Whitsunday great hail and high waters, the like of long time had not been seen. The extreme violence of this tempest made London's streets more fresh and fair than ever was seen before.

1599. May 16. *Shakespeare listed in an inventory of property as part-owner of the Globe*

1599. Alarm
In the month of August by the Queen's appointment (politickly to prevent dangerous annoyance of her estate then

feared to happen but not expressed), the citizens of London were charged with the furniture and setting forth to sea of twelve ships, since increased to sixteen, etc. Also with six thousand men and furniture for the wars, which men with all speed were made in a readiness. Three thousand of them were daily trained in the field under captains, citizens of the same city, from the 6 of August, etc. The other three thousand appointed to attend upon her royal person were also likewise trained under captains in brave furniture, for they were householders of account. All which their charges was partly borne by themselves, the residue performed by subsidies levied of the citizens.

In this meantime, to wit, on the 5 of August at night, by commandment from Her Majesty, the chains were drawn thwart the streets and lanes of the city and lanterns with light of candles were hanged, one at every man's door, there to burn all the night. And so from night to night, and great watches kept in the streets, which so continued a long time. The city and citizens kept unusual watch and ward, and all sorts of people were much amazed and frightened, as well by reason of preparation for wars, not knowing any cause, as also by the sudden strange and terrible rumors and reports of the Spaniards' fierce approach.

Also many thousands of horsemen and footmen, chosen persons, well appointed for the wars, trained up in armor with brave liveries under valiant captains in divers shires, were brought up to London, where they were lodged in the suburbs, towns, and villages near adjoining from the 8 of August till the 20 or 23. In which time the horsemen were showed in Saint James Field and the footmen trained in other grounds about the city, and then all discharged homewards with charge to be always ready at an hour's warning. And so it followed that on the 25 of August at night, posts were sent after them to recall the horsemen presently to return to London with all speed possible, which charge they prepared to perform. But on the 27 of August the said posts were likewise sent to stay them at home, or to return them back, whose forwardness in service of the Queen was such as the like hath not been seen or heard of towards any prince of this realm, such was the dutifulness of her loving and obedient subjects. The 26 of August, being Sunday, in the morning before six o'clock, by the commandment from the Queen, the three thousand soldiers trained up by the citizens were all in armor in the open streets, attending on their captains till past seven o'clock. At what time, being thoroughly wet by a great shower of rain, were sent home again for that day. On the next morrow, being the 27, the other three thousand citizens, householders, and subsidy men showed on the Miles End, where they trained all that day and other until the 4 of September and so ceased they training. And whatsoever had been foreseen and wisely prevented by the Queen and her nobility (whereof the commonalty were utterly ignorant for that time), a good peace within this realm has since followed, which may God long continue among us.

1599. September 21.   *Thomas Platter sees JULIUS CAESAR at the Globe* (see p. 27)

1600.   Friar's Weed

The 19 of January sixteen priests and four laymen were removed out of divers prisons in and about London and sent to the castle of Wisbeck in Cambridgeshire, whereof one was a Bishop of Ireland and another was a Franciscan friar of the rule of the Capuchins, which wore his friar's weed all the way as he went, a thing not seen in England many years before.

1600.   The Earl of Essex

The 5 of June the earl of Essex was called before the Lords of the Council at the Lord Keeper's where, for matters laid to his charge, he was suspended from use of divers offices till Her Majesty's pleasure to the contrary, to keep to his house as before. Whereat the people still murmured.

1600. August 4.   *AS YOU LIKE IT, HENRY V, and MUCH ADO ABOUT NOTHING registered*

1600. August 23.   *HENRY IV registered*

1600.   Soldiers

In the month of September soldiers prest in and about the city of London to the number of 350, and likewise out of divers shires, were sent towards Ireland, whereof divers running from their captains and colors were afterward taken and hanged for example to others.

1600. Jousts

The 17 of November there were most princely jousts performed at Whitehall in honor of the Queen's holy day by three earls, four lords, seven knights, and nine gentlemen, Her Majesty's Pensioners. At these jousts was so great an assembly of people as the like hath not been seen in that place before. There were also present sundry ambassadors, as, namely, from the French king, the king of Barbary and Fez, and the emperor of Russia.

1601. The Earl of Essex

Sunday, the 8 of February, about ten o'clock before noon, Robert Devereux, Earl of Essex, assisted by sundry noblemen and gentlemen, in warlike manner entered the city of London at the Temple Bar, crying for the Queen, till they came to Fenchurch Street, and there entered the house of Mr. Thomas Smith, one of the sheriffs of London, who finding himself not master of his own house (by means of the strength the earl brought with him) and being ignorant of his intent and purposes, conveyed himself out at a back gate to the mayor. Whereupon the earl with his troop turned into Grace Street. And there, perceiving himself with his assistants to be proclaimed traitors, also the citizens to be raised in arms against him, he with his followers wandering up and down the city, towards evening would have passed at Ludgate, which was closed against him so that he was forced to return to Queen Hithe and from thence by water to his house by the Strand, which he fortified. He understanding that great ordinance was brought to have beat it down, he yielded and was conveyed to the Tower about midnight.

1601. The Earl of Essex

The 19 of February, the earl of Essex and the earl of Southampton were both arraigned at Westminster and found guilty of high treason.

1601. The Earl of Essex

Ash Wednesday, the 25 of February, the earl of Essex was beheaded in the Tower between the hours of seven and eight o'clock in the morning, being present the earls of Hertford and Cumberland, the Lord Thomas Howard, Constable of the Tower for that time, and not passing sixty or seventy persons more. The hangman was beaten as he returned

thence so that the sheriffs of London were sent for to assist
and rescue him from such as would have murdered him.

1601. September 8.   *Burial of John Shakespeare, William's
father*

1602. January 18.   *MERRY WIVES OF WINDSOR registered*

1602. May 1.   *Shakespeare buys 107 acres of arable land in
old Stratford for 320 pounds*

1602.   Proclamation to Pull Down Houses
   The 22 of June, proclamation was published for the pulling
down of late-built houses and the avoiding of inmates in the
city of London, Westminster, and for the space of three miles
distant of both these cities. But little hurt was done, and
small effect followed more than an act of Parliament made
to that purpose. Those cities are still increased and pestered
with cottages and inmates to the great infection of them
both.

1602. July 26.   *HAMLET registered*

1603. February 7.   *TROILUS AND CRESSIDA registered*

1603.   Death of Queen Elizabeth I and Accession of James I
   In the month of March the Queen, lying at Richmond dan-
gerously sick, straight watches were kept in London with
warding at the gates, lanterns with lights hanged out all
night, at which news the people were sore perplexed.
   Thursday, the 24 of March, about 2 o'clock in the morning deceased Queen Elizabeth at her manor of Richmond in
Surrey, being then aged seventy years and had reigned forty-
four years, five months, and odd days. Whose corpse was
privily conveyed to Whitehall, and there remained till the 28
of April, and then buried at Westminster.
   The same day aforesaid the nobility and Privy Councilors
of Estate, with as great peace, prudence, and providence as
the heart of man could imagine, assembled themselves together and far beyond the general imagination of all men,
being a matter most remarkable, took speedy order as well
for the instant manifesting the Queen's death as in publishing
to the whole realm for their lasting comfort the true and
lawful successor. And about eleven o'clock the same Thurs-

day in the forenoon, which according to the computation of the Church of England is the last day of the year 1602, being accompanied with the Lord Mayor, aldermen and sheriffs of London, and very many others of most reverend and honorable quality, at the high cross in Cheapside proclaimed James the sixth of that name, King of Scotland, to be the right king of England, Scotland, France, and Ireland, Defender of the Faith, being lineally descended from Margaret, the eldest daughter to King Henry VII, by Elizabeth his wife, which was the eldest daughter of King Edward IV. The said Margaret was married to King James, the fourth of that name, King of Scotland, in the year of our redemption 1503, who had issue James V, who was the father to Mary, Queen of Scotland. And the said Mary was mother to James VI, now sole monarch of the whole Island of Great Britain and King of France and Ireland. This forenamed proclamation was most distinctly and audibly read by Sir Robert Cecil, principal secretary unto Queen Elizabeth. Also the Lords and Privy Councilors of Estate with great diligence sent speedily condign messengers unto His Majesty into Scotland, who manifested their whole proceeding with tender of their zealous love and duty and the people's universal joy and great desire to see their king. Which His Majesty most graciously accepted, approved all their proceedings, and returned them all princely thanks, authorizing the Lords and others late Privy Councilors of Estate to the Queen to persist as they had begun until he came personally unto them.

This change was very plausible, and well pleasing to the nobility and gentry and generally to all the commons of this realm, among whom the name of a king was then so strange as few could remember or had seen a king before except they were aged persons, considering that the government of the realm had continued near the space of 50 years under the reign of two queens, which is the far greater part of an old man's age. But tidings hereof being brought to the King in Scotland, he called a council to him, and taking order for settling all things in his realm of Scotland, he began his voyage towards England.

1603. March 17.   *The Lord Chamberlain's Men become the King's Men.*

1603. Preservation of Game

The 16 of May, proclamation was made to prohibit all

manner of persons from killing of deer and all wild fowl according to the tenor of divers statutes for preservation of the King's game of hunting and hawking.

1603. To Court When House Was Infected

The 1 of June there was one whipped through London for presuming to come to the Court having his house infected.

1603. Sir Walter Raleigh

The 4 of November the Lord Cobham, the Lord Grey of Wilton were conveyed from London Tower unto Winchester to be arraigned. And to that purpose the 19 of November were also conveyed from the Tower to Winchester Sir Walter Raleigh, Sir Griffin Markham, knights; George Brooke, brother to the Lord Cobham; Anthony Copley, gentleman; William Watson and William Clearke, priests. And the same day out of the gatehouse at Westminster went Sir Edward Parham, knight, and Brooksby Esquire of Leicestershire. They were all condemned of high treason save only Sir Edward Parham, who was acquitted by the jury. The 29 of November were executed the two priests and six days after was George Brooke hanged. And the 9 of December, Sir Griffin Markham and two barons, after they had been severally brought upon the scaffold in the castle of Winchester and had made their confessions and prepared themselves likewise severally to die, upon the sudden the King's warrant written with his own hand was there delivered to Sir Benjamin Tichborne, High Sheriff of Hampshire, commanding him to stay execution. These three and Sir Walter Raleigh were returned prisoners to the Tower the 15 of December.

1603. Plague

From the 23 of December 1602 unto the 22 of December 1603 there died of all diseases within London and the liberties 38,244, whereof of the plague, 30,578. And the next year following London was clear of that infection, and then were all the shires in England grievously visited. Note the work of God.

1604. The King's Entry into London

The 15 of March the King, Queen, and Prince, with the Lords spiritual and temporal, the gentry, and all officers as well of honor and arms as otherwise, passed most triumphantly from the Tower through the high streets of His Highness' Royal Chamber of London to Westminster. And all the way he went, even from his first entrance into the city until he came to Temple Bar, His Majesty was received and attended by the Lord Mayor in a robe of crimson velvet bearing a golden scepter in his hand; and the grave citizens of every company in their liveries standing in their stalls with great state, having their banners and bannerets displayed on the one side of the streets, and the other side very strongly railed to give free passage and keep back the violent pressing of the multitudes of people, which at that time exceeded as well in houses as otherwise. And at this time the former gates of pageants—seven in number—were all most sumptuously beautified and adorned with solemn orations, melodious harmony, and divers ingenious devices. The first pageant stood in Fenchurch Street, the second in Gracious Street, the third in Cornhill, the fourth at the east end of Cheapside. And at the east side of the high cross in Cheape was erected a low gallery, wherein stood aldermen, the chamberlain, the town clerk, with the council of the city, where Sir Henry Mountegue, Recorder of London, after his oration in the behalf of the Lord Mayor and the whole body of the city, presented three cups of gold; one for the King, the second for the Queen, and the third for the Prince. The fifth pageant stood at the west end of Cheape, the sixth in Fleet Street, and the seventh at Temple Bar. At this time all the chief conduits ran claret wine. There was another pageant erected in the Strand at the charges of the inhabitants thereabouts.

1604. Peace

The 5 of August arrived Don John de Velasco, Constable of Castile, being sent from Philip III, King of Spain, to take the oath of the King of England for ratification of the Articles of Peace, then agreed upon by certain English lords, authorized by the King and by former commissioners sent the last year from Spain and the archduke. Which said Don John with all the commissioners upon Sunday, the 19 of August, were more royally entertained and feasted at Whitehall. And the same forenoon the King in his own chapel was sworn unto the foresaid Articles, and in the afternoon the Peace was proclaimed with Spain and the archduke at the Court and in London. And this month the archduke won the strong town of Ostend in Flanders after it had been besieged with all extremity for three years and three months.

1604. November 1. *OTHELLO performed at Court*

1604. December 26. *MEASURE FOR MEASURE performed at Court*

1605. The Gunpowder Plot

Thomas Percy, Robert Catesby, Thomas Winter, and others, in the last year of the reign of Queen Elizabeth by the instigation of certain Jesuits practiced [plotted] with the king of Spain to send a well-furnished army upon England, promising him great aid to entertain them at their arrival at Milford Haven. And to that purpose the king promised to send them 50,000 pounds for levying of horse and foot and preparation of munitions in England to second them. But whilst this was in a manner concluded, Queen Elizabeth died, and the king of Spain, upon certain knowledge that King James established, dispatched his ambassadors and commissioners for England for confirmation of a lasting peace between them. Yet nevertheless the said Robert Catesby sent Thomas Winter again to the king of Spain to resolicit their former project, but the king answered him, "Your old queen is dead, with whom I had wars, and you have a new king with whom I have ever been in good peace and amity, and for continuance thereof I have sent my special commissioners, and until I see what will become thereof I will not hearken unto any other course whatsoever." When Winter returned and made this known unto Catesby, Percy, and the rest, then they began to cast about what they might do of themselves to advance the Roman Catholic religion. But first they would see the event [outcome] of the first Parliament, if that would mitigate any former laws, and try what good the conclusion of peace with Spain would do unto them before they attempted any further. But when they perceived that neither Parliament nor public peace sorted in any part to their desire, and that the peace concluded was rather a more ready means for the law to proceed against them than otherwise, because the peace concerned only the amity of Christian princes for the general good of Christendom without any particular or private respect, then Catesby told the rest he had a device in his head that should free them and the rest of the English Catholics from their oppressions. And when he had found out fit ministers for execution of his device, after they had taken oath and sacrament for secrecy, he told them he had devised the mean to undermine and blow up the Parliament house at the instant when the King, Queen, Prince, Peers, and Commons were all assembled. Which project they presently embraced, and forthwith Percy hired certain lodgings close to the Parliament house. And then they appointed miners who with great difficulty dug and undermined a part of the wall. But after awhile they understood that the vault right under the Parliament house was to be let to hire; then Guy Fawkes went and hired it. This Fawkes was of late a soldier in Flanders, and for this purpose was sent for, who by consent of the rest changed his name and was called John Johnson, Mr. Percy's man. After they had hired the vault they secretly conveyed into it thirty-six barrels of powder and covered them all over with billets [firewood] and fagots.

About ten days before the Parliament should begin an unknown party in the evening met a servant of the Lord Monteagle in the street and delivered to him a letter, charging him to give it speedily unto the lord, which he did. When his lord had read it and observed the dangerous contents, with a special caveat not to appear the first day of Parliament, he was amazed and forthwith delivered it to the earl of Salisbury, the King's principal secretary, a chief Councilor of Estate. When the earl had judiciously observed the strange phrase and tenor thereof, with the terrible threats therein against the whole State, he acquainted the Lord Chamberlain therewith. And then they conjoined unto them the Lord Admiral, the earls of Worcester and Northampton, who instantly consulted what was fittest to be done, omitting neither time, diligence, nor industry. All which not withstanding, they could not as yet find out the depth of this mystery and were therefore much troubled in mind because the appointed day of Parliament drew near, which was Tuesday, the 5 of November. Upon the Saturday before, the King being returned from hunting, the said lords acquainted His Highness with what had passed. And when His Majesty had well noted the strange contents of the letter, which purported the sudden ruin of the State, the King said, notwithstanding the slight regard which might be given to scattered libels, yet this was more quick and pithy than was usual in libels, and willed them to search in all places, as well those not daily frequented as of usual repair. And concerning any foreign disturbance or invasion, he well knew the present force and preparation of all Christian princes, and that whatsoever practice of treason was now in hand, it must be performed in some unsuspected place and by some homebred traitors. Thereupon new search was made in all places about the Court and the Parliament house, but could not as yet find anything worthy their labors. All which searches were performed with such silence and discretion that there rose no manner of suspicion either in Court or city.

The Lord Chamberlain, whose office it most concerned, never rested day nor night, and the night before the Parliament as Sir Thomas Knyvet with others scouted about the Parliament house, espied a fellow standing in a corner very suspiciously and asked him his name, what he was, and what he did there so late. Who answered very bluntly his name was John Johnson, Mr. Percy's man and keeper of his lodgings. Sir Thomas Knyvet continued still his search in all places thereabouts, and returning thither again found him lingering there still, searched him, and found under his cloak a close lantern, and a burning candle in it and about him other signs of suspicion that he stood not there for any good. Then the knight entered the vault where they found the powder covered with billets and fagots as aforesaid. And then the Lord Chamberlain caused the traitor to be bound, and being now about three o'clock in the morning, he went unto the King and with exceeding gladness told His Majesty the treason was discovered and prevented and the traitor in hold. The King desired to see Fawkes, who when he came before the King used like traitorous and audacious speeches as he did at first apprehension, affirming himself was the only man to perform this treason, saying it sore vexed him that the deed was not done. And for that time would not confess anything touching the rest of the conspirators, but that himself only and alone was the contriver and practicer of this treason.

Between five and six o'clock in the morning the Council gave order to the Lord Mayor of London to look to the city, and in very calm manner to set civil watch at the city gates, signifying therewithall that there was a plot of treason discovered and that the King would not go to Parliament that day. And the same day in the afternoon the manner of the treason was by proclamation made known unto the people, for joy whereof there was that night as many bonfires in and about London as the streets could permit, and the people gave humble and hearty thanks unto Almighty God for their King and country's right blessed escape.

Within three days after two other proclamations were made, signifying unto the people who were the chief conspirators, with commandment to apprehend Percy and Catesby and to take them alive if it were possible. Which said Percy and Catesby were gone to Holbach in Warwickshire to meet Winter, Grant, and others, where under pretense of a great hunting, they meant to raise the country and surprise the Lady Elizabeth from the Lord Harington, whom they meant to proclaim Queen and in whose name they meant to enter into arms, being persuaded that the King, the Prince, and Duke of York were by the time blown up in the Parliament house. But when they knew that their treason was known and prevented, and saw the King's forces round about the house so as they could not escape, Percy and Catesby very desperately issued forth and fighting back to back were both slain with one musket shot.

1605. June 5. *Stratford Marriage Register: "John Hall, gentleman, and Susanna Shakespeare"*

1605. July 24. *Shakespeare invests 440 pounds in the tithes of Stratford and neighborhood*

1606. Rumor

Saturday, the 22 of March, between six and seven o'clock in the forenoon, a rumor was suddenly spread throughout the Court and the city of London that for certain the King that morning was slain as he was hunting in Okeeing Park twenty miles from London. Which dreadful news still increased until nine o'clock, being seconded by infinite suggestions, by reason whereof it was generally received for truth. And thereupon the Court gates were kept shut; the Lord Mayor began to set guard at the city gates and to raise their trained soldiers; Sir William Wade, Lieutenant of the Tower, did the like with his hamlets within his liberties; and the Parliament was greatly amazed. But by eleven o'clock the joyful news of the King's good health was made known in London by proclamation, as it had been an hour before at the Court gate. Whereat the people began to revive their vexed spirits which until then were wondrously surcharged with heart's grief. Yea, men and women, old matrons and young virgins made exceeding great lamentation. This flying terror went three days journey into the country before it was fully suppressed.

1606. December 26. *KING LEAR "played before the King's Majesty at Whitehall upon St. Stephen's Night at Christmas last by His Majesty's Servants, playing usually at the Globe on the Bankside."*

1607. Flood

The 20 of January it pleased God to send a mighty west wind which continued sixteen hours, which brought in the sea. By reason whereof and of high spring tides, both which encountered the land waters. After, a great rain which caused the river of Severn, beginning as far as the mount in Cornwall, to overflow her banks all along on both sides up into Somersetshire and Gloucestershire. In some places the waters overflowed their banks three foot, in others places five foot, and some places seven foot. By means of which sudden inundation much people and cattle were drowned and divers churches and villages borne down and spoiled, and some utterly destroyed. And in Wales in divers places it did most harm in manner as aforesaid, the like whereof in England is not known to be mentioned in any chronicle.

1607. Enclosures

About the middle of May certain common persons assembled themselves in Northamptonshire, Warwickshire, and Leicestershire. They cut and broke down hedges, filled up ditches, and laid open all such enclosures of commons and other grounds as they found enclosed, which of ancient time had been open and employed to tillage. And the last of May they were straightly commanded by proclamation to surcease their disorder, but yet ceased not. Whereupon the sheriffs and justices had authority given them to suppress them by force. And after that the King sent certain noblemen and judges to punish the willful offenders according to law. And the 28 of June the King made another proclamation, signifying his great unwillingness to have proceeded against them either by martial law or civil justice if lenity or gentle admonition might any way have prevailed with them to desist from their turbulent rebellions and traitorous practice.

1607. Frost

The 8 of December began a hard frost and continued until

the 15 of the same and then thawed. And the 22 of December it began again to freeze violently so that divers persons went halfway over the Thames upon the ice. And the 30 of December at every ebb many people went quite over the Thames in divers places, and so continued from that day until the 3 of January. The people passed daily between London and the Bankside at every half ebb, for the flood removed the ice and forced the people daily to tread new paths, except only between Lambeth and the ferry at Westminster, the which by incessant treading became very firm and free passage until the great thaw. And from Sunday, the 10 of January, until the 15 of the same the frost grew extreme so as the ice became firm and removed not. Then all sorts of men, women, and children went boldly upon the ice in most parts; some shot at pricks, others bowled and danced, with other variable pastimes. By reason of which concourse of people there were many that set up booths and standings upon the ice, as fruit sellers, victualers that sold beer and wine, shoemakers, and a barber's tent, etc. Every of them had fire near their beings. The 15 of January it began somewhat to thaw and so continued four days all together. Yet nevertheless the great ice upon the Thames held firm and passable, and became somewhat smooth, like as in the last great frost in the year 1564, which till then were very craggy and uncertain. The 19 of January the frost began again, but not violently until Sunday, the 24 of January, and then held on until the 30 of the same. The 1 of February the ice began to break by little and little, and the next day in the afternoon all the ice was quite dissolved and clean gone so as no sign remained thereof. Many bridges were spoiled by this frost and much fowl perished, especially small birds which in many places were found frozen to death. This frost was more grievous in Ireland and France than in England.

1608. February 21. *Christened: "Elizabeth, daughter to John Hall, gentleman"*

1608. May 20. *PERICLES and ANTONY AND CLEOPATRA registered*

1608. September 9. *Burial of "Mary Shakespeare, widow"*

1609. May 20. *SONNETS registered*

1609.   Bear, Lion, and Horse

The 23 of June the King, Queen, and Prince, with divers great lords and many others, came to the Tower to make trial of the lions' single valor and to have the lions kill a great fierce bear which had killed a child. But the lions being tried by one and one at a time, and lastly by two together which were bred in that open yard where the bear was put loose for combat, yet would none of them assail him but fled from him and sought to return into their dens. After the first lion was put forth then was there a stone horse [stallion] put in to the bear and lion who, when he had gazed upon them a little, fell to grazing standing in the midst between them both. And whereas at first there was but two mastiffs let in who fought boldly with the lion, there was now six dogs let in who flew all upon the horse, being most in their sight at their first entrance, and would soon have worried the horse to death but that suddenly, even as the King wished, there entered in three stout bearwards who wondrous valiantly rescued the horse and brought away the dogs while the lion and bear stood staring upon them. And the 5 of July this bear, according to the King's express commandment, was baited to death with dogs upon a stage, and the mother of the murdered child had twenty pound given her out of the money given by the people to see the death of the bear.

1610.   Prince Henry at Barriers

The 6 of January at the Court of Whitehall in the presence of the King and Queen, and the ambassadors of Spain and Venice, and of all the peers and great ladies of the land, and of many thousand of others: there the Prince performed his first feats of arms, *viz.*, at barriers against all comers, being assisted only with six others, viz., the duke of Lenox, the earl of Arundel, the earl of Southampton, the Lord Hay, Sir Thomas Somerset, and Sir Richard Preston, who shortly after was created Lord Dingwell. Against these challengers came fifty-six brave defendants, consisting of earls, barons, knights, and esquires. Every challenger fought with eight several defendants two several combats at two several weapons, viz., at push of pike and with single sword. The Prince performed this challenge with wondrous skill and courage to the great joy and admiration of all the beholders, the Prince not being full sixteen years of age until the 19 of February. These feats of arms with sundry stately shows and ingenious devices began before ten o'clock at night and continued until three o'clock next morning, being Sunday. And that day the Prince feasted all the combatants at Saint James house, and then gave three rich prizes unto three of the best deservers, defendants, *viz.*, unto the earl of Montgomery, Mr. Thomas Darcy, son and heir to the Lord Darcy of Chichester, and unto Sir Robert Gordon.

1611. January 1.   Masque

Upon New Year's night the Prince of Wales being accompanied with twelve others, viz., two earls, three barons, five knights, and two esquires, they performed a very stately masque, in which there was an excellent scene, ingenious speeches, and rare songs, and with great variety of most delicate music.

1611. April 20.   *Simon Forman sees MACBETH at the Globe*

1611. May 15.   *Simon Forman sees THE WINTER'S TALE at the Globe*

1611.   *Simon Forman sees CYMBELINE at the Globe*

1612.   Lent

This year upon sundry apparent reasons of present ensuing famine, the fast of Lent was straightly commanded to be strictly kept and that all persons should utterly abstain from killing and eating of all manner of butcher's flesh, which course took good effect.

1613.   *Shakespeare buys a house in Blackfriars for 140 pounds*

1613.   Prodigies, Globe Burned

The 17 of April 1613 at Alington in Lancashire was born a maiden child having four legs, four arms, two bellies joined to one back, one head with two faces, the one before and the other behind. And this year likewise was great shipwreck by violent tempests. There happened also sundry inundations and strange accidents, and much damage done by fire in divers places. And upon Saint Peter's Day the Globe on the Bankside was burned.

1616. *Stratford Marriage Register: "Thomas Quiney to Judith Shakespeare"*

1616. April 25. *Stratford Burial Register: "William Shakespeare, gentleman"*

—John Stow and Edmund Howes, *The Abridgement of the English Chronicle* (1618). The editor has interpolated in italics the documented facts of Shakespeare's life.

A COURTIER'S LIFE IN COURT AND COUNTRY

Sir John Harington

I came home to Kelston and found my Mall, my children, and my cattle all well fed, well taught, and well beloved. 'Tis not so at court; ill breeding with ill feeding, and no love but that of the lusty god of gallantry, Asmodeus. I am to send good store of news from the country for Her Highness' entertainment.

The Queen stood up and bade me reach forth my arm to rest her thereon. Oh, what sweet burden to my next song! Petrarch shall eke out good matter for this business.

In August I was much troubled at sundry grievances from divers men in high states, but envy doth haunt many and breed jealousy. I will bid adieu to good company and leave suing and seeking at Court. For if I have no more friends nor better at Heaven's court than at this, I shall begin to think somewhat of brief damnation.

The Queen did once ask my wife, in merry sort, "how she kept my good will and love, which I did always maintain to be truly good towards her and my children?" My Mall in wise and discrete manner told Her Highness, "she had confidence in her husband's understanding and courage, well founded on her own stedfastness not to offend or thwart but to cherish and obey; hereby did she persuade her husband of her own affection and in so doing did command his." "Go to, go to mistress," said the Queen, "you are wisely bent I find. After such sort do I keep the good will of all my husbands, my good people. For if they did not rest assured of some special love toward them, they would not readily yield me such good obedience." This deserves noting as being both wise and pleasant.

It resteth with me in opinion that ambition thwarted in its

career doth speedily lead on to madness. Herein I am strengthened by what I learn in my lord of Essex, who shifteth from sorrow and repentance to rage and rebellion so suddenly as well proveth him devoid of good reason or right mind. In my last discourse he uttered strange words bordering on such strange designs that made me hasten forth and leave his presence. Thank heaven! I am safe at home, and if I go in such troubles again, I deserve the gallows for a meddling fool. His speeches of the Queen become no man who hath *mens sana in corpore sano*. He hath ill advisers, and much evil has sprung from this source. The Queen well knoweth how to humble the haughty spirit; the haughty spirit knoweth not how to yield, and the man's soul seemeth tossed to and fro like the waves of a troubled sea.

I hear much (by private means) of strange plots by Cobham, Grey, Raleigh, and others. I have no concerns of this sort, save that my man Ralph hath stolen two cheeses from my dairy house. I wish he were choked herewith! And yet the fellow hath five children. I will not sue him if he repenteth and amendeth.

I have not seen Her Highness save twice since Easter last, both of which times she spoke vehemently and with great wrath of her servant the Lady Mary Howard for as much as she had refused to bear her mantle at the hour Her Highness is wonted to air in the garden, and on small rebuke did vent such unseemly answer as did breed much choler in her mistress. Again, on another occasion she was not ready to carry the cup of grace during the dinner in the Privy Chamber nor was she attending at the hour of Her Majesty's going to prayer. All which doth now so disquiet Her Highness that she swore she would no more show her any countenance but out with all such ungracious flouting wenches because, forsooth, she hath much favor and marks of love from the young earl, which is not so pleasing to the Queen who doth still much exhort all her women to remain in virgin state as much as may be. I adventured to say as far as discretion did go in defense of our friend, and did urge much in behalf of youth and enticing love, which did often abate of right measures in fair ladies; and, moreover, related whatever might appease the Queen, touching the confession of her great kindness to her sister Jane before her marriage. All which did nothing to soothe Her Highness' anger, saying, "I have made her my servant and she will now make herself my mistress; but in good faith, William, she shall not and so tell her."

I am now setting forth for the country where I will read Petrarch, Ariosto, Horace, and such wise ones. I will make verses on the maidens and give my wine to the masters, but it shall be such as I do love and do love me. I do much delight to meet my good friends and discourse of getting rid of our foes. Each night do I spend, or much better part thereof, in counsel with the ancient examples of learning. I con over their histories, their poetry, their instructions, and thence glean my own proper conduct in matters both of merriment or discretion. Otherwise, my good Lord, I ne'er had overcome the rugged paths of Ariosto nor won the high palm of glory which you brought unto me (I venture to say it), namely, our late Queen's approbation, esteem, and reward. How my poetry may be relished in time to come, I will not hazard to say. Thus much I have lived to see and (in good sooth) feel too, that honest prose will never better a man's purse at Court. And had not my fortune been in *terra firma*, I might, even for my verses, have danced barefoot with Clio and her schoolfellows until I did sweat, and then have gotten nothing to slake my thirst but a pitcher of Helicon's well. E'en let the beardless god Apollo dip his own chin in such drink, a hair of my face shall have better entertainment.

Kelston, 1603. Here now will I rest my troubled mind and tend my sheep like an Arcadian swain that hath lost his fair mistress. For, in sooth, I have lost the best and fairest love that ever shepherd knew, even my gracious Queen. And sith my good mistress is gone, I shall not hastily put forth for a new master.

I came here a day or two before the Danish king came and from the day he did come until this hour I have been well-nigh overwhelmed with carousal and sports of all kinds. The sports began each day in such manner and such sort as well-nigh persuaded me of Mahomet's paradise. We had women, and indeed wine too, of such plenty as would have astonished each sober beholder. Our feasts were magnificent and the two royal guests did most lovingly embrace each other at table. I think the Dane hath strangely wrought on our good English nobles, for those whom I never could get to taste good liquor now follow the fashion and wallow in beastly delights. The ladies abandon their sobriety and are seen to roll about in intoxication. In good sooth, the Parliament did kindly to provide His Majesty so seasonably with money, for there hath been no lack of good living: shows, sights, and banquetings from morn to eve.

One day a great feast was held, and after dinner the representation of Solomon's Temple and the coming of the Queen of Sheba was made or (as I may better say) was meant to have been made, before their majesties by device of the earl of Salisbury and others. But alas! as all earthly things do fail to poor mortals in enjoyment, so did prove our presentment hereof. The lady who did play the Queen's part did carry most precious gifts to both their majesties but, forgetting the steps arising to the canopy, overset her caskets into His Danish Majesty's lap and fell at his feet, though I rather think it was in his face. Much was the hurry and confusion; cloths and napkins were at hand to make all clean. His Majesty then got up and would dance with the Queen of Sheba, but he fell down and humbled himself before her and was carried to an inner chamber and laid on a bed of state, which was not a little defiled with the presents of the Queen which had been bestowed on his garments, such as wine, cream, jelly, beverage, cakes, spices, and other good matters. The entertainment and show went forward and most of the presenters went backward or fell down, wine did so occupy their upper chambers. Now did appear in rich dress Hope, Faith, and Charity. Hope did assay to speak but wine rendered her endeavors so feeble that she withdrew and hoped the King would excuse her brevity. Faith then was all alone, for I am certain she was not joined with good works, and left the Court in a staggering condition. Charity came to the King's feet and seemed to cover the multitude of sins her sisters had committed. In some sort she made obeisance and brought gifts, but said she would return home again as there was no gift which heaven had not already given His Majesty. She then returned to Hope and Faith, who were both sick and spewing in the lower hall. Next came Victory in bright armor and presented a rich sword to the King, who did not accept it but put it by with his hand, and by a strange medley of versification did endeavor to make suit to the King. But Victory did not triumph long, for after much lamentable utterance she was led away like a silly captive and laid to sleep in the outer steps of the antechamber. Now did Peace make entry and strive to get foremost to the King, but I grieve to tell how great wrath she did discover unto those of her attendants and, much the contrary to her semblance, most rudely made war with her olive branch and laid on the pates of those who opposed her coming.

I have much marveled at these strange pageantries, and they do bring to my remembrance what passed of this sort in our Queen's days, of which I was sometime an humble presenter and assistant. But I ne'er did see such lack of good order, discretion, and sobriety as I have now done. I have passed much time in seeing the royal sports of hunting and hawking, where the manners were such as made me devise the beasts were pursuing the sober creation, and not man in quest of exercise or food. I will now, in good sooth, declare to you who will not blab, that the gunpowder fright is got out of all our heads and we are going on hereabouts as if the devil was contriving that every man should blow up himself by wild riot, excess, and devastation of time and temperance. The great ladies do go well masked, and indeed it be the only show of their modesty to conceal their countenance, but, alack, they meet with such countenance to uphold their strange doings that I marvel not at aught that happens.

Lord Thomas Howard to Sir John Harington

If you have good will and good health to perform what I shall commend, you may set forward for Court whenever it suiteth your own convenience. The King hath often enquired after you and would readily see and converse again with the "merry blade," as he hath oft called you since you were here. I will now premise certain things to be observed by you toward well gaining our Prince's good affection. He doth wondrously covet learned discourse, of which you can furnish out ample means. He doth admire good fashion in clothes, I pray you give good heed hereunto. Strange devices oft come into man's conceit, someone regardeth the endowments of the inward sort, wit, valor, or virtue; and another hath, perchance, special affection towards outward things, clothes, deportment, and good countenance. I would wish you to be well trimmed; get a new jerkin well bordered and not too short, the King saith he liketh a flowing garment. Be sure it be not all of one sort but diversely colored, the collar falling somewhat down, and your ruff well stiffened and bushy. We have lately had many gallants who failed in their suits for want of due observance of these matters. The King is nicely heedful of such points and dwelleth on good looks and handsome accouterments. Eighteen servants were lately discharged and many more will be discarded, who are not to his liking in these matters. I wish you to follow my directions as I wish you to gain all you desire. Robert Carr is now most likely to win the Prince's affection and doth it wondrously in a little time. The Prince leaneth on his arm, pinches his cheek, smooths his ruffled garment and, when he looketh at Carr, directeth discourse to divers others. This young man doth much study all art and device. He hath changed his tailors and tiremen many times, and all to please the Prince, who laugheth at the long-grown fashion of our young courtiers and wisheth for change every day. You must see Carr before you go to the King, as he was with him a boy in Scotland and knoweth his taste and what pleaseth him. In your discourse you must not dwell too long on any one subject and touch but lightly on religion. Do not of yourself say, "This is good or bad," but, "If it were Your Majesty's good opinion, I myself should think so and so." Ask no more questions than what may serve to know the Prince's thought. In private discourse the King seldom speaketh of any man's temper, discretion, or good virtues, so meddle not at all but find out a clue to guide you to the heart and most delightful subject of his mind. I will advise one thing, the roan jennet whereon the King rideth every day must not be forgotten to be praised, and the good furniture above all, which lost a great man much notice the other day. A noble did come in suit of a place and saw the King mounting the roan; delivered his petition, which was heeded and read, but no answer was given. The noble departed and came to Court the next day and got no answer again. The Lord Treasurer was then pressed to move the King's pleasure touching the petition. When the King was asked for answer thereto, he said in some wrath, "Shall a king give heed to a dirty paper when a beggar noteth not his gilt stirrups?" Now it fell out that the King had new furniture when the noble saw him in the courtyard but he was overcharged with confusion and passed by admiring the dressing of the horse. Thus, good knight, our noble failed in his suit. I could relate and offer some other remarks on these matters but silence and discretion should be linked together like dog and bitch, for of them is gendered security. I am certain it proveth so at this place. You have lived to see the trim of old times and what passed in the

Queen's days. These things are no more the same. Your
Queen did talk of her subjects' love and good affections, and
in good truth she aimed well. Our King talketh of his subjects' fear and subjection, and herein I think he doth well
too, as long as it holdeth good. Carr hath all favors, as I told
you before. The King teacheth him Latin every morning, and
I think someone should teach him English too, for as he is a
Scottish lad he hath much need of better language. The King
doth much covet his presence; the ladies too are not behind
hand in their admiration, for I tell you, good knight, this
fellow is straight-limbed, well-favored, strong-shouldered, and
smooth-faced, with some sort of cunning and show of modesty, though, God wot, he well knoweth when to show his
impudence. You are not young, you are not handsome, you
are not finely, and yet will you come to Court and think to
be well-favored? Why, I say again, good knight, that your
learning may somewhat prove worthy hereunto; your Latin
and your Greek, your Italian, your Spanish tongues, your wit
and discretion may be well looked unto for a while as
strangers at such a place, but these are not the things men
live by nowadays. Will you say the moon shineth all the
summer, that the stars are bright jewels fit for Carr's ears,
that the roan jennet surpasseth Bucephalus and is worthy to
be bestridden by Alexander, that his eyes are fire, his tail is
Berenice's locks, and a few more such fancies worthy your
noticing? Your lady is virtuous and somewhat of a good
housewife, has lived in a court in her time, and I believe you
may venture her forth again. But I know those would not
quietly rest were Carr to leer on their wives as some do
perceive, yea, and like it well too they should be so noticed. If
any mischance be to be wished, 'tis breaking a leg in the
King's presence, for this fellow owes all his favor to that
bout. I think he hath better reason to speak well of his own
horse than the King's roan jennet. We are almost worn out in
our endeavors to keep pace with this fellow in his duty and
labor to gain favor, but all in vain. Where it endeth I cannot
guess, but honors are talked of speedily for him. I trust this
by my own son that no danger may happen from our free-
doms. If you come here, God speed your ploughing at the
Court; I know you do it rarely at home. So adieu, my good
knight, and I will always write me

Your truly loving old friend,
T. HOWARD

—Thomas Park, ed., *Nugae Antiquae* (1804).

GOSSIP, RUMOR, AND FACT (1600–1615)

DISGUISE

1600. December 22. The French king kept the solemnity
of his marriage at Lyons the 23 of the last, and saw not the
great duchess nor the duchess of Mantua, who went into
Lorraine another way, because they espied his humor that he
lingered at the camp for the nonce only to avoid charges and
gave them no presents. His misery and ambition is much
misliked of all, and the clergy will in no wise be well
persuaded of him. He was so desirous and hasty to see his
Queen that he went disguised as a private gentleman with
others (that he had appointed) to see her dine, and caused a
letter from himself to be delivered her in his presence (unknown yet), which she received with such humbleness that it
was praised of everybody and pleased him not a little. He
could not tarry the solemnity but went that night to her
unknown, and one of his minions demanding what he meant,
told him he went to do that he never did in his life—to lie
that night with an honest woman.

CHALLENGE ALL COMERS

1601. February 3. We have daily here many new experi-
ments made, as the last week one came hopping from Char-
ing Cross into Paul's bound in a sack; and this morning
another carried up a horse and rode upon him on the top of
Paul's steeple; with divers other such wagers, and among the
rest Green, that was lately your cousin Lytton's man, hath set
up a printed paper and doth challenge all comers at wrest-
ling.

SUICIDE FOR LOVE

1601. July 8. One Sir ... Radney of Somersetshire (neph-
ew to Sir Edward Dyer) that went out of his wits about
Christmas for Mrs. Pranell (lately married to the earl of

Hertford), coming by the place where she dwells, cut his own throat as an earnest of his love.

RECRUITING SOLDIERS

1602. April 26. Sir Francis Vere is here soliciting for men; he sent his forerunners before him, who came down into the country with the Council's letters to take up voluntaries, but in most places with drumming and all they could do, they scant got two men in three days. So that seeing it will not fadge [succeed] that way, it is said we shall have a press and send him away with three thousand men.

FALL OF THE GREAT

1602. November 4. Now coming so fresh from reading your letters and discourses of Byron, I cannot go on without touching a point or two *en passant*. Let the French twattle what they list of his dying *en soldat*, I cannot perceive by aught I have seen or heard but that he died very timorously and childishly, which shows that his valor was rather a French fury than true fortitude. Another observation came to my remembrance in reading his process: of three strange disasters, befallen three great men, in three neighbor countries, in three years successively (this, you see, passes *tres sequuntur tria*); and all their cases so intricate—especially the two strangers—and their persons and services so magnified that a great part of the world rests unsatisfied in their deaths and will not be persuaded against their deserts by any understandings, but *mundus vult decipi* and so let it go.

APPARITION

1602. November 4. We have much talk of an apparition in Wales not far from Chester, of great troops of horse and foot in battle array, seen upon a mountain by sixteen or eighteen persons of credit; but when they came to discover what they were, suddenly vanished.

EXORCISM

1602. November 4. The young Lady North is brought to bed of a son, and the common report is that Dr. Dee hath delivered the Lady Sandys of a devil or of some other strange possession.

RUMOR

1602. November 19. Yesterday here was a running report that the French king was slain by a friar. It was very current and took fire like a train or a squib. I never knew any news spread so suddenly, for in less than three hours it was all over the town, but this day it cools again, and we cannot learn how it should rise. Though at the hottest I did not thoroughly believe it, yet did it more appall me than any public news I heard these seven years.

OMINOUS WEATHER

1603. July 10. Mr. Winwood was married on Tuesday with much thunder, lightning, and rain; the ominous weather and dismal day put together might have made a superstitious man startle but he turned all to the best, and so may it prove!

RANK AND PUNISHMENT

1605. October 24. Yesterday a goldsmith in Cheapside was fined in the Star Chamber for arresting the countess of Rutland upon an execution, and it was thoroughly argued how far noble men and women are privileged in their persons from arrests. The week before there was a purveyor censured, for misdemeanor in his place, to ride with his face to the horse tail, wherein one of his judges dissented from the rest and would rather have it upon an ass, and that for two reasons: first, it would be more wonderment and gather more boys about him; and secondly the slow pace of the ass would prolong his punishment.

TRIAL BY COMBAT

1611. December 4. There was an appeal brought this term in the King's Bench by young Egerton against one Robinson, that was second to his brother when he was slain by Morgan upon weak and malicious surmises. Morgan was brought to arraignment before, and avoided the indictment by skill in law; and though this man might easily have found some such trick (the principal not being tried), yet he took such indignation that his own kinsman should use him thus, that openly at the bar he protested that as long as he could die with his sword in his hand he would never put his life upon a lawyer's mercenary tongue, and then challenge the combat of him, which could not be denied him in law, and so was granted to be tried in Easter term.

MOLL CUTPURSE

1612. February 12. The other week a young minion of Sir Pexall Brockhurst did penance at Paul's Cross, whom he had entertained and abused since she was twelve years old; and this last Sunday Moll Cutpurse, a notorious baggage (that used to go in man's apparel and challenged the field of divers gallants), was brought to the same place, where she wept bitterly and seemed very penitent; but it is since doubted she was maudlin drunk, being discovered to have tippled of three quarts of sack before she came to her penance. She had the daintiest preacher or ghostly father that ever I saw in pulpit, one Ratcliffe of Brasenose in Oxford, a likelier man to have led the revels in some Inn of Court than to be where he was; but the best is he did extreme badly, and so wearied the audience that the best part went away and the rest tarried rather to hear Moll Cutpurse than him.

LAST HERETIC BURNED

1612. February 26. The same day one Legate, an Arian, being sentenced and excommunicated in the consistory, was delivered over to the sheriffs of London; but we hear not yet of his execution. He hath been long forborne and mildly dealt withal, but continuing obstinate and holding thirteen heretical positions against the divinity of our Savior Christ the King, would have the bishops proceed against him; and though some lawyers are of opinion that we have no law to execute heretics, and that whatsoever was done in that kind in Queen Elizabeth's time was done *de facto* and not *de jure*, yet the King says if he be so desperate to deny Christ to be God he will adventure to burn him with a good conscience.

LONG WEDDED, NOT BEDDED

1612. November 3. The Lord Walden, that hath been now a good while wedded to the Lord of Dunbar's daughter, was not bedded with her till the last week, and that by special commandment.

DISGUISE

1612. November 12. The Lady Elizabeth is much afflicted with this loss [Prince Henry], and not without good cause, for he did extraordinarily affect her, and during his sickness inquired still after her, and the last words he spake in good sense (they say) were, "Where is my dear sister?" She was as desirous to visit him, and went once or twice in the evening disguised for the purpose, but could not be admitted because his disease was doubted to be contagious.

INSANE GHOST

1612. November 19. The same day sevennight he [Prince Henry] died, there fell out a very ridiculous accident. A very handsome young fellow, much about his age and not altogether unlike him, came stark naked to St. James whiles they were at supper, saying he was the Prince's ghost come from heaven with a message to the King; but by no manner of examination or threatening could they get any more out of him, or who set him awork. Some say he is simple, others mad. He belongs to one of the Chancery. All the penance they gave him was two or three lashes, (which he endured as it seemed without sense) and keeping him naked as he was all night and the next day in the porter's lodge, where thousands came to see him. The King sent to have him dismissed without more ado or inquiry.

HORN-SICKNESS

1613. March 25. Langley, our townclerk, is lately dead of the horn-sickness, for taking his wife tardy with one of his men. It drove him into such a distemper of melancholy and frenzy that within four or five days made an end of him.

ELECTION OR SUCCESSION

1613. March 25. The King is very angry and out of love with our Cambridge men for their questions at the Palsgrave's being there, especially whether *electio* or *succes-*

sio were to be preferred in kingdoms, and is out of patience that it should be so much as argued in schools.

LIBEL

1613. May 13. There was a little box sealed up cast in the court not long since with this superscription, "The life and death of the late Lord Treasurer, to be delivered to the King's own hands," as they say it was; but upon the view there was other scandalous matter and it proved a shameless libel.

PRIVATE QUARRELS

1613. September 6. Though there be in show a settled peace in these parts of the world, yet the many private quarrels among the great ones prognosticate troubled humors, which may breed dangerous diseases if they be not purged and prevented.

SEX

1613. September 6. The main blow for the divorce [of Lady Essex] will be given the 18 of this month when the commissioners are to give up their opinions. It is very likely to go forward, which in some sort were pity, as well for the example and consequence as for that I have heard from some that may know, that all this business rises from willfulness and vain idle vows on both sides. When as upon her forwardness and untowardness at their first meetings or coming together, he grew to that impatience that he prayed God to damn him if ever he offered her any such kindness till she called for it, and she in the like heat wished to be damned if ever she did. Perhaps I am overbold with you in this plain manner of dealing, but if you knew what indecent words and deeds have passed in the course of this suit, you would excuse it and think me modest. For what would you say if you should hear a churchman in open audience demand of him and desire to be resolved, whether he had affection, erection, application, penetration, ejaculation, with a great deal of amplification upon every one of these points?

THE WHIRLIGIG OF COURT

1614. January 5. This is what I can certify you that passes here [at Court] *de facto,* but what may be or shall be or will be, he were a cunning man could divine; for here is such discoursing, such working, plotting, and supplanting that what stands right today is awry tomorrow, and every day brings new alterations, so that they are driven to hammer and square out new projects, which not succeeding *mutant quadrata rotundis,* and turn the bias another way. They say it is a pleasure for a man not interested to look upon gamesters, but in good faith I am so wearied with these varieties of discourse that I think it a miserable distraction and torture both of body and of mind.

PLAYS AT COURT

1615. January 5. I never knew any Christmas bring forth less variety of occurence. The world is in motion round about us, and yet we have no news; here at home we pass on with a slow pace, and nothing fallen out worth the remembrance. They have plays at court every night, both holy days and working days, wherein they show great patience, being for the most part such poor stuff that instead of delight they send the auditory away with discontent. Indeed our poets' brains and invention are grown very dry insomuch that of five new plays there is not one pleases, and therefore they are driven to furbish over their old, which stand them in best stead and bring them most profit. Tomorrow night there is a masque at court, but the common voice and preparations promise so little that it breeds no great expectation.

—John Chamberlain, *The Letters of John Chamberlain,* Vol. 1, ed. by Norman Egbert McClure (Philadelphia, 1939), pp. 112-567 passim.

PART III

Some Ideas and Values

GOD (1594)

Our God is one, or rather very Oneness and mere unity, having nothing but itself in itself, and not consisting, as all things do besides God, of many things. In which essential Unity of God a Trinity personal nevertheless subsisteth, after a manner far exceeding the possibility of man's conceit. The works which outwardly are of God, they are in such sort of him being one that each Person hath in them somewhat peculiar and proper. For being Three, and they all subsisting in the essence of one Deity, from the Father, by the Son, through the Spirit all things are. That which the Son doth hear of the Father, and which the Spirit doth receive of the Father and the Son, the same we have at the hands of the Spirit as being the last and therefore the nearest unto us in order, although in power the same with the second and the first.

—Richard Hooker, *Of the Laws of Ecclesiastical Polity*, 1. 2. 2.

"TAKE BUT DEGREE AWAY, UNTUNE THAT STRING" (1547)

Almighty God hath created and appointed all things, in heaven, earth and waters, in a most excellent and perfect order. In heaven he hath appointed distinct orders and states of archangels and angels. In the earth he hath assigned kings, princes, with other governors under them, all in good and necessary order. The water above is kept and raineth down in due time and season. The sun, moon, stars, rainbow, thunder, lightning, clouds, and all birds of the air, do keep their order. The earth, trees, seeds, plants, herbs, and corn, grass and all manner of beasts keep them in their order. All the parts of the whole year, as winter, summer, months, nights and days, continue in their order. All kinds of fishes in the sea, rivers and waters, with all fountains, springs, yea, the seas themselves keep their comely course and order.

And man himself hath also all his parts, both within and without, as soul, heart, mind, memory, understanding, reason, speech, with all and singular corporal members of his body, in a profitable, necessary and pleasant order. Every degree of people, in their vocation, calling and office, hath appointed to them their duty and order. Some are in high degree, some in low, some kings and princes, some inferiors and subjects, priests and laymen, masters and servants, fathers and children, husbands and wives, rich and poor, and every one hath need of other, so that in all things is to be lauded and praised the goodly order of God, without the which no house, no city, no commonwealth can continue and endure. For where there is no right order, there reigneth all abuse, carnal liberty, enormity, sin and Babylonical confusion. Take away kings, princes, rulers, magistrates, judges, and such states of God's order, no man shall ride or go by the highway unrobbed, no man shall sleep in his own house or bed unkilled, no man shall keep his wife, children, and possesions in quietness. All things shall be common, and there must needs follow all mischief and utter destruction, both of souls, bodies, goods and commonwealths.

—Sermon of Obedience

REBELLION (1598?)

ALL: Peace, peace!

MORE: Look, what you do offend you cry upon:
That is, the peace. Not one of you here present,
Had there such fellows lived when you were babes,
That could have topped the peace as now you would.

The peace wherein you have till now grown up
Had been ta'en from you, and the bloody times
Could not have brought you to the state of men.
Alas, poor things, what is it you have got
Although we grant you get the thing you seek?

BETTS: Marry, the removing of strangers, which cannot choose but much advantage the poor handicrafts of the city.

MORE: Grant them removed, and grant that this your noise
Hath chid down all the majesty of England;
Imagine that you see the wretched strangers,
Their babies at their backs, and their poor luggage,
Plodding to th' ports and coasts for transportation,
And that you sit as kings in your desires,
Authority quite silenced by your brawl,
And you in ruff of your opinions clothed,
What had you got? I'll tell you: you had taught
How insolence and strong hand should prevail,
How order should be quelled, and by this pattern
Not one of you should live an aged man:
For other ruffians, as their fancies wrought,
With self-same hand, self reasons, and self right,
Would shark on you, and men, like ravenous fishes,
Would feed on one another.

DOLL: Before God, that's as true as the gospel.

LINCOLN: Nay, this is a sound fellow, I tell you. Let's mark him.

MORE: Let me set up before your thoughts, good friends,
One supposition which, if you will mark,
You shall perceive how horrible a shape
Your innovation bears. First, 'tis a sin
Which oft the apostle did forewarn us of,
Urging obedience to authority;
And 'twere no error if I told you all
You were in arms 'gainst God.

ALL: Marry, God forbid that!

MORE: Nay, certainly you are;
For to the King God hath his office lent
Of dread, of justice, power, and command,
Hath bid him rule and willed you to obey;
And to add ampler majesty to this,
He hath not only lent the King his figure,
His throne and sword, but given him His own name,
Calls him a God on earth. What do you then,
Rising 'gainst him that God himself installs,
But rise 'gainst God? What do you to your souls
In doing this, oh desparate as you are?
Wash your foul minds with tears; and those same hands
That you, like rebels, lift against the peace,
Lift up for peace; and your unreverent knees,
Make them your feet to kneel to be forgiven.
Tell me but this: what rebel captain,
As mutinies are incident, by his name
Can still the rout? Who will obey a traitor?
Or how can well that proclamation sound
When there is no addition but a rebel
To qualify a rebel? You'll put down strangers,
Kill them, cut their throats, possess their houses,
And lead the majesty of law in lyam
To slip him like a hound. Say now the King,
As he is clement if the offender mourn,
Should so much come too short of your great trespass
As but to banish you, whither would you go?
What country, by the nature of your error,
Should give you harbor? Go you to France or Flanders,
To any German province, Spain or Portugal,
Nay, anywhere that not adheres to England,
Why, you must needs be strangers. Would you be pleased
To find a nation of such barbarous temper
That, breaking out in hideous violence,
Would not afford you an abode on earth,
Whet their detested knives against your throats,
Spurn you like dogs, and like as if that God
Owed not nor made not you, nor that the elements
Were not all appropriate to your comforts,
But chartered unto them? What would you think
To be thus used? This is the strangers' case,
And this your momtanish inhumanity.

ALL: Faith, he says true. Let's us do as we may be done by.

LINCOLN: We'll be ruled by you, Mr. More, if you'll stand our friend to procure our pardon.

MORE: Submit you to these noble gentlemen,
Entreat their mediation to the King,
Give up yourself to form, obey the magistrate,
And there's no doubt but mercy may be found
If you so seek it.

—William Shakespeare (?), *Sir Thomas More.*

BLASPHEMY (1590)

Nature that framed us of four elements,
Warring within our breasts for regiment,
Doth teach us all to have aspiring minds.
Our souls, whose faculties can comprehend
The wonderous architecture of the world
And measure every wandering planet's course,
Still climbing after knowledge infinite,
And always moving as the restless spheres,
Wills us to wear ourselves and never rest
Until we reach the ripest fruit of all,
That perfect bliss and sole felicity,
The sweet fruition of an earthly[1] crown.

—Christopher Marlowe, *1 Tamburlaine,* 2. 7. 18-29.

[1] Read *heavenly* and the passage is eloquent orthodoxy.

"THE WHEEL IS COME FULL CIRCLE" (1592)

Base Fortune, now I see that in thy wheel
There is a point, to which when men aspire,
They tumble headlong down. That point I touched,
And, seeing there was no place to mount up higher,
Why should I grieve at my declining fall?
Farewell fair Queen, weep not for Mortimer
That scorns the world and as a traveller
Goes to discover countries yet unknown.

—Christopher Marlowe, *Edward II*, 5. 6. 58–65.

"I AM DETERMINED TO PROVE A VILLAIN"
(1601)

Some, first, are perfectly incorporated with evil; they reason
themselves into it. Their resolutions and the whole bent of
their wills are fixed entirely in its interests, or else long
custom hath got such a perfect mastery over them that they
cannot disengage themselves. These miserable wretches are
utterly abandoned; their very understanding is vitiated, sees,
consents to, and approves the evil. And this usually is the
case when vice and debauchery meets with a strong and
vigorous mind, and hath taken such deep root in it that it
comes at last to be naturalized and of a piece with it. All the
faculties are tinctured, it is corrupted throughout, and vice so
closely interwoven as to become a part of its temper and
constitution.

Others, secondly, have their intervals of folly only. They

are wicked now and then by fits, just as any violent gush of a temptation disturbs or puts them out of their course, or some impetuous passion drives them headlong upon the rocks. So that these men are surprised and carried away forcibly by a current too strong for them to stem.

The third sort are betwixt these two extremes. They have a right notion of vice considered in itself, and when they reflect upon their fault abstractedly do severely accuse and condemn themselves for it. And thus they differ from the first sort, who are advanced even to the desperate degree of a good liking of wickedness. But then they have not the violence or surprise of passions or temptations to qualify and extenuate their crime, and in this respect they differ from the second sort, too. But these men go to work in cold blood and with great deliberation. They weigh circumstances and drive a bargain, as it were; observe well the heinousness of the sin, and then put the pleasure or profit it brings into the contrary scale. And thus they barter away their souls, and are content to be wicked for a certain price and for such as they think a valuable consideration.

—Pierre Charron, *Of Wisdom.*

"THE HUMOROUS MAN":

True (Malvolio) and Affected (Osric) Humor (1601)

MITIS. In faith this humour will come ill to some,
You will be thought to be too peremptory.
ASPER. This humour? good! and why this humour,
Mitis?
Nay, do not turn, but answer.
MITIS. Answer what?
ASPER. I will not stir your patience, pardon me,
I urged it for some reasons, and the rather

To give these ignorant well-spoken days
Some taste of their abuse of this word humour.
  COR. O, do not let your purpose fall, good Asper;
It cannot but arrive most acceptable,
Chiefly to such as have the happiness
Daily to see how the poor innocent word
Is rack'd and tortured.
  MITIS. Ay, I pray you proceed.
  ASPER. Ha, what? What is't?
  COR. For the abuse of humour.
  ASPER. O, I crave pardon, I had lost my thoughts.
Why, humour, as 'tis *ens*, we thus define it,
To be a quality of air, or water,
And in itself holds these two properties,
Moisture and fluxure: as, for demonstration,
Pour water on this floor, 'twill wet and run:
Likewise the air, forced through a horn or trumpet,
Flows instantly away, and leaves behind
A kind of dew; and hence we do conclude,
That whatsoe'er hath fluxure and humidity,
As wanting power to contain itself,
Is humour. So in every human body,
The choler, melancholy, phlegm, and blood,
By reason that they flow continually
In some one part, and are not continent,
Receive the name of humours. Now thus far
It may, by metaphor, apply itself
Unto the general disposition:
As when some one peculiar quality
Doth so possess a man, that it doth draw
All his affects, his spirits, and his powers,
In their confluctions, all to run one way,
This may be truly said to be a humour.
But that a rook, by wearing a pied feather,
The cable hatband, or the three-piled ruff,
A yard of shoe-tye, or the Switzer's knot
On his French garters, should affect a humour!
O, it is more than most ridiculous.
  COR. He speaks pure truth; now if an idiot
Have but an apish or fantastic strain,
It is his humour.
  ASPER. Well, I will scourge those apes,
And to these courteous eyes oppose a mirror,

As large as is the stage whereon we act;
Where they shall see the time's deformity
Anatomized in every nerve, and sinew,
With constant courage, and contempt of fear.

—Ben Jonson, *Every Man Out of His Humour.*

"MY TABLES,—MEET IT IS I SET IT DOWN"
(1600)

Memorable Lines (Sententiae) *from a Book of Quotations,
Arranged under such Headings as "God" and "Death."*

God will control when mortal men have done.

Heaven works our fall, but yet the fault is ours.

In vain do men contend against the stars.

When *hope* and hap, when health and wealth is highest,
Then woe and wrack, disease and need is nighest.

They *love* indeed that dare not say they love.

Whoever loved that loved not at first sight?

Chastity is bright honor's glorious crown.

To play the fool well is good sign of *wit.*

Divided *kingdoms* make divided hearts.

Sleepless suspicion, pale distrust, cold fear
Always with princes company doth bear.

Kingdoms are fortune's fatal tennis balls.

Law with extremity is extreme wrong.

Bloodshed by bloodshed still is nourished. [Of *war*]

All *men* to some peculiar [special] vice incline.

Man is but mere calamity itself.

What cannot *women* do that know their power?

Usurping rule is held by *tyranny*.

Gold, that makes all men false, is true itself.

Death is far sweeter than the *fear* of death.

Whiles timorous knowledge stands considering,
Audacious ignorance performs the deed.

Fortune oft hurts when most she seems to help.

A chance may win what by mischance was lost.

Unlooked-for things do happen soonest of all.

The cards once dealt, it boots not ask, Why so?

It lies not in our power to love or hate,
For will in us is overruled by *fate*.

What happens me this day may you the next.

Too much preciseness savors of *self-love*.

Choose few friends, try them, *flatterers* speak fair.

We see the *good* but yet we choose the ill.

Nothing is *evil* that is necessary.

Too many *great* one kingdom cannot hold.

Times change, and we in them do alter still.

So some men *live* they care not how they live.

To *die* is all as common as to live.

Near death he stands that stands too near a crown.

—Bodenham's *Belvedere, or The Garden of the Muses.*

FROM THE *ESSAYS* (1625)

Francis Bacon

OF TRUTH

A mixture of a lie doth ever add pleasure. Doth any man doubt that if there were taken out of men's minds vain opinions, flattering hopes, false valuations, imaginations as one would, and the like, but it would leave the minds of a number of men poor shrunken things, full of melancholy and indisposition, and unpleasing to themselves?

OF DEATH

It is worthy the observing that there is no passion in the mind of man so weak but it mates and masters the fear of death. And therefore death is no such terrible enemy when a man hath so many attendants about him that can win the combat of him. Revenge triumphs over death, love slights it, honor aspireth to it, grief flieth to it, fear pre-occupateth it.

OF REVENGE

Revenge is a kind of wild justice.

OF LOVE

The stage is more beholding to love than the life of man. For as to the stage, love is ever matter of comedies, and now and then, of tragedies; but in life it doth much mischief, sometimes like a siren, sometimes like a fury.

OF NOBILITY

We will speak of nobility first as a portion of an estate; then as a condition of particular persons. A monarchy where there is no nobility at all, is ever a pure and absolute tyranny; as that of the Turks. For nobility attempers sovereignty, and draws the eyes of the people somewhat aside from the line royal. But for democracies, they need it not; and they are commonly more quiet and less subject to sedition, than where there are stirps of nobles. For men's eyes are upon the business, and not upon the persons; or if upon the persons, it is for the business sake, as fittest, and not for flags and pedigree. We see the Switzers last well, notwithstanding their diversity of religion and of cantons. For utility is their bond, and not respects. The united provinces of the Low Countries in their government excel; for where there is an equality, the consultations are more indifferent, and the payments and tributes more cheerful. A great and potent nobility addeth majesty to a monarch, but diminisheth power; and putteth life and spirit into the people, but presseth their fortune. It is well when nobles are not too great for sovereignty nor for justice; and yet maintained in that height, as the insolency of inferiors may be broken upon them before it come on too fast upon the majesty of kings. A numerous nobility causeth poverty and inconvenience in a state; for it is a surcharge of expense; and besides, it being a necessity that many of the nobility fall in time to be weak in fortune, it maketh a kind of disproportion between honour and means.

As for nobility in particular persons; it is a reverend thing to see an ancient castle or building not in decay; or to see a fair timber tree sound and perfect. How much more to behold an ancient noble family, which hath stood against the waves and weathers of time. For new nobility is but the act of power, but ancient nobility is the act of time.

OF THE TRUE GREATNESS OF KINGDOMS

But above all, for empire and greatness, it importeth most that a nation do profess arms as their principal honor, study, and occupation. . . . It is enough to point at it: that no nation that doth not directly profess arms may look to have great-

1. existence before essence

2. Reason alone is insufficient—
   only *involvement* can
   invest meaning.

3. Man is alienated—from
   God, fellow man, nature,
   himself.

4. Anguish of decision making.

5. Man's encounter with
   nothingness.

6. *Freedom and responsibility*
   of whatever he is.

ness fall into their mouths. .... And those that have professed arms but for an age have notwithstanding commonly attained that greatness in that age which maintained them long after when their profession and exercise of arms hath grown to decay....

No body can be healthful without exercise, neither natural body nor politic. And certainly to a kingdom or estate a just and honorable war is the true exercise. A civil war, indeed, is like the heat of a fever, but a foreign war is like the heat of exercise, and serveth to keep the body in health, for in a slothful peace both courages will effeminate and manners corrupt. But howsoever it be for happiness, without all question for greatness it maketh to be still for the most part in arms. And the strength of a veteran army, though it be a chargeable business, always on foot, is that which commonly giveth the law, or at least the reputation, amongst all neighbor states, as may well be seen in Spain which hath had, in one part or other, a veteran army almost continually now by the space of six-score years.

PART IV

Literary-Dramatic Criticism:
The Tradition

Ideas Available in Latin and Italian or in Conversation to
Shakespeare and His Contemporaries

ON POETRY AND THE EMOTIONS

Plato

A Dialogue Between Socrates, who Speaks First, and Glaucon

Then must we not infer that all these poetical individuals, beginning with Homer, are only imitators; they copy images of virtue and the like, but the truth they never reach? The poet is like a painter who, as we have already observed, will make a likeness of a cobbler though he understands nothing of cobbling; and his picture is good enough for those who know no more than he does, and judge only by colors and figures.

Quite so.

In like manner the poet with his words and phrases may be said to lay on the colors of the several arts, himself understanding their nature only enough to imitate them; and other people, who are as ignorant as he is, and judge only from his words, imagine that if he speaks of cobbling, or of military tactics, or of anything else, in meter and harmony and rhythm, he speaks very well—such is the sweet influence which melody and rhythm by nature have. And I think that you must have observed again and again what a poor appearance the tales of poets make when stripped of the colors which music puts upon them, and recited in simple prose.

The best of us, as I conceive, when we listen to a passage of Homer or one of the tragedians, in which he represents some pitiful hero who is drawling out his sorrows in a long oration, or weeping, and smiting his breast—the best of us, you know, delight in giving way to sympathy, and are in raptures at the excellence of the poet who stirs our feelings most.

Yes, of course I know.

But when any sorrow of our own happens to us, then you may observe that we pride ourselves on the opposite quality—

we would fain be quiet and patient; this is the manly part, and the other which delighted us in the recitation is now deemed to be the part of a woman.

Very true, he said.

Now can we be right in praising and admiring another who is doing that which any one of us would abominate and be ashamed of in his own person?

No, he said, that is certainly not reasonable.

Nay, I said, quite reasonable from one point of view.

What point of view?

If you consider, I said, that when in misfortune we feel a natural hunger and desire to relieve our sorrow by weeping and lamentation, and that this feeling which is kept under control in our own calamities is satisfied and delighted by the poets—the better nature in each of us, not having been sufficiently trained by reason or habit, allows the sympathetic element to break loose because the sorrow is another's; and the spectator fancies that there can be no disgrace to himself in praising and pitying any one who comes telling him what a good man he is, and making a fuss about his troubles; he thinks that the pleasure is a gain, and why should he be supercilious and lose this and the poem too? Few persons ever reflect, as I should imagine, that from the evil of other men something of evil is communicated to themselves. And so the feeling of sorrow which has gathered strength at the sight of the misfortunes of others is with difficulty repressed in our own.

How very true!

And does not the same hold also of the ridiculous? There are jests which you would be ashamed to make yourself, and yet on the comic stage, or indeed in private, when you hear them, you are greatly amused by them, and are not at all disgusted at their unseemliness;—the case of pity is repeated;—there is a principle in human nature which is disposed to raise a laugh, and this which you once restrained by reason, because you were afraid of being thought a buffoon, is now let out again; and having stimulated the risible faculty at the theater, you are betrayed unconsciously to yourself into playing the comic poet at home.

Quite true, he said.

And the same may be said of lust and anger and all the other affections, of desire and pain and pleasure, which are held to be inseparable from every action—in all of them poetry feeds and waters the passions instead of drying them up; she lets them rule, although they ought to be controlled, if mankind are ever to increase in happiness and virtue.

I cannot deny it.

Therefore, Glaucon, I said, whenever you meet with any of the eulogists of Homer declaring that he has been the educator of Hellas, and that he is profitable for education and for the ordering of human things, and that you should take him up again and again and get to know him and regulate your whole life according to him, we may love and honor those who say these things—they are excellent people, as far as their lights extend; and we are ready to acknowledge that Homer is the greatest of poets and first of tragedy writers; but we must remain firm in our conviction that hymns to the gods and praises of famous men are the only poetry which ought to be admitted into our state. For if you go beyond this and allow the honeyed muse to enter, either in epic or lyric verse, not law and the reason of mankind, which by common consent have ever been deemed best, but pleasure and pain will be the rulers in our state.

—*The Republic, X,* trans. by Benjamin Jowett, 600-1, 605-7.

ON COMEDY, TRAGEDY, AND THE EPIC

Aristotle

COMEDY

Comedy, as was said before, is an imitation of bad characters; bad, not with respect to every sort of vice, but to the ridiculous only, as being a species of turpitude or deformity; since it may be defined to be a fault or deformity of such a sort as is neither painful nor destructive. A ridiculous face, for example, is something ugly and distorted, but not so as to cause pain.

TRAGEDY

Tragedy, then, is an imitation of some action that is important, entire, and of a proper magnitude—by language, embellished and rendered pleasurable, but by different means in different parts—in the way, not of narration, but of action—effecting through pity and terror the correction and refinement of such passions.

By pleasurable language I mean a language that has the embellishments of rhythm, melody, and meter. And I add, by different means in different parts, because in some parts meter alone is employed, in others, melody.

Now as tragedy imitates by acting, what is seen,[2] in the first place, must necessarily be one of its parts: then the *melopoeia* (or music) and the diction; for these last include the means of tragic imitation. By diction I mean the metrical compositon. The meaning of *melopoeia* is obvious to every one.

Again, tragedy being an imitation of an action, and the persons employed in that action being necessarily characterized by their manners and their sentiments [thoughts], since it is from these that actions themselves derive their character, it follows that there must also be manners and sentiments as the two causes of actions, and, consequently, of the happiness or unhappiness of all men. The imitation of the action is the fable: for by fable[3] I now mean the contexture of incidents, or the plot. By manners, I mean whatever marks the characters of the persons; by sentiments, whatever they say, whether proving anything, or delivering a general sentiment, etc.

Hence all tragedy must necessarily contain six parts, which together constitute its peculiar character or quality: fable, manners, diction, sentiments, what is seen, and music. Of these parts, two relate to the means, one to the manner, and three to the object of imitation. And these are all. These specific parts, if we may so call them, have been employed by most poets, and are all to be found in almost every tragedy.

---

[2] For the translator's *decoration* for ὄψις the editor has substituted *what is seen* and *spectacle*.
[3] For *fabula* (fable) in the sense of "plot," see the following selection, Cicero, *On Narrative*.

But of all these parts the most important is the combination of incidents or the fable. Because tragedy is an imitation, not of men, but of actions—of life, of happiness and unhappiness; for happiness consists in action, and the supreme good itself, the very end of life, is action of a certain kind—not quality. Now the manners of men constitute only their quality or characters; but it is by their actions that they are happy, or the contrary. Tragedy, therefore, does not imitate action for the sake of imitating manners, but in the imitation of action that of manners is of course involved. So that the action and the fable are the end of tragedy; and in everything the end is of principal importance.

Again, tragedy cannot subsist without action; without manners it may. The tragedies of most modern poets have this defect; a defect common, indeed, among poets in general. As among painters also, this is the case with Zeuxis, compared with Polygnotus: the latter excels in the expression of the manners; there is no such expression in the pictures of Zeuxis.

Further, suppose any one to string together a number of speeches in which the manners are strongly marked, the language and the sentiments well turned; this will not be sufficient to produce the proper effect of tragedy: that end will much rather be answered by a piece, defective in each of those particulars, but furnished with a proper fable and contexture of incidents. Just as in painting, the most brilliant colors, spread at random and without design, will give far less pleasure than the simplest outline of a figure.

Add to this, that those parts of tragedy by means of which it becomes most interesting and affecting are parts of the fable; I mean reversals[4] and discoveries.

As a further proof, adventurers in tragic writing are sooner able to arrive at excellence in the language and the manners than in the construction of a plot; as appears from almost all our earlier poets.

The fable, then, is the principal part—the soul, as it were—of tragedy, and the manners are next in rank; tragedy being an imitation of an action, and through that principally of the agents.

In the third place stand the sentiments. To this part it belongs to say such things as are true and proper; which, in the dialogue, depends on the political and rhetorical arts: for

[4] The translator's term is *revolution*.

the ancients made their characters speak in the style of political and popular eloquence; but now the rhetorical manner prevails.

The manners are whatever manifests the disposition of the speaker. There are speeches, therefore, which are without manners or characters, as not containing anything by which the propensities or aversions of the person who delivers them can be known. The sentiments comprehend whatever is said, whether proving anything affirmatively or negatively, or expressing some general reflection, etc.

Fourth in order is the diction; that is, as I have already said, the expression of the sentiments by words; the power and effect of which is the same, whether in verse or prose.

Of the remaining two parts the music stands next; of all the pleasurable accompaniments and embellishments of tragedy the most delightful.

What is seen has also a great effect, but of all the parts is most foreign to the art. For the power of tragedy is felt without representation and actors; and the beauty of what is seen depends more on the art of the mechanic than on that of the poet.

These things being thus adjusted, let us go on to examine in what manner the fable should be constructed; since this is the first and most important part of tragedy.

Now we have defined tragedy to be an imitation of an action that is complete and entire; and that has also a certain magnitude; for a thing may be entire and a whole, and yet not be of any magnitude.

1. By entire I mean that which has a beginning, a middle, and an end. A beginning is that which does not necessarily suppose anything before it, but which requires something to follow it. An end, on the contrary, is that which supposes something to precede it, either necessarily or probably, but which nothing is required to follow. A middle is that which both supposes something to precede and requires something to follow. The poet, therefore, who would construct his fable properly is not at liberty to begin or end where he pleases, but must conform to these definitions.

2. Again, whatever is beautiful, whether it be an animal, or any other thing composed of different parts, must not only have those parts arranged in a certain manner, but must also be of a certain magnitude; for beauty consists in magnitude and order. Hence it is that no very minute animal can be beautiful: the eye comprehends the whole too instantaneously

to distinguish and compare the parts. Neither, on the contrary, can one of a prodigious size be beautiful; because, as all its parts cannot be seen at once, the whole, the unity of object, is lost to the spectator; as it would be, for example, if he were surveying an animal of many miles in length. As, therefore, in animals and other objects, a certain magnitude is requisite, but that magnitude must be such as to present a whole easily comprehended by the eye; so in the fable a certain length is requisite, but that length must be such as to present a whole easily comprehended by the memory.

With respect to the measure of this length—if referred to actual representation in the dramatic contests, it is a matter foreign to the art itself. For if a hundred tragedies were to be exhibited in concurrence, the length of each performance must be regulated by the hourglass; a practice of which, it is said, there have formerly been instances. But if we determine this measure by the nature of the thing itself, the more extensive the fable, consistently with the clear and easy comprehension of the whole, the more beautiful will it be, with respect to magnitude. In general, we may say that an action is sufficiently extended when it is long enough to admit of a change of fortune, from happy to unhappy, or the reverse, brought about by a succession, necessary or probable, of well-connected incidents.

A fable is not one, as some conceive it to be, merely because the hero of it is one. For numberless events happen to one man, many of which are such as cannot be connected into one event; and so, likewise, there are many actions of one man which cannot be connected into any one action. Hence appears the mistake of all those poets who have composed *Herculeids, Theseids,* and other poems of that kind. They conclude that because Hercules was one, so also must be the fable of which he is the subject. But Homer, among his many other excellences, seems also to have been perfectly aware of this mistake, either from art or genius. For when he composed his *Odyssey,* he did not introduce all the events of his hero's life—such, for instance, as the wound he received upon Parnassus; his feigned madness when the Grecian army was assembling, etc.—events not connected, either by necessary or probable consequence, with each other; but he comprehended those only which have relation to one action; for such we call that of the *Odyssey.* And in the same manner he composed his *Iliad.*

As, therefore, in other mimetic arts, one imitation is an

imitation of one thing, so here the fable, being an imitation of an action, should be an imitation of an action that is one and entire, the parts of it being so connected that if any one of them be either transposed or taken away the whole will be destroyed or changed; for whatever may be either retained or omitted, without making any sensible difference, is not properly a part.

It appears, further, from what has been said, that it is not the poet's province to relate such things as have actually happened, but such as might have happened—such as are possible, according either to probable or necessary consequence.

For it is not by writing in verse or prose that the historian and the poet are distinguished: the work of Herodotus might be versified, but it would still be a species of history, no less with meter than without. They are distinguished by this, that the one relates what has been, the other what might be. On this account poetry is a more philosophical and a more excellent thing than history: for poetry is chiefly conversant about general truth, history about particular. In what manner, for example, any person of a certain character would speak or act, probably or necessarily—this is general; and this is the object of poetry, even while it makes use of particular names. But what Alcibiades did, or what happened to him—this is particular truth.

With respect to comedy this is now become obvious; for here the poet, when he has formed his plot of probable incidents, gives to his characters whatever names he pleases; and is not, like the iambic poets, particular and personal.

Tragedy, indeed, retains the use of real names; and the reason is that what we are disposed to believe, we must think possible. Now, what has never actually happened we are not apt to regard as possible; but what has been is unquestionably so, or it could not have been at all. There are, however, some tragedies in which one or two of the names are historical, and the rest feigned: there are even some in which none of the names are historical; such is Agathon's tragedy called *The Flower*; for in that all is invention, both incidents and names; and yet it pleases. It is by no means, therefore, essential that a poet should confine himself to the known and established subjects of tragedy. Such a restraint would, indeed, be ridiculous; since even those subjects that are known are known comparatively but to a few, and yet are interesting to all.

From all this it is manifest that a poet should be a poet or maker of fables, rather than of verses; since it is imitation that constitutes the poet, and of this imitation actions are the object: nor is he the less a poet, though the incidents of his fable should chance to be such as have actually happened; for nothing hinders, but that some true events may possess that probability, the invention of which entitles him to the name of poet.

Of simple fables or actions, the episodic are the worst. I call that an episodic fable, the episodes of which follow each other without any probable or necessary connection; a fault into which bad poets are betrayed by their want of skill, and good poets by the players: for in order to accommodate their pieces to the purposes of rival performers in the dramatic contests, they spin out the action beyond their powers, and are thus frequently forced to break the connection and continuity of its parts.

But tragedy is an imitation, not only of a complete action, but also of an action exciting terror and pity. Now that purpose is best answered by such events as are not only unexpected, but unexpected consequences of each other: for, by this means, they will have more of the wonderful than if they appeared to be the effects of chance; since we find that, among events merely casual, those are the most wonderful and striking which seem to imply design: as when, for instance, the statue of Mitys at Argos killed the very man who had murdered Mitys, by falling down upon him as he was surveying it; events of this kind not having the appearance of accident. It follows, then, that such fables as are formed on these principles must be the best.

Fables are of two sorts, simple and complicated; for so also are the actions themselves of which they are imitations. An action (having the continuity and unity prescribed) I call simple, when its catastrophe is produced without either reversal or discovery; complicated when with one or both. And these should arise from the structure of the fable itself, so as to be the natural consequences, necessary or probable, of what has preceded in the action. For there is a wide difference between incidents that follow from, and incidents that follow only after, each other.

A reversal is a change (such as has already been mentioned) into the reverse of what is expected from the circumstances of the action; and that produced, as we have said, by probable or necessary consequence.

Thus, in the *Oedipus*, the messenger, meaning to make

Oedipus happy, and to relieve him from the dread he was under with respect to his mother, by making known to him his real birth, produces an effect directly contrary to his intention. Thus also in the tragedy of *Lynceus,* Lynceus is led to suffer death, Danaus follows to inflict it; but the event, resulting from the course of the incidents, is that Danaus is killed and Lynceus saved.

A discovery—as, indeed, the word implies—is a change from unknown to known, happening between those characters whose happiness or unhappiness forms the catastrophe of the drama, and terminating in friendship or enmity.

The best sort of discovery is that which is accompanied by reversal as in the *Oedipus.*

There are also other discoveries; for inanimate things of any kind may be recognized in the same manner, and we may discover whether such a particular thing was, or was not, done by such a person. But the discovery most appropriated to the fable and the action is that above defined; because such discoveries and reversals must excite either pity or terror, and tragedy we have defined to be an imitation of pitiable and terrible actions: and because, also, by them the event, happy or unhappy, is produced.

Now discoveries, being relative things, are sometimes of one of the persons only, the other being already known; and sometimes they are reciprocal: thus, Iphigenia is discovered to Orestes by the letter which she charges him to deliver, and Orestes is obliged, by other means, to make himself known to her.

These, then, are two parts of the fable—reversal and discovery. There is a third, which we denominate disasters. The two former have been explained. Disasters comprehend all painful or destructive actions: the exhibition of death, bodily anguish, wounds, and everything of that kind.

The parts of tragedy which are necessary to constitute its quality have been already enumerated. Its parts of quantity—the distinct parts into which it is divided—are these: prologue, episode, exode, and chorus; which last is also divided into the parode and the *stasimon.* These are common to all tragedies. The *commoi* are found in some only.

The prologue is all that part of a tragedy which precedes the parode of the chorus; the episode, all that part which is included between entire choral odes; the exode, that part which has no choral ode after it.

Of the choral part, the parode is the first speech of the

whole chorus; the *stasimon* includes all those choral odes that are without anapaests and trochees.

The *commos* is a general lamentation of the chorus and the actors together.

Such are the separate parts into which tragedy is divided. Its parts of quality were before explained.

The order of the subject leads us to consider, in the next place, what the poet should aim at and what avoid in the construction of his fables; and by what means the purpose of tragedy may be best effected.

Now since it is requisite to the perfection of a tragedy that its plot should be of the complicated, not of the simple kind, and that it should imitate such actions as excite terror and pity (this being the peculiar property of the tragic imitation), it follows evidently, in the first place, that the change from prosperity to adversity should not be represented as happening to a virtuous character; for this raises disgust rather than terror or compassion. Neither should the contrary change, from adversity to prosperity, be exhibited in a vicious character: this, of all plans, is the most opposite to the genius of tragedy, having no one property that it ought to have; for it is neither gratifying in a moral view, nor affecting, nor terrible. Nor, again, should the fall of a very bad man from prosperous to adverse fortune be represented: because, though such a subject may be pleasing from its moral tendency, it will produce neither pity, nor terror. For our pity is excited by misfortunes undeservedly suffered, and our terror by some resemblance between the sufferer and ourselves. Neither of these effects will, therefore, be produced by such an event.

There remains, then, for our choice, the character between these extremes: that of a person neither eminently virtuous or just, nor yet involved in misfortune by deliberate vice or villainy, but by some error of human frailty; and this person should also be someone of high fame and flourishing prosperity. For example, Oedipus, Thyestes, or other illustrious men of such families.

Hence it appears that, to be well constructed, a fable, contrary to the opinion of some, should be single rather than double; that the change of fortune should not be from adverse to prosperous, but the reverse; and that it should be the consequence, not of vice, but of some great frailty, in a character such as has been described, or better rather than worse. . . .

The most perfect tragedy, then, according to the principles of the art, is of this construction. . . .

I place in the second rank that kind of fable to which some assign the first: that which is of a double construction like the *Odyssey*, and also ends in two opposite events, to the good and to the bad characters. That this passes for the best is owing to the weakness of the spectators, to whose wishes the poets accommodate their productions. This kind of pleasure, however, is not the proper pleasure of tragedy, but belongs rather to comedy; for there, if even the bitterest enemies, like Orestes and Aegisthus, are introduced, they quit the the scene at last in perfect friendship, and no blood is shed on either side.

Terror and pity may be raised by what is seen—the mere spectacle; but they may also arise from the circumstances of the action itself; which is far preferable and shows a superior poet. For the fable should be so constructed that, without the assistance of the sight, its incidents may excite horror and commiseration in those who hear them only: an effect which every one who hears the fable of the *Oedipus* must experience. But to produce this effect by means of spectacle discovers want of art in the poet; who must also be supplied by the public with an expensive apparatus.

As to those poets who make use of spectacle in order to produce, not the terrible, but the marvelous only, their purpose has nothing in common with that of tragedy. For we are not to seek for every sort of pleasure from tragedy, but for that only which is proper to the species.

Since, therefore, it is the business of the tragic poet to give that pleasure which arises from pity and terror, through imitation, it is evident that he ought to produce that effect by the circumstances of the action itself.

Let us, then, see of what kind those incidents are which appear most terrible or piteous.

Now such actions must, of necessity, happen between persons who are either friends, or enemies, or indifferent to each other. If an enemy kills, or purposes to kill, an enemy, in neither case is any commiseration raised in us, beyond what necessarily arises from the nature of the action itself.

The case is the same when the persons are neither friends nor enemies. But when such disasters happen between friends —when, for instance, the brother kills, or is going to kill, his brother, the son his father, the mother her son, or the reverse—these, and others of a similar kind, are the proper incidents for the poet's choice. The received tragic subjects, therefore, he is not at liberty essentially to alter; Clytaemnestra must die by the hand of Orestes, and Eriphyle by that of Alcmaeon; but it is his province to invent other subjects, and to make a skilful use of those which he finds already established. What I mean by a skilful use I proceed to explain.

The atrocious action may be perpetrated knowingly and intentionally, as was usual with the earlier poets, and as Euripides, also, has represented Medea destroying her children.

It may, likewise, be perpetrated by those who are ignorant at the time of the connection between them and the injured person, which they afterward discover; like Oedipus, in Sophocles. There, indeed, the action itself does not make a part of the drama: the *Alcmaeon* of Astydamas, and Telegonus in the *Ulysses Wounded*, furnish instances within the tragedy.

There is yet a third way, where a person upon the point of perpetrating, through ignorance, some dreadful deed, is prevented by a sudden discovery.

Besides these, there is no other proper way. For the action must of necessity be either done or not done, and that either with knowledge or without: but of all these ways, that of being ready to execute knowingly, and yet not executing, is the worst; for this is, at the same time, shocking and yet not tragic, because it exhibits no disastrous event. It is, therefore, never, or very rarely, made use of. The attempt of Haemon to kill Creon in the *Antigone* is an example.

Next to this is the actual execution of the purpose.

To execute through ignorance, and afterwards to discover, is better: for thus the shocking atrociousness is avoided, and, at the same time, the discovery is striking.

But the best of all these ways is the last. Thus, in the tragedy of *Cresphontes*, Merope, in the very act of putting her son to death, discovers him, and is prevented. In the *Iphigenia*, the sister in the same manner discovers her brother; and in the *Helle*, the son discovers his mother at the instant when he was going to betray her.

On this account it is that the subjects of tragedy, as before remarked, are confined to a small number of families. For it was not to art, but to fortune, that poets applied themselves to find incidents of this nature. Hence the necessity of having recourse to those families in which such calamities have happened.

Of the plot or fable and its requisites enough has now been said.

With respect to the manners, four things are to be attended to by the poet.

First, and principally, they should be good. Now manners, or character, belong, as we have said before, to any speech or action that manifests a certain disposition; and they are bad or good as the disposition manifested is bad or good. This goodness of manners may be found in persons of every description: the manners of a woman or a slave may be good; though, in general, women are, perhaps, rather bad than good, and slaves altogether bad.

The second requisite of the manners is propriety.

There is a manly character of bravery and fierceness which cannot, with propriety, be given to a woman.

The third requisite is resemblance; for this is a different thing from their being good and proper, as above described.

The fourth is uniformity; for even though the model of the poet's imitation be some person of ununiform manners, still that person must be represented as uniformly ununiform.

We have an example of manners unnecessarily bad in the character of Menelaus in the tragedy of *Orestes*: of improper and unbecoming manners in the lamentation of Ulysses in *Scylla*, and in the speech of Menalippe: of ununiform manners in the *Iphigenia at Aulis*; for there the Iphigenia who supplicates for life has no resemblance to the Iphigenia of the conclusion.

In the manners, as in the fable, the poet should always aim either at what is necessary or what is probable; so that such a character shall appear to speak or act, necessarily or probably, in such a manner, and this event to be the necessary or probable consequence of that. Hence it is evident that the development also of a fable should arise out of the fable itself, and not depend upon machinery as in the *Medea,* or in the incidents relative to the return of the Greeks in the *Iliad.* The proper application of machinery is to such circumstances as are extraneous to the drama; such as either happened before the time of the action, and could not by human means be known; or are to happen after, and require to be foretold: for to the Gods we attribute the knowledge of all things. But nothing improbable should be admitted in the incidents of the fable; or, if it cannot be avoided, it should, at least, be confined to such as are without the tragedy itself; as in the *Oedipus* of Sophocles.

Since tragedy is an imitation of what is best, we should follow the example of skillful portrait-painters; who, while they express the peculiar lineaments, and produce a likeness, at the same time improve upon the original. And thus, too, the poet, when he imitates the manners of passionate men (or of indolent, or any other similar kind), should draw an example approaching rather to a good than to a hard and ferocious character: as Achilles is drawn by Agathon and by Homer. These things the poet should keep in view; and besides these, whatever relates to those senses which have a necessary connection with poetry: for here, also, he may often err. But of this enough has been said in the treatises already published.

What is meant by a discovery has already been explained. Its kinds are the following:

First, the most inartificial of all, and to which, from poverty of invention, the generality of poets have recourse—the discovery by visible signs. Of these signs, some are natural; as the lance with which the family of earth-born Thebans were marked, or the stars which Carcinus has made use of in his *Thyestes*: others are adventitious; and of those some are corporal, as scars; some external, as necklaces, bracelets, etc., or the little boat by which the discovery is made in the tragedy of *Tyro*. Even these, however, may be employed with more or less skill. The discovery of Ulysses, for example, to his nurse by means of his scar, is very different from his discovery by the same means to the herdsmen. For all those discoveries, in which the sign is produced by way of proof, are inartificial. Those which, like that in the "Washing of Ulysses" happen suddenly and casually are better.

Secondly, discoveries invented at pleasure by the poet, and on that account still inartificial. For example, in the *Iphigenia*, Orestes, after having discovered his sister, discovers himself to her. She, indeed, is discovered by the letter; but Orestes by verbal proofs, and these are such as the poet chooses to make him produce, not such as arise from the circumstances of the fable. This kind of discovery, therefore, borders upon the fault of that first mentioned; for some of the things from which those proofs are drawn are even such as might have been actually produced as visible signs.

Another instance is the discovery by the sound of the shuttle in the *Tereus* of Sophocles.

Thirdly, the discovery occasioned by memory; as when some recollection is excited by the view of a particular object. Thus, in the *Cyprians* of Dicaeogenes, a discovery is produced by tears shed at the sight of a picture: and thus, in the "Tale of Alcinous," Ulysses, listening to the bard, recollects, weeps, and is discovered.

Fourthly, the discovery occasioned by reasoning or inference; such as that in the *Choephorae*: "The person who is arrived resembles me—no one resembles me but Orestes—it must be he!" And that of Polyides the Sophist, in his *Iphigenia*; for the conclusion of Orestes was natural: "It had been his sister's lot to be sacrificed, and it was now his own!" That also, in the *Tydeus* of Theodectes: "He came to find his son and he himself must perish!" And thus, the daughters of Phineus, in the tragedy denominated from them, viewing the place to which they were led, infer their fate: "there they were to die, for there they were exposed!" There is also a compound sort of discovery arising from false inference in the audience; as in *Ulysses the False Messenger*: he asserts that he shall know the bow which he had not seen; the audience falsely infer that a discovery by that means will follow.

But of all discoveries the best is that which arises from the action itself, and in which a striking effect is produced by probable incidents. Such is that in the *Oedipus* of Sophocles: and that in the *Iphigenia*; for nothing more natural than her desire of conveying the letter. Such discoveries are the best, because they alone are effected without the help of invented proofs or bracelets, etc.

Next to these are the discoveries by inference.

The poet, both when he plans and when he writes his tragedy, should put himself as much as possible in the place of a spectator; for by this means, seeing everything distinctly as if present at the action, he will discern what is proper, and no inconsistencies will escape him. The fault objected to Carcinus is a proof of this. Amphiaraus had left the temple: this the poet, for want of conceiving the action to pass before his eyes, over-looked; but in the representation the audience were disgusted, and the piece condemned.

In composing, the poet should even, as much as possible, be an actor: for, by natural sympathy, they are most persuasive and affecting who are under the influence of actual passion. We share the agitation of those who appear to be truly agitated—the anger of those who appear to be truly angry.

Hence it is that poetry demands either great natural

quickness of parts, or an enthusiasm allied to madness. By the first of these we mould ourselves with facility to the imitation of every form; by the other, transported out of ourselves, we become what we imagine.

When the poet invents a subject, he should first draw a general sketch of it, and afterwards give it the detail of its episodes and extend it. The general argument, for instance, of the *Iphigenia* should be considered in this way: "A virgin on the point of being sacrificed is imperceptibly conveyed away from the altar, and transported to another country where it was the custom to sacrifice all strangers to Diana. Of these rites she is appointed priestess. It happens, some time after, that her brother arrives there." But why?— because an oracle had commanded him, for some reason exterior to the general plan. For what purpose? This also is exterior to the plan. "He arrives, is seized, and at the instant that he is going to be sacrificed the discovery is made." And this may be, either in the way of Euripides or, like that of Polyides, by the natural reflection of Orestes that "it was his fate also as it had been his sister's to be sacrificed"; by which exclamation he is saved.

After this, the poet, when he has given names to his characters, should proceed to the episodes of his action; and he must take care that these belong properly to the subject; like that of the madness of Orestes, which occasions his being taken, and his escape by means of the ablution. In dramatic poetry the episodes are short; but in the epic they are the means of drawing out the poem to its proper length. The general story of the *Odyssey*, for example, lies in a small compass: "A certain man is supposed to be absent from his own country for many years; he is persecuted by Neptune, deprived of all his companions, and left alone. At home his affairs are in disorder—the suitors of his wife dissipating his wealth and plotting the destruction of his son. Tossed by many tempests, he at length arrives, and making himself known to some of his family attacks his enemies, destroys them, and remains himself in safety." This is essential; the rest is episode.

Every tragedy consists of two parts—the complication and the development. The complication is often formed by incidents supposed prior to the action, and by a part, also, of those that are within the action; the rest form the development. I call complication all that is between the beginning of the piece and the last part, where the change of fortune commences; development all between the beginning of that change and the conclusion. Thus, in the *Lynceus* of Theodectes, the events antecedent to the action and the seizure of the child constitute the complication; the development is from the accusation of murder to the end.

There are four kinds of tragedy, deducible from so many parts, which have been mentioned. One kind is the complicated, where all depends on reversal and discovery; another is the disastrous, such as those on the subject of Ajax or Ixion; another, the moral, as the *Phthiotides* and the *Peleus*; and fourthly, the simple, such as the *Phorcides*, the *Prometheus*, and all those tragedies the scene of which is laid in the infernal regions.

It should be the poet's aim to make himself master of all these manners; or as many of them, at least, as possible, and those the best: especially considering the captious criticism to which in these days he is exposed. For the public, having now seen different poets excel in each of these different kinds, expect every single poet to unite in himself, and to surpass, the peculiar excellences of them all.

One tragedy may justly be considered as the same with another or different, not according as the subjects, but rather according as the complication and development are the same or different. Many poets, when they have complicated well, develop badly. They should endeavour to deserve equal applause in both.

We must also be attentive to what has been often mentioned, and not construct a tragedy upon an epic plan. By an epic plan I mean a fable composed of many fables; as if any one, for instance, should take the entire fable of the *Iliad* for the subject of a tragedy. In the epic poem the length of the whole admits of a proper magnitude in the parts; but in the drama the effect of such a plan is far different from what is expected. As a proof of this, those poets who have formed the whole of the destruction of Troy into a tragedy, instead of confining themselves (as Euripides, but not Aeschylus, has done in the story of Niobe) to a part, have either been condemned in the representation or have contended without success. Even Agathon has failed on this account and on this only; for in reversals, and in actions also of the simple kind, these poets succeed wonderfully in what they aim at; and that is the union of tragic effect with moral tendency; as when, for example, a character of great wisdom, but without integrity, is deceived, like Sisyphus; or a brave but unjust man conquered. Such events, as Agathon says, are probable, "as it is probable, in general, that many things should happen contrary to probability."

TRAGEDY AND EPIC

The surprising is necessary in tragedy; but the epic poem goes further and admits even the improbable and incredible, from which the highest degree of the surprising results, because there the action is not seen. The circumstances, for example, of the pursuit of Hector by Achilles, are such as, upon the stage, would appear ridiculous—the Grecian army standing still and taking no part in the pursuit, and Achilles making signs to them by the motion of his head not to interfere. But in the epic poem this escapes our notice. Now the wonderful always pleases, as is evident from the additions which men always make in relating anything in order to gratify the hearers.

It is from Homer principally that other poets have learned the art of feigning well. It consists in a sort of sophism. When one thing is observed to be constantly accompanied or followed by another, men are apt to conclude that if the latter is, or has happened, the former must also be, or must have happened. But this is an error. For knowing the latter to be true, the mind is betrayed into the false inference that the first is true also.

The poet should prefer impossibilities which appear probable to such things as, though possible, appear improbable. Far from producing a plan made up of improbable incidents, he should, if possible, admit no one circumstance of that kind; or, if he does, it should be exterior to the action itself, like the ignorance of Oedipus concerning the manner in which Laius died; not within the drama, like the narrative of what happened at the Pythian games in the *Electra*; or in the *Mysians*, the man who travels from Tegea to Mysia without speaking. To say that without these circumstances the fable would have been destroyed is a ridiculous excuse: the poet should take care, from the first, not to construct his fable in that manner. If, however, anything of this kind has been admitted, and yet is made to pass under some color of probability, it may be allowed, though even in itself absurd. Thus in the *Odyssey*, the improbable account of the manner in which Ulysses was landed upon the shore of Ithaca is such as in the hands of an ordinary poet would evidently have been intolerable; but here the absurdity is concealed under the various beauties of other kinds with which the poet has embellished it.

The diction should be most labored in the idle parts of the poem—those in which neither manners nor sentiments prevail; for the manners and the sentiments are only obscured by too splendid a diction.

HOW TO ANSWER CRITICAL OBJECTIONS

For, in the first place, suppose the poet to have represented things impossible with respect to some other art. This is certainly a fault. Yet it may be an excusable fault, provided the end of the poet's art be more effectually obtained by it; that is, according to what has already been said of that end, if by this means that, or any other part, of the poem is made to produce a more striking effect. The pursuit of Hector is an instance. If, indeed, this end might as well, or nearly as well, have been attained without departing from the principles of the particular art in question, the fault, in that case, could not be justified, since faults of every kind should, if possible, be avoided.

Still, we are to consider further whether a fault be in things essential to the poetic art, or foreign and incidental to it; for it is a far more pardonable fault to be ignorant, for instance, that a hind has no horns, than to paint one badly.

Further, if it be objected to the poet that he has not represented things conformably to truth, he may answer that he has represented them as they should be. This was the answer of Sophocles, that "he drew mankind such as they should be; Euripides, such as they are." And this is the proper answer.

But if the poet has represented things in neither of these ways, he may answer that he has represented them as they are said and believed to be. Of this kind are the poetical descriptions of the Gods. It cannot, perhaps, be said that they are either what is best or what is true; but, as Xenophanes says, opinions "taken up at random"; these are things, however, not "clearly known."

Again, what the poet has exhibited is, perhaps, not what is best, but it is the fact; as in the passage about the arms of the sleeping soldiers:

... fixed upright in the earth
Their spears stood by.

For such was the custom at that time, as it is now among the Illyrians.

In order to judge whether what is said or done by any character be well or ill, we are not to consider that speech or action alone, whether in itself it be good or bad, but also by whom it is spoken or done, to whom, at what time, in what manner, or for what end—whether, for instance, in order to obtain some greater good or to avoid some greater evil.

TRAGEDY SUPERIOR TO THE EPIC

Tragedy has the advantage in the following respects: It possesses all that is possessed by the epic; it might even adopt its meter; and to this it makes no inconsiderable addition, in the music and what is seen; by the latter of which the illusion is heightened, and the pleasure arising from the action is rendered more sensible and striking.

It has the advantage of greater clearness and distinctness of impression, as well in reading as in representation.

It has also that of attaining the end of its imitation in a shorter compass: for the effect is more pleasurable when produced by a short and close series of impressions, than when weakened by diffusion through a long extent of time; as the *Oedipus* of Sophocles, for example, would be if it were drawn out to the length of the *Iliad*.

Further, there is less unity in all epic imitation, as appears from this—that any epic poem will furnish matter for several tragedies. For, supposing the poet to choose a fable strictly one, the consequence must be either that his poem, if proportionably contracted, will appear curtailed and defective, or, if extended to the usual length, will become weak and, as it were, diluted. If, on the other hand, we suppose him to employ several fables—that is, a fable composed of several actions—his imitation is no longer strictly one. The *Iliad*, for example, and the *Odyssey* contain many such subordinate parts, each of which has a certain magnitude and unity of its own; yet is the construction of those poems as perfect, and as nearly approaching to the imitation of a single action, as possible.

If, then, tragedy be superior to the epic in all these respects, and also in the peculiar end at which it aims (for each species ought to afford, not any sort of pleasure indiscriminately, but such only as has been pointed out), it evidently follows that tragedy, as it attains more effectually the end of the art itself, must deserve the preference.

—*The Poetics*, trans. by Thomas Twining (1789, 1812), from chaps. 5, 6-18, 24, and 25.

ON NARRATIVE

Cicero

The *narrative* is an exposition of events that have occurred or are supposed to have occurred. There are three kinds: one which contains just the case and the whole reason for the dispute; a second in which a digression is made beyond the strict limits of the case for the purpose of attacking somebody, or of making a comparison, or of amusing the audience in a way not incongruous with the business in hand, or for amplification. The third kind is wholly unconnected with public issues, and is recited or written solely for amusement but at the same time provides valuable training. It is subdivided into two classes: one concerned with events, the other principally with persons. That which consists of an exposition of events has three forms: *fabula, historia, argumentum.*

Fabula is the term applied to a narrative in which the events are not true and have no verisimilitude, for example: "Huge winged dragons yoked to a car." *Historia* is an account of actual occurrences remote from the recollection of our own age, as: "War on men of Carthage Appius decreed." *Argumentum* is a fictitious narrative which nevertheless could have occurred. An example may be quoted from Terence: "For after he had left the school of youth."

But the form of narrative which is concerned with persons is of such a sort that in it can be seen not only events but also the conversation and mental attitude of the characters.

For example: "He comes to me perpetually, crying, 'What are you about, Micio? Why are you bringing the boy to ruin on our hands? Why the license? Why these drinking parties? Why do you pile him up the guineas for such a life and let

Reprinted by permission of the publishers and THE LOEB CLASSICAL LIBRARY from H. M. Hubbell, translator, Cicero, *De Inventione,* Cambridge, Mass.: Harvard University Press.

him spend so much at the tailor's? It's extremely silly of you.' He himself is extremely hard, past right and sense." This form of narrative should possess great vivacity, resulting from fluctuations of fortune, contrast of characters, severity, gentleness, hope, fear, suspicion, desire, dissimulation, delusion, pity, sudden change of fortune, unexpected disaster, sudden pleasure, a happy ending to the story. But these embellishments will be drawn from what will be said later about the rules of style.

Now it seems necessary to speak of that form of narrative which contains an exposition of a case at law. It ought to possess three qualities: it should be brief, clear, and plausible. It will be brief if it begins with what needs to be said, and is not carried back to the most remote events; if it does not include details when it is sufficient to have stated the substance of the story—for often it is sufficient to say what happened, so that you do not need to tell how it happened—and if the narrative is not carried farther than is needed, and if it does not digress to another story. Brevity may be gained if the story is told in such a way that at times something which has not been mentioned can be gathered from what has been said; also if not only what is prejudicial is omitted but also what is neither prejudicial nor helpful; and if each thing is mentioned once and once only, and if it does not begin all over again at the point at which it has just stopped. Many are deceived by an appearance of brevity so that they are prolix when they think they are brief. This occurs when they try to say many things in a brief compass, rather than saying very few or not more than is necessary. Many, for example, think that one is speaking briefly who speaks as follows: "I went to his house, I called the slave. He answered. I asked for his master. He said that he was not at home." Here, although so many things could not be said more briefly, still because it was sufficient to say, "He said he was not at home," it is made too long by the abundance of details. Therefore in this section of the speech too, a false brevity is to be avoided, and one must refrain no less from an excess of superfluous facts than from an excess of words.

It will be possible to make the narrative clear if the events are presented one after another as they occurred, and the order of events in time is preserved so that the story is told as it will prove to have happened or will seem possible to have happened. On this point care must be taken not to say anything in a confused and intricate style, not to shift to another subject, not to go back to ultimate beginnings nor to go on too far, and not to omit anything pertinent to the case. In general the rules about brevity are to be followed in seeking clarity also. For often a case is misunderstood more from excessive length of the narrative than from obscurity. The diction must also be perspicuous; this topic must be discussed among the rules for style.

The narrative will be plausible if it seems to embody characteristics which are accustomed to appear in real life; if the proper qualities of the character are maintained, if reasons for their actions are plain, if there seems to have been ability to do the deed, if it can be shown that the time was opportune, the space sufficient and the place suitable for the events about to be narrated; if the story fits in with the nature of the actors in it, the habits of ordinary people and the beliefs of the audience. Verisimilitude can be secured by following these principles.

ON THE LAUGHABLE

Cicero

Concerning laughter, there are five things which are subjects of consideration: one, what it is; another, whence it originates; a third, whether it becomes the orator to wish to excite laughter; a fourth, to what degree; a fifth, what are the several kinds of the ridiculous? As to the first, what laughter itself is, by what means it is excited, where it lies, how it arises and bursts forth so suddenly that we are unable, though we desire, to restrain it, and how it affects at once the sides, the face, the veins, the countenance, the eyes, let Democritus consider; for all this has nothing to do with my remarks, and if it had to do with them, I should not be ashamed to say that I am ignorant of that which not even they understand who profess to explain it. But the seat and as it were province of what is laughed at (for that is the next point of inquiry), lies in a certain offensiveness and deformity; for those sayings are laughed at solely or chiefly which point out and designate something offensive in an inoffensive manner. But, to come to the third point, it certainly becomes the orator to excite laughter, either because mirth itself attracts favor to him by whom it is raised; or because all admire wit, which is often comprised in a single word, especially in him who replies and sometimes in him who attacks; or because it overthrows the adversary, or hampers him, or makes light of him, or discourages, or refutes him; or because it proves the orator himself to be a man of taste, or learning, or polish; but chiefly because it mitigates and relaxes gravity and severity and often, by a joke or a laugh, breaks the force of offensive remarks, which cannot easily be overthrown by arguments. But to what degree the laughable should be carried by the orator requires very diligent consideration, a point which we placed as the fourth subject of inquiry; for neither great vice, such as is united with crime, nor great misery is a subject for ridicule and laughter, since people will have those guilty of enormous crimes attacked with more forcible weapons than ridicule and do not like the miserable to be derided, unless perhaps when they are insolent; and you must be considerate too of the feelings of mankind, lest you rashly speak against those who are personally beloved.

Such is the caution that must be principally observed in joking. Those subjects accordingly are most readily jested upon which are neither provocative of violent aversion nor of extreme compassion. All matter for ridicule is therefore found to lie in such defects as are to be observed in the characters of men not in universal esteem, nor in calamitous circumstances, and who do not appear deserving to be dragged to punishment for their crimes; such topics nicely managed create laughter. In deformity also and bodily defects is found fair enough matter for ridicule, but we have to ask the same question here as is asked on other points, How far the ridicule may be carried? In this respect it is not only directed that the orator should say nothing impertinently but also that, even if he can say anything very ridiculously, he should avoid both errors, lest his jokes become either buffoonery or mimicry, qualities of which we shall better understand the nature when we come to consider the different species of the ridiculous.

There are two sorts of jokes, one of which is excited by things, the other by words. By things whenever any matter is told in the way of a story ...[5] whether you have any true story to tell (which however must be interspersed with fictitious circumstances), or whether you merely invent. The excellence of such jesting is that you can describe things as occurring in such a way that the manners, the language, and every look of the person of whom you speak may be represented so that the occurrence may seem to the audience to pass and take place at the very time when you address them. Another kind of jest taken from things is that which is derived from a depraved sort of imitation or mimicry. ... Of this species is Roscius' imitation of an old man; when he says, "For you, my Antipho, I plant these trees," it is old age itself that seems to speak while I listen to him. But all this department of ridicule is of such a nature that it must be attempted with the greatest caution. For if the imitation is too extravagant, it becomes, like indecency, the part of players in pantomime and farce; the orator should be moderate in imitation that the audience may conceive more than they can see represented by him; he ought also to give proof of ingenuousness and modesty by avoiding everything offensive or unbecoming in word or act.

These, therefore, are the two kinds of the ridiculous which is drawn from things; and they suit well with continuous pieces of humor in which the manners of mankind are so described and expressed that, either by means of some narrative their character is exactly understood, or by throwing in a little mimicry they may be convicted of some impropriety remarkable enough for ridicule. But in words, the ridiculous is that which is excited by the point of a particular expression or thought; but as in the former kind, both in narration and imitation, all resemblance to the players of pantomime should be avoided, so in this all scurrilous buffoonery is to be studiously shunned by the orator. ... A regard, therefore, to proper times, moderation and forbearance in jesting, and a

[5] The ellipses indicate that some illustrative jokes which are now unintelligible have been omitted.

limitation in the number of jokes will distinguish the orator from the buffoon; and the circumstance, besides, that we joke with an object, not that we may appear to be jesters but that we may gain some advantage, while they joke all day without any purpose whatever. . . . The proper season, then, for jesting we must determine by our own prudence and judgment, in the exercise of which I wish that we had some body of rules to direct us, but nature is the sovereign guide.

Let us now consider briefly the sorts of jests that chiefly excite laughter. Let this, then, be our first division, that whatever is expressed wittily consists sometimes in a thought, sometimes in the mere language, but that men are most delighted with a joke when the laugh is raised by the thought and the language in conjunction. But remember this, that whatever topics I shall touch upon from which ridicule may be drawn, from almost the same topics serious thoughts may be derived; there is only this difference, that seriousness is used on dignified subjects with gravity, joking on such as are in some degree unbecoming and as it were grotesque; for instance, we may with the very same words commend a thrifty servant and jest upon one that is extravagant. That old saying of Nero about a thieving servant is humorous enough, That he was the only one from whom nothing in the house was sealed or locked up, a thing which is not only said of a good servant but in the very same words. . . .

Those smart sayings which spring from some ambiguity are thought extremely ingenious, but they are not always employed to express jests but often even grave thoughts. What Publius Licinus Varus said to Africanus the elder, when he was endeavoring to fit a chaplet to his head at an entertainment and it broke several times, "Do not wonder if it does not fit you, for you have a great head," was a fine and noble thought. . . . Not to be tedious, there is no subject for jest from which serious and grave reflections may not be drawn. It is also to be observed that everything which is ridiculous is not witty, for what can be so ridiculous as a buffoon. But it is by his face, his appearance, his look, his mimicry, his voice, and, in fine, by his whole figure that he excites laughter. I might, indeed, call him witty, but not in such a way that I would have an orator, but an actor in pantomime, to be witty.

This kind of jesting, above all, then, though it powerfully excites laughter, is not suited to us; it represents the morose, the superstitious, the suspicious, the vainglorious, the foolish—

habits of mind which are in themselves ridiculous—and such kind of characters we are to expose, not to assume. There is another kind of jesting which is extremely ludicrous, namely mimicry; but it is allowable only in us to attempt it cautiously, if ever we do attempt it, and but for a moment, otherwise it is far from becoming to a man of education. A third is distortion of features, utterly unworthy of us. A fourth is indecency in language, a disgrace not only to the forum but to any company of well-bred people. So many things, then, being deducted from this part of oratory, the kinds of jesting which remain are (as I distinguished them before) such as consist in thought or in expression. That which, in whatever terms you express it, is still wit consists in the thought, that which by a change of words loses its spirit has no wit but what depends on expression.

Plays on ambiguous words are extremely ingenious but depend wholly on the expression not on the matter. They seldom, however, excite much laughter but are rather commended as jests of elegance and scholarship, as that about Titius, whom, being a great tennis player and at the same time suspected of having broken the sacred images by night, Terentius Vespa excused when his companions inquired for him, as he did not come to the Campus Martius, by saying that he had broken an arm. . . . And if you were to ask me, I should say that he who is called a jester excels chiefly in jokes of this kind, but that other jests excite laughter in a greater degree. The ambiguous gains great admiration, as I observed before, from its nature, for it appears the part of a wit to be able to turn the force of a word to quite another sense than that in which other people take it, but it excites surprise rather than laughter unless when it happens to be joined with some other sorts of jesting.

Some of these sorts of jesting I will now run over; but you are aware that that is the most common kind of joke, when we expect one thing and another is said, in which case our own disappointed expectation makes us laugh. But if something of the ambiguous is thrown in with it, the wit is heightened. . . . But as there are several sorts of ambiguity, with regard to which accurate study is necessary, we should be attentive and on the watch for words; and thus, though we may avoid frigid witticisms (for we must be cautious that a jest be not thought far-fetched), we shall hit upon many acute sayings. Another kind is that which consists in a slight change in a word, which, when produced by the alteration of a letter, the Greeks call *paranomasia*, as Cato called *nobilior mobilior*. . . .

All such jokes lie in a single word. Often too a verse is humorously introduced either just as it is, or with some little alteration, or some part of a verse. . . . To the same purpose proverbs may be applied. . . . Such jokes, as they cannot, if any change is made in the words of them, retain the same grace, are necessarily considered as turning not on the matter but on the mere expression.

There is also a kind of joke, not at all absurd, which lies in expression, when you seem to understand a thing literally and not in its obvious meaning, in which kind it was that Tutor, the old mimic, an exceedingly laughable actor, exclusively distinguished himself. But I have nothing to do with actors; I only wished this kind of jesting to be illustrated by some notable example. Of this kind was your answer lately, Crassus, to one who asked you whether he should be troublesome if he came to you some time before it was light, and you said, "You will not be troublesome.'" when he rejoined, "You will order yourself to be waked then?" to which you replied, "Surely I said that you would not be troublesome. . . ." Such jests may be insipid, or are witty only when another answer is expected; for our surprise (as I before observed) naturally amuses us, and thus, when we are deceived, as it were, in our expectation, we laugh.

Those jests also lie in words which spring from some allegorical phraseology, or from a metaphorical use of some word, or from using words ironically. From allegorical phraseology: as when Rusca in old times proposed the law to fix the ages of candidates for offices, and Marcus Servillius, who opposed the law, said to him, "Tell me, Marcus Pinarius Rusca, if I speak against you, will you speak ill of me as you have spoken of others?" "As you shall sow," replied he, "so you shall reap." From the use of a single word in a metaphorical sense: as when the elder Scipio said to the Corinthians, who offered to put up a statue of him in the place where those of other commanders were, That he did not like such comrades. From the ironical use of words: as when Crassus spoke for Aculeo before Marcus Perperna as judge, and Lucius Aelius Lama appeared for Gratidianus against Aculeo, and Lama, who was deformed, as you know, offered impertinent interruptions, Crassus said, "Let us hear this beautiful youth." When a laugh followed, "I could not form my own shape," said Lamia, "but I could form my understand-

ing." "Then," said Crassus, "let us hear this able orator,"
when a greater laugh than before ensued. Such jests are
agreeable as well in grave as in humorous speeches. For I
observed a little while ago, that the subjects for jests and for
gravity are distinct, but that the same form of expression will
serve for grave remarks as for jokes. Words antithetically
used are a great ornament to language, and the same mode
of using them is often also humorous; thus, when the well-
known Servius Galba carried to Lucius Scribonius the tribune
a list of his own intimates to be appointed as judges, and
Libo said, "What, Galba, will you never go out of your own
dining room?" "Yes," replied Galba, "when you go out of
other men's bedchambers. . . ."

Such kinds of jokes as lie in words I think that I have now
sufficiently discussed, but such as relate to things are more
numerous and excite more laughter, as I observed before.
Among them is narrative, a matter of exceeding difficulty;
for such things are to be described and set before the eyes as
may seem to be probable, which is the excellence of narration, and such also as are grotesque, which is the peculiar
province of the ridiculous. . . . To this head we may assign
the narratives given in fables. Allusions are also drawn
from history. . . . Such jests are also derived from similitudes,
which include either comparison or something of bodily representation. . . . There are jokes too from things being exten-
uated or exaggerated hyperbolically and to astonish, as you,
Crassus, said in a speech to the people, that Memmius fancied himself so great a man that as he came into the forum
he stooped his head at the arch of Fabius. . . . There is also
frequently acuteness shown when something obscure and not
commonly known is illustrated by a slight circumstance and
often by a single word, as when Publius Cornelius, a man, as
was suspected, of a covetous and rapacious disposition but of
great courage and an able commander, thanked Caius Fabricius for having, though he was his enemy, made him consul,
especially during a difficult and important war. "You have no
reason to thank me," returned Fabricius, "if I had rather be
pillaged than sold for a slave. . . ."

Ironical dissimulation has also an agreeable effect when
you say something different from what you think, not after
the manner to which I alluded before when you say the exact
reverse of what you mean, as Crassus said to Lamia, but
when through the whole course of a speech you are seriously
jocose, your thoughts being different from your words. . . .

According to what those say who know these matters better than myself, I conceive that Socrates for irony and dissimulation far excelled all other men in the wit and genius which he displayed. It is an elegant kind of humor, satirical with a mixture of gravity, and adapted to oratory as well as to polite conversation. Indeed all the kinds of humor of which I have spoken are seasonings not more appropriate to law-pleadings in the forum than to any other kind of discourse. . . .

But I will pursue the remainder of my subject. It is a kind of joking similar to a sort of dissimulation when anything disgraceful is designated by an honorable term, as when Africanus the censor removed from his tribe that centurion who absented himself from the battle in which Paulus commanded, alleging that he had remained in the camp to guard it and inquiring why he had such a mark of ignomy set upon him, "I do not like," replied Africanus, "over vigilant people." It is an excellent joke too when you take any part of another person's words in a different sense from that which is intended, as Fabius Maximus did with Livius Salinator when, on Tarentum being lost, Livius had still preserved the citadel and had made many successful sallies from it, and Fabius, some years afterwards, having retaken the town, Livius begged him to remember that it was owing to him that Tarentum was retaken. "How can I do otherwise than remember," said Fabius, "for I should never have retaken it if you had not lost it." Such jokes as the following, too, are, though rather absurd, often on that very account extremely amusing and very apposite not only to characters in plays but also to us orators:

The foolish man!
As soon as he had come to wealth, he died.

This kind of jokes is rather trifling and, as I said, fit for actors in farces, but sometimes it finds a proper place with us, as even one who is not a fool may express himself like a fool in a humorous way. . . . Such jests excite great laughter, and in truth all sayings that are uttered by men of sense with a degree of absurdity and sarcasm under the pretence of not understanding what is said to them. A joke of this kind is not to seem to comprehend what you comprehend very well, as when Pontidius, being asked, "What do you think of him who is taken in adultery?" replied, "That he is slow. . . ." It is a very happy stroke, too, when he who has uttered a sarcasm is jested upon in the same strain in which he has attacked another, as when Quintus Opimius, a man of consular dignity who had the report of having been licentious in his youth, said to Egilius, a man of wit who seemed to be an effeminate person but was in reality not so, "How do you do, my Egilia, when will you pay me a visit with your distaff and spindle?" and Egilius replied, "I certainly dare not, for my mother forbade me to visit women of bad character."

There are witty sayings also which carry a concealed suspicion of ridicule, of which sort is that of the Sicilian, who, when a friend of his made lamentation to him saying that his wife had hanged herself upon a fig tree, said, "I beseech you give me some shoots of that tree that I may plant them." Of the same sort is what Catulus said to a certain bad orator, who, when he imagined that he had excited compassion at the close of a speech, asked our friend here, after he had sat down, whether he appeared to have raised pity in the audience, "Very great pity," replied Crassus, "for I believe there is no one here so hard-hearted but that your speech seemed pitiable to him." Those jests amuse me extremely which are expressed in passion and as it were with moroseness, not when they are uttered by a person really morose, for in that case it is not the wit but the natural temper that is laughed at. . . . Contrasted with this there is a patient and cool species of the humorous, as when Cato received a stroke from a man carrying a trunk, who afterwards called to him to take care, he asked him whether he carried anything else besides the trunk. There is also a witty mode of exposing folly, as when the Sicilian to whom Scipio, when praetor, assigned his host for an advocate in some cause, a man of rank but extremely stupid, said, "I beseech you, praetor, give this advocate to my adversary and give me none." Explanations of things, too, are amusing which are given from conjecture in a sense far different from that which they are intended to convey but with ingenuity and aptness. . . .

A union of discordant particulars is laughable, as, "What is wanting to him, except fortune and virtue." A familiar reproof of a person as if he were in error is also amusing. . . . Similar to this is friendly admonition by way of giving advice, as when Granius persuaded a bad pleader, who had made himself hoarse with speaking, to drink a cold mixture of honey and wine as soon as he got home, "I shall ruin my voice," said he, "if I do so." "It will be better," said Granius,

"than to ruin your clients." It is a happy hit too when
something is said that is peculiarly applicable to the character
of some particular person. . . . But of all jokes none create
greater laughter than something said contrary to expectation,
of which there are examples without number. . . . Nothing
could be more witty than the joke of our friend Crassus.
When Silus, a witness, was injuring the cause of Piso by
something that he said he had heard against him, "It is
possible," said he, "Silus, that the person from whom you
heard this said it in anger." Silus assented. "It is possible too
that you did not rightly understand him." To this also he
assented with the lowest of bows, expressing entire agreement
with Crassus. "It is also possible," continued Crassus, "that
what you say you have heard you never heard at all." This
was so different from what was expected that the witness was
overwhelmed by a general laugh.

You may often also humorously grant to your adversary
what he wishes to detract from you, as Caius Laelius, when a
man of disreputable family told him that he was unworthy of
his ancestors, replied, "But, by Hercules, you are worthy of
yours." Jokes too are frequently uttered in a sententious
manner, as Marcus Cincius, on the day when he proposed his
law about gifts and presents, and Caius Cento stood forth
and asked him with some scorn, "What are you proposing,
little Cincius?" replied, "That you, Caius, may pay for what
you wish to use." Things also which are impossible are often
wished for with much wit, as Marcus Lepidus, when he lay
down upon the grass while others were taking their exercise
in the Campus Martius, exclaimed, "I wish this were labor."
It is an excellent joke also to give inquisitive people who
tease you as it were a calm answer of such a nature as they
do not expect, as Lepidus the censor, when he deprived
Antistius of Pyrgi of his horse,[6] and his friends called out to
him and inquired what reason Antistius could give his father
why his horse was taken from him when he was an excellent,
industrious, modest, frugal member of the colony, rejoined,
"That I believe not a word of it." Some other sorts of jests
are enumerated by the Greeks, as execrations, expressions of
admiration, threats. But I think that I have divided these
matters into too many heads already, for such as lie in the
force and meaning of a word are commonly easy to settle
and define, but in general, as I observed before, they are
heard rather with approbation than laughter. Jokes, however,

[6] From the rank of knights.

which lie in the subject and thought are, though infinite in their varieties, reducible under a very few general heads; for it is by deceiving expectation, by satirising the tempers of others, by playing humorously on our own, by comparing a thing with something worse, by dissembling, by uttering apparent absurdities, and by reproving folly that laughter is excited; and he who would be a facetious speaker must be endowed with a natural genius for such kinds of wit as well as with personal qualifications, so that his very look may adapt itself to every species of the ridiculous; and the graver and more serious such a person is, as is the case with you, Crassus, so much more humorous do the sayings which fall from him generally appear.

> —Cicero, *De Oratore*, trans by George Barnes (1762), revised by J. S. Watson (1876), 2. 58. 235-2. 71. 289.

FAMOUS TAGS FROM *THE ART OF POETRY*

Horace

THE PURPLE PATCH

In grave beginnings and great things professed
Ye have ofttimes, that may o'ershine the rest,
A scarlet piece or two stitched in.

14–16

BREVIS ESSE LABORO

Myself for shortness labor and I grow
Obscure. This, striving to run smooth and flow,
Hath neither soul nor sinews. Lofty he,
Professing greatness, swells; that, low by lee,
Creeps on the ground, too safe, too afraid of storms.

25–28

So shunning faults to greater fault doth lead.

31

LUCIDUS ORDO

Take, therefore, you that write, still matter fit
Unto your strength and long examine it
Upon your shoulders. Prove what they will bear
And what they will not. Him whose choice doth rear
His matter to his power in all he makes,
Nor language nor clear order e'er forsakes.

38–41

CALLIDA IUNCTURA

Then thou speakest to me
Most worthy praise when words that common grew
Are by thy cunning placing made mere new.

47–48

DEBEMUR MORTI NOS NOSTRAQUE

It hath been ever free,
And ever will, to utter terms that be
Stamped to the time. As woods whose change appears
Still in their leaves throughout the sliding years,
The first born dying, so the aged state
Of words decay, and phrases born but late
Like tender buds shoot up and freshly grow.
Ourselves and all that's ours to death we owe.

58–63

IUS ET NORMA LOQUENDI

Much phrase that now is dead shall be revived,
And much shall die that now is nobly lived
If custom please, at whose disposing will
The power and rule of speaking resteth still.

70–72

DECORUM

The comic matter will not be expressed
In tragic verse, no less Thyestes' feast
Abhors low numbers.

89–91

Yet sometime doth the comedy excite
Her voice and angry Chremes chafes outright
With swelling throat, and oft the tragic wight
Complains in humble phrase. Both Telephus
And Peleus, if they seek to heart-strike us
That are spectators with their misery
When they are poor and banished, must throw by
Their bombard-phrase and foot-and-half-foot words.

                                                    93–96

SI VIS ME FLERE

If thou wouldst have me weep, be thou first drowned
Thyself in tears.

                                                    102–103

AUT FAMAM SEQUERE

Or follow fame, thou that dost write, or feign
Things in themselves agreeing. If again
Honored Achilles chance by thee be seized,
Keep him still active, angry, unappeased

                                                    119–121

SERVETUR AND IMUM

If something strange, that never yet was had,
Unto the scene thou bringst and darest create
A mere new person, look he keep his state
Unto the last as when he first went forth,
Still to be like himself and hold his worth.

                                                    125–127

PROPRIE COMMUNIA DICERE

'Tis hard to speak things common properly.

                                                    128

RIDICULUS MUS

The mountains travailed and brought forth
A scorned mouse!

                                                    139

IN MEDIAS RES

Nor from the brand with which the life did burn
Of Meleager brings he the return
Of Diomede, nor Troy's sad war begins
From the two eggs that did disclose the twins.
He ever hastens to the end and so,
As if he knew it, raps his hearer to
The middle of his matter.

146–149

THE AGES OF MAN

The customs of each age thou must observe
And give their years and natures, as they swerve,
Fit rites. The child, that now knows how to say
And can tread firm, longs with like lads to play;
Soon angry and soon pleased, is sweet or sour,
He knows not why, and changeth every hour.
The unbearded youth, his guardian once being gone,
Loves dogs and horses and is ever one
In the open field, is wax-like to be wrought
To every vice as hardly to be brought
To endure counsel, a provider slow
For his own good, a careless letter-go
Of money, haughty, to desire soon moved,
And then as swift to leave what he hath loved.
These studies alter now in one grown man;
His bettered mind seeks wealth and friendship, then
Looks after honors, and bewares to act
What straightway he must labor to retract.
The old man many evils do girt round,
Either because he seeks and, having found,
Doth wretchedly the use of things forbear,
Or does all business coldly and with fear;
A great deferrer, long in hope, grown numb
With sloth yet greedy still of what's to come,
Froward, complaining, a commender glad
Of the times past when he was a young lad,
And still correcting youth and censuring.
Man's coming years much good with them do bring,
At his departing take much thence. Lest then
The parts of age to youth be given, or men

To children, we must always dwell and stay
In fitting proper adjuncts to each day.

156–178

VIOLENCE OFFSTAGE

Medea must not kill
Her sons before the people.

185

FIVE ACTS

Nor must the fable, that would hope the fate
Once seen to be again called for and played,
Have more or less than just five acts, nor laid
To have a god come in except a knot
Worth his untying happen there.

189–192

TANTUM SERIES IUNCTURAQUE POLLET

I can out of known gear a fable frame
And so as every man may hope the same,
Yet he that offers at it may sweat much
And toil in vain, the excellence is such
Of order and connection.

250–243

SCRIBENDI RECTE

The very root of writing well, and spring,
Is to be wise, thy matter first to know,
Which the Socratic writings best can show.
And where the matter is provided, still
There words will follow, not against their will.
He that hath studied well the debt and knows
What to his country, what his friends he owes,
What height of love a parent will fit best,
What brethren, what a stranger, and his guest,
Can tell a statesman's duty, what the arts
And office of a judge are, what the parts
Of a brave chief sent to the wars, he can
Indeed give fitting dues to every man.
And I still bid the learned maker look

On life and manners and make those his book,
Thence draw forth true expressions. For sometimes
A poem of no grace, weight, art, in rhymes
With specious places and being humored right
More strongly takes the people with delight
And better stays them there than all fine noise
Of verse mere matterless and tinkling toys.

309–322

AUT PRODESSE . . . AUT DELECTARE

Poets would either profit or delight,
Or mixing sweet and fit, teach life the right.

333–334

PROXIMA VERIS

Let what thou feignst for pleasure's sake be near
The truth, nor let thy fable think what e'er
It would must be.

338–339

SOMETIMES EVEN HOMER NODS

There are yet faults which we would well forgive,
For neither doth the string still yield that sound
The hand and mind would, but it will resound
Ofttimes a sharp when we require a flat;
Nor always doth the loosed bow hit that
Which it doth threaten. Therefore, where I see
Much in the poem shine, I will not be
Offended with few spots which negligence
Hath shed or human frailty not kept thence.

347–353

Sometimes I hear good Homer snore.

359

UT PICTURA POESIS

As painting so is poesy. Some man's hand
Will take you more the nearer that you stand.
As some the farther off; this loves the dark;

This, fearing not the subtlest judge's mark,
Will in the light be viewed; this once the sight
Doth please; this ten times over will delight.

361–365

NONUM IN ANNUM

But if hereafter thou shalt write, not fear
To send it to be judged by Metius' ear
And to your father's and to mine; though it be
Nine years kept in your papers by, you're free
To change and mend what you not forth do set.
The writ once out never returned yet.

386–390

NATURE OR ART

'Tis now inquired which makes the nobler verse,
Nature or art. My judgment will not pierce
Into the profits what a mere rude brain
Can or all toil without a wealthy vein;
So doth the one the other's help require
And friendly should unto one end conspire.

408–411

—Translated by Ben Jonson.

ON COMEDY AND TRAGEDY (fourth century)

Diomedes

Tragedy involves the full cycle of fortune turning to adversity
in characters of the heroic age—this is Theophrastus' definition. . . . Comedy—we render the Greek definition—involves
a full cycle in the fortune of private citizens but never the
danger of death. . . . The fortunes involved in comedy are
those of little streets and unimportant households, not as in
tragedy of princes and men of state. . . . The distinctions

between comedy and tragedy are these: the characters of tragedy are semidivine, leaders of the state, kings; those of comedy are unimportant and private persons. The subjects of tragedy are woes, exiles, deaths; of comedy, love affairs and seductions. Finally, the movement of events in tragedy is almost always from happy circumstances to bitter deaths, accompanied at the end with the perception that the fortunes of the house involved have gone to ruin. Hence comedy and tragedy are by definition distinct: the one a full cycle of harmless incident, the other a reversal of great fortunes. Sorrow, then, is characteristic of tragedy.

—Diomedes, *Ars Grammatica,* trans. by J. V. Cunningham.

ON COMEDY AND TRAGEDY (twelfth century)

Donatus

There are many differences between tragedy and comedy, but the principal difference is that in comedies the characters are of moderate estate, the difficulties that arise are slight, and the outcome of it all is joyful; but the marks of tragedy are precisely the opposite: the characters are great, the actions fearful in the extreme, and the outcome is sad and involves deaths. Again, in comedy all is disturbed at the beginning and tranquil at the close; in tragedy the order of progression is exactly reversed. The moral of tragedy is that life should be rejected; of comedy, that it should be embraced. And, finally, in comedy the story is always made up; in tragedy the story is commonly true and based on history.

—Evanthius, *Donatus on Terence,* trans. by J. V. Cunningham.

ON TRAGEDY

Averroës

Tragedy is the imitative representation of a notable action, brought to completion by a voluntary decision, and having in it a certain force of generalization with respect to matters of some import, as distinguished from a particular proposition about some individual fact. By means of this imitative representation there is induced in the minds of the audience a rightness of feeling which springs from the pity and terror which the representation begets in them.

—Averroës, *Commentary on Aristotle's "Poetics,"* trans. by J. V. Cunningham.

ON TEACHING COMPOSITION AND LITERATURE (1511)

Erasmus

THE IMPORTANCE OF THE ART OF COMPOSITION; ITS METHOD SET OUT

When this time has arrived [for regular exercises in prose and verse], care must be taken to propound themes not only worthy in subject but suitable, as being within the range of the boy's interests. For in this way he may acquire not only training in style but also a certain store of facts and ideas for future use. For example, such a subject as the following would prove attractive: "The rash self-confidence of Marcellus imperiled the fortunes of Rome; they were retrieved by the caution of Fabius." Here we see the underlying sentiment, that reckless counsels hasten toward disaster. Here is another: "Which of the two shewed less wisdom, Crates who cast his gold onto the sea, or Midas who cherished it as his supreme good?" Or: "Eloquence too little restrained brought Demosthenes and Cicero to their ruin." One more: "No encomium can exceed the deserts of Codrus, who held that the safety of his subjects claimed even the life of the King himself." But Valerius Maximus will provide you with ample choice of such themes. At first these may be set in the vernacular.

Mythology and fable will also serve your purpose. "Hercules gained immortal fame as the destroyer of monsters." "The Muses delight in the fountain and the grove; they shrink from the crowded haunts of men." "One should not burden a friend with a difficulty which it is a duty to solve ourselves." "All men are conscious of the wallet which hangs in front, but ignore that which they carry behind them." Proverb and moral will suggest such themes as these: "It is not everyone's good fortune to visit Corinth." "How far above the type of today was he who counted a man worthy not for his wealth but for his manhood!" "Socrates despises those who live in order to eat; he applauds those who eat in order to live." My book *Adagia* will supply you with instances enough. Other themes may be suggested from the properties of natural objects, such as the attraction of the magnet or the mimicry of the polypus. Similes, also, allegories, sententious sayings, smart turns of expression, will lend themselves to exercises in composition. The master in the course of his reading will be careful to note instances which present themselves as models suitable for imitation.

The pupil will now have attained a certain facility in speaking and in writing Latin. He will be ready, therefore, to proceed to a more advanced stage in grammar, which must be learnt by means of rules aptly illustrated by quotations: the rules being expressed as tersely as may be consistent with clearness. I would add that in all that concerns Greek constructions we should do well to follow the guidance of Gaza's grammar.

THE METHODS TO BE PURSUED IN WRITING ADVANCED EXERCISES IN COMPOSITION

But I must repeat that when once the simpler rules of composition, in prose and verse, and the commoner figures of speech have been mastered, the whole stress of teaching must be laid upon a close yet wide study of the greater writers. Fortified with this the student can produce *original* work in prose, under the criticism (this is most important) of a thoroughly skilled instructor.

Practice in the epistolary style, both in Greek and Latin, may be gained by writing to an argument propounded in the vernacular. This will come first. Then the whole range of rhetorical prose is open to the student who must gain acquaintance with the different varieties of style; for instance, that demanded in the production of the fable, of the moral commonplace, or the short story, or the dilemma; the art of expressing an encomium, or a denunciation; a parallel, a simile, a description. Another exercise will take the form of paraphrasing poetry into prose and the reverse process. There is also much advantage in attempting the same subject, say an epistle, in two diverse styles. Or one motive may be expressed in four or five different meters. Further, an identical topic may be propounded both for verse and for prose, alike in Latin and in Greek. An affirmation may be set to be proved by three or four differing lines of argument. Perhaps the most useful exercise of all consists in construing from Greek into Latin, practice in which demands diligent attention. For in this exercise we are committed to three distinct operations: first, we have to analyse the construction of the passage in the older tongue; next, we are forced to appreciate carefully the peculiar genius of each language and to note the principles which are common to both; thirdly, in producing an accurate rendering from the Greek we are exercised in moving freely amidst the resources of Roman vocabulary and sentence structure. So exacting a task claims whatever stimulus, encouragement, and skilled aid the master has to offer to the pupil, who will further find inspiration in the reading of model passages of a similar theme to that which he has in hand.

ORIGINAL COMPOSITION; ITS VARIETY; THE METHOD OF AIDING THE STUDENT; CORRECTION OF EXERCISES

It is now time to call for original composition, in which we leave the task of developing a stated theme to the taste and industry of the pupil himself. The right choice of subjects for such exercises is a test of the master's talent. Suppose an epistle to be required—say, of congratulation or of condolence or expostulation or of some other recognised type—the master should limit himself to indicating certain characteristics of structure or phrasing, common to each variety, and then those which may be specially appropriate to the kind of letter actually proposed. The same method will apply to exercises in formal oratory—a declamation in praise of Socrates or in denunciation of Caesar; against reliance on riches or in favor of Greek Letters; for the married life or against it; against pilgrimages or in praise of them.

This will lead to the study of the art of oratory as laid down by Cicero and Quintilian. For the subjects proposed as above must be treated in accordance with accepted methods. The master should suggest the number of propositions to be set out on a given theme, of the arguments to be employed, and of the proofs to be adduced in support of each; and the sources from which these may be drawn. This constitutes a kind of skeleton form of the oration, to be filled in to suit the actual subject selected. Further, the pupil should be led to consider the various methods by which he may adorn his treatment of the argument, such as simile and contrast, parallel cases, moral reflection, adages, anecdotes, parables, and so on; and he should have some guidance in choice of figure and metaphor as aids to ornament in style. In regard to the logical ordering of argument as a whole, the student should be taught to attend to the niceties of exposition—the exordium, the transition, the peroration; for each of these has its own peculiar excellence, and each, moreover, admits of the merit not only of precision but also of elegance.

Seven or eight exercises of this kind done under careful supervision should be sufficient to enable the pupil to lay out matter for original prose composition without help. Amongst suitable subjects for the purpose are those drawn from legend and ancient history, such as these: "Menelaus before a Trojan assembly claims the restoration of Helen"; "Phalaris presses the priests of Delphi to accept his Brazen Bull as an offering to the god"; "Cicero is warned to reject the offers of Mark Antony." As regards the correction of compositions, the master will note his approval of passages which show ingenuity in selection of material, and in its treatment, and in imitation. He will censure omission or bad arrangement of matter, exaggerations, carelessness, awkwardness of expression. He will at the same time point out how corrections may be suitably made, and ask for a rewriting of the exercise. Yet, after all, his chief aim will be to stimulate his pupils by calling attention to the progress made by this one or by the other, thus arousing the spirit of emulation in the class.

THE BEST METHODS OF PROCEDURE IN READING AN
AUTHOR IN CLASS

In reading a classic let the master avoid the practice, common to inferior teachers, of taking it as the text for universal and irrelevant commentary. Respect the writer, and let it be your rule to rest content with explaining and illustrating his meaning. This would be the method I advise, say, in taking a class through a play of Terence. You begin by offering an appreciation of the author, and state what is necessary concerning his life and surroundings, his talent, and the characteristics of his style. You next consider comedy as an example of a particular form of literature, and its interest for the student: the origin and meaning of the term itself, the varieties of comedy, and the Terentian prosody. Now you proceed to treat briefly and clearly the argument of the play, taking each situation in due course. Side by side with this you will handle the diction of the writer; noting any conspicuous elegance, or such particularities as archaism, novel usage, Graecisms; bringing out anything that is involved or obscure in phrases or sentence forms; marking, where necessary, derivations and orthography, metaphors and other rhetorical artifices. Parallel passages should next be brought under notice, similarities and contrasts in treatment observed, and direct borrowings traced—no difficult task when we are comparing a Latin poet with his Greek predecessors. The last factor in the lesson consists in the moral applications which it suggests; the story of Orestes and Pylades, or of Tantalus, are obvious examples.

It may be wise in some cases to open the reading of a fresh book by arousing interest in its broader significance. For instance, the "Second Eclogue" of Vergil must be treated as something more than a purely grammatical or literary exercise. "The essence of friendship," the master would begin, "lies in similarity. Violently contradictory natures are incapable of mutual affection. The stronger and the more numerous the ties of taste and interest the more durable is the bond." This, amplified by apt adages and wise reflections, of which literature is full, will serve to draw the pupil's thought to the more general aspects of his reading. But it is only a master of ability, insight, and wide culture, to whom such a method is possible. A store of pertinent quotations is the product of careful reading. For instance, in illustration of this particular theme, he will adduce such quotations as this: *"cascus cascam ducit; balbus balbum rectius intelligit; semper graculus arridet graculo,"* and others of the same import. Again, the master will have learnt from his knowledge of men that extreme differences of fortunes or of intellectual tastes do not consist with abiding friendship, that a fool laughs at a man of education, a boor has nothing in common with a courtier. He knows that there is a complete lack of sympathy between the Stoic and the Epicurean, the philosopher and the attorney, the poet and the divine, the orator and the recluse. See, too, what advantage learning gives to the master in enforcing the same theme from tradition and from history. He can refer to Castor and Pollux, to Romulus and Remus, to Cain and Abel. The beautiful myth of Narcissus will, in able hands, prove a parable of striking force. What has more likeness to ourselves than our own reflection? Thus, when one man of learning feels drawn to another, is he not in truth attracted by the reflection of himself? And so of a man of wise temperance, or a man of integrity, conscious of similar excellence in another. Upon such recognition of identical qualities is friendship based—I mean the frank, open and abiding friendship which alone deserves the name. The Platonic myth of the two types of Aphrodite, the celestial and the profane, may be adduced to prove that true affection can subsist between the good alone. For where excellence is only upon one side, friendship is but a fleeting and insecure thing. Now it is as a parable of unstable friendship that the master should treat this eclogue. Alexis is of the town, Corydon a countryman; Corydon a shepherd, Alexis a man of society. Alexis cultivated, young, graceful; Corydon rude, crippled, his youth far behind him. Hence the impossibility of a true friendship. The lesson finally left on the mind of the pupil is that it is the prudent part to choose friends among those whose tastes and characters agree with our own. Such methods of treating a classical story, by forcing attention to the moral to be deduced from it, will serve to counteract any harm which a more literal interpretation might possibly convey. After all, it is what a reader brings to a passage rather than what he finds there which is the real source of mischief.

AN INTRODUCTION TO LITERARY CRITICISM IS AFFORDED BY SUCH A METHOD OF CLASSICAL INSTRUCTION

Speaking generally, it is advisable to introduce every new

book read by indicating its chief characteristics, and then setting out its argument. The characteristics of epigram are aptness and point; of tragedy emotion, the various types of which and their exciting causes must be distinguished. In a great play the argument of each speech, the logical fence of the dialogue, the scene where the action is laid, the period, and the surroundings call for attention in due order. Comedy suggests a different method of introductory treatment; a more familiar setting, lighter, less strenuous emotions, are common to every comedy, though each play will require its own prefatory discussion. In beginning the *Andria*, the master will note the contrast of Chremes and Simo, as types of old age, of Pamphilus and Charinus as examples of young men. And so through other plays. The *Eclogues* of Vergil will be shown to have their setting in a Golden Age; their ideas, similes, comparisons, are drawn from pastoral life; the emotions depicted are far from complex; the shepherd's delight is in simple melody and the wisdom of maxim and proverb, his reverence is for traditional lore and augury. A historical book, epic or satire, dialogue or fable, will be introduced each in its appropriate way, before the text is touched upon, and the excellence or the defect of the piece emphasized.

Most important is it that the student be brought to learn for himself the true method of such criticism, that he may distinguish good literature from mediocrity. Hence the value of acquaintance with the judgments to be found in the oratorical writings of Cicero and Quintilian; in Seneca and in the old grammarians such as Donatus. Once acquired, this power of insight into the mind of the great writers will lead to a habit of general criticism of character and situation. The student will put such questions to himself as these. Why did Cicero feign to be afraid in his defence of Milo? Why did Vergil depict Turnus as a second hero? But enough to indicate what I mean by literary criticism.

—Desiderius Erasmus, *Upon the Right Method of Instruction*, a paraphrastic translation by William Harrison Woodward.

ITALIAN CRITICISM
OF THE SIXTEENTH CENTURY
Trissino (1563)

RHYME

Since we have spoken of all the modes of making rhymed verses and of all the species of poems that are made with them, it will be well to lay them aside, because verses without rhyme, that is without agreement of the termination of the last words, are more fitted to all sorts of poetry than those with rhyme. It is true that in the choruses of tragedies and comedies and in poems whose matter is love or praise, where sweetness and attractiveness are especially desirable, rhymes with their rules are not to be given up, but ought to be received and adopted as principal causes of this attractiveness and sweetness; and perhaps for this reason alone that period of antiquity, in which as though through some heavenly influence not merely literature but all the fine arts were brought down to the lowest point, adopted rhyme with great eagerness, so that in the time of the decay of the Latin language men of unpolished abilities pursued it with great zeal, as the hymns of the church clearly show.

SENTENTIAE

The sentences or wise sayings in which not merely tragedy but also heroic poetry, comedy, and the other poems ought to abound are speeches short, moral, conclusive, and full of meaning, which the Greek call *gnomai*, and they exhort either to do or not to do something; some are affirmative, some simple, some compound, some credible, some true, some hyperbolical. The exhortations to act are like this of Dante:

Aye to that truth which has the face of falsehood,
A man should close his lips as far as may be,
Because without his fault it causes shame.

—*Literary Criticism: Plato to Dryden,* trans. by Alan H. Gilbert, 1940. Reprinted with permission from Wayne State University Press.

The exhortations not to do something are like this from my *Italy Liberated from the Goths*:

> He should never sleep the entire night
> Who stands at the helm of a nation.

The affirmatives are such as this from Petrarch: "It is less shameful to err in youth." The simple are as is this line from him: "Ever sighing relieves naught." The compound are like this one from the same author: "The end crowns a life and the evening a day." The credible are like this from Dante: "Love, that exempts no one beloved from loving." The true are like the following from the *Sofonisba*: "This mortal life cannot run its course without sorrow." The hyperbolic are like this line from Petrarch: "Infinite in number is the troop of the fools." It should be noted that nothing forbids the same sentence to have two, three, or four of the qualities mentioned, that is, it can be at the same time an exhortation to a deed, and simple, and true, and affirmative, and so it is with the other qualities, provided they are not opposites and contraries, for the same sentence cannot be at the same time an exhortation to act and not to act, both simple and compound, and both hyperbolic and true. . . .

Cinthio (1543)

NUMBER OF ACTORS

In regard to the fourth objection, that on the number of the speakers, it is manifest that in ancient tragedies their number is not certain and defined, for some of them have six, some seven, and sometimes eight and nine are seen, and sometimes ten and eleven, nor are those lacking which have twelve and thirteen; this has led me to think that the interlocutors can be as many as suffice to develop the parts of the plot to an end magnificently and without confusion. And I am the more confirmed in this opinion when I see that the ancients who have given their judgment on the Greek tragedies praise highly those that carry with them the largest number of persons; the reason for this number, as it seems to me, is that regal actions are on a grand scale and individuals of various conditions appear in them on the side of him who suffers as much of him who is the cause of the action; such actions cannot be carried to an end without a great deal of speaking by the characters. Therefore it seems to me that the number of persons introduced represents in large measure the majesty of the action, if only that number of persons is judiciously brought in. This is especially true when the kings of divers nations with their courts appear on the stage, for I know that Your Excellency saw in the time of your illustrious father how unhappily that comedy turned out that was represented with but five actors, and with what great difficulty (though the argument was pleasing) it was carried to its conclusion, for the spectators were bored by having the same persons in their eyes and ears all the time. And if this monotony appears strange in comedy, where actions of the common people only and of not much importance are seen, how clearly should it be rejected in the presentation of regal affairs, and especially in our times, when the courts of great princes are crowded with a multitude of the most noble persons. Therefore, so long as unnecessary actors are not introduced and they do not make confusion but take the parts and produce the effects suitable to them, plenty rather than poverty of persons will make the conduct of the stage appear always more magnificent and more pleasing.

OEDIPUS

I will turn to respond to the sixth objection that he has made against me, that is that the *Dido* is not like the *Oedipus Tyrannus*. And this I concede to him without question, with respect to the material, since the subject of the *Oedipus Tyrannus* is such that one like it has never existed before, does not now, and probably never will again. And if Aristotle selected this play as a sort of Idea for the composition of tragedy, he did it with the judgment he has used in all his other compositions, for this material is truly unique among the others. And he who was the author of the drama shows without any doubt a marvelous acuteness of ability, because the plot is excellently knit and loosed. And Sophocles found the material so disposed and had little trouble in making it into a tragedy, and needed only to ornament it with words fitting the subject. But if we wish to respect the judgment of this slanderer we shall be obliged to say that all the tragedies that have been composed before and after the *Oedipus Tyrannus* are of no value, for there is none that is like it in subject.

DOUBLE PLOT

And here it should be understood that though double

tragedies are little praised by Aristotle (though some think otherwise) double structure is nonetheless to be much praised in comedy and has made the plays of Terence succeed wonderfully. I call that plot double which has in its action diverse kinds of persons of the same station in life, as two lovers of different character, two old men of varied nature, two servants of opposite morals, and other such things, as they may be seen in the *Andria* and in the other plots of the same poet, where it is clear that these like persons of unlike habits make the knot and the solution of the plot very pleasing. And I believe that if this should be well imitated in tragedy by a good poet, and the knot so arranged that its solution will not bring confusion, double structure in tragedy will not be less pleasing (always remembering the reverence due to Aristotle) than it is in comedy. If there have been those who have favored this method and held an opinion unlike that of Aristotle, they are not, I think, to be blamed, especially if the tragedy has a happy end, for this kind of end is much like that of comedy, and therefore such a tragedy can be like comedy in its imitation of the action. . . .

MEN OF HIGHEST RANK

The illustrious actions of tragedy are so called not because they are praiseworthy or virtuous but because they are enacted by men of the highest rank. They must be chosen and arranged, if the work is well done, in accord with the demands of the times in which the poet writes, as regards the thoughts expressed, the characteristics of the persons presented, his fitness in general, and other circumstances.

FIVE ACTS

The Latins have held that a plot should be divided into five acts. In the first the argument should be contained. In the second the things contained in the argument begin to move toward their end. In the third come impediments and perturbations. In the fourth begins to appear a way to remedy what is causing trouble. In the fifth is given the expected end with a fitting solution for all the argument. These reasons serve only for comedy, but with the proper changes can serve also for tragedy, and this division has been common to both tragedy and comedy.

FROM *THE DEFENSE OF POESIE* (1595)

Sir Philip Sidney

"TRAGICAL-COMICAL-HISTORICAL-PASTORAL"

Now in his parts, kinds, or species, as you list to term
them, it is to be noted that some poesies have coupled
together two or three kinds, as the tragical and comical,
whereupon is risen the tragi-comical. Some, in the like manner, have mingled prose and verse, as Sannazaro and Boethi-
us. Some have mingled matters heroical and pastoral. But
that cometh all to one in this question, for, if severed they be
good, the conjunction cannot be hurtful.

COMEDY AND TRAGEDY

No, perchance it is the comic, whom naughty play-makers
and stage-keepers have justly made odious. To the arguments
of abuse I will after answer. Only thus much now is to be
said, that the comedy is an imitation of the common errors
of our life, which he representeth in the most ridiculous and
scornful sort that may be, so as it is impossible that any
beholder can be content to be such a one. Now, as in
geometry the oblique must be known as well as the right, and
in arithmetic the odd as well as the even, so in the actions of
our life who seeth not the filthiness of evil wanteth a great
foil to perceive the beauty of virtue. This doth the comedy
handle so in our private and domestical matters, as with
hearing it we get as it were an experience, what is to be
looked for of a niggardly Demea, of a crafty Davus, of a
flattering Gnatho, of a vainglorious Thraso; and not only to
know what effects are to be expected, but to know who be
such, by the signifying badge given them by the comedian.
And little reason hath any man to say that men learn evil by
seeing it so set out; since, as I said before, there is no man
living but, by the force truth hath in nature, no sooner seeth

151

these men play their parts, but wisheth them in *pistrinum;* although perchance the sack of his own faults lie so behind his back that he seeth not himself dance the same measure; whereto yet nothing can more open his eyes than to see his own actions contemptibly set forth.

So that the right use of comedy will (I think) by nobody be blamed; and much less of the high and excellent tragedy, that openeth the greatest wounds, and showeth forth the ulcers that are covered with tissue, that maketh kings fear to be tyrants, and tyrants manifest their tyrannical humors; that with stirring the affects of admiration and commiseration teacheth the uncertainty of this world, and upon how weak foundations gilden roofs are builded, that maketh us know.

> *Qui sceptra saevus duro imperio regit,*
> *Timet timentes, metus in auctorem redit.*

But how much it can move, Plutarch yieldeth a notable testimony of the abominable tyrant Alexander Phéraeus, from whose eyes a tragedy, well made and represented, drew abundance of tears, who without all pity had murdered infinite numbers, and some of his own blood, so as he that was not ashamed to make matters for tragedies yet could not resist the sweet violence of a tragedy. And if it wrought no further good in him, it was that he, in despite of himself, withdrew himself from hearkening to that which might mollify his hardened heart. But it is not the tragedy they do mislike; for it were to absurd to cast out so excellent a representation of whatsoever is most worthy to be learned.

OUR TRAGEDIES AND COMEDIES

Our tragedies and comedies not without cause cried out against, observing rules neither of honest civility nor skillful poetry, excepting *Gorboduc* (again, I say, of those that I have seen), which notwithstanding, as it is full of stately speeches and well-sounding phrases, climbing to the height of Seneca's style, and as full of notable morality, which it doth most delightfully teach, and so obtain the very end of poesy, yet in truth it is very defectious in the circumstances, which grieves me, because it might not remain as an exact model of all tragedies. For it is faulty both in place and time, the two necessary companions of all corporal actions. For where the stage should always represent but one place, and the uttermost time presupposed in it should be, both by Aristotle's precept and common reason, but one day, there is both many days and many places, inartificially imagined. But if it be so in *Gorboduc*, how much more in all the rest, where you shall have Asia of the one side and Afric of the other, and so many other under-kingdoms, that the player, when he comes in, must ever begin with telling where he is, or else the tale will not be conceived? Now ye shall have three ladies walk to gather flowers, and then we must believe the stage to be a garden. By and by we hear news of shipwreck in the same place, and then we are to blame if we accept it not for a rock. Upon the back of that comes out a hideous monster, with fire and smoke, and then the miserable beholders are bound to take it for a cave. While in the meantime two armies fly in, represented with four swords and bucklers, and then what hard heart will not receive it for a pitched field? Now of time they are much more liberal, for ordinary it is that two young princes fall in love. After many traverses, she is got with a child, delivered of a fair boy; he is lost, groweth a man, falleth in love, and is ready to get another child; and all this in two hours' space; which how absurd it is in sense, even sense may imagine, and art hath taught, and all ancient examples justified, and, at this day, the ordinary players in Italy will not err in. Yet will some bring in an example of *Eunuchus* in Terence, that containeth matter of two days, yet far short of twenty years. True it is, and so was it to be played in two days, and so fitted to the time it set forth. And though Plautus have in one place done amiss, let us hit with him, and not miss with him. But they will say, How then shall we set forth a story, which contains both many places and many times? And do they not know that a tragedy is tied to the laws of poesy, and not of history; not bound to follow the story, but having liberty either to feign a quite new matter or to frame the history to the most tragical conveniency? Again, many things may be told which cannot be showed, if they know the difference betwixt reporting and representing. As for example, I may speak (though I am here) of Peru, and in speech digress from that to the description of Calicut; but in action I cannot represent it without Pacolet's horse. And so was the manner the ancients took, by some *Nuntius* to recount things done in former time or other place. Lastly, if they will represent an history, they must not (as Horace saith) begin *ab ovo*, but they must come to the principal point of that one action which they will represent.

By example this will be best expressed. I have a story of young Polydorus, delivered for safety's sake, with great riches, by his father Priam to Polymnestor, king of Thrace, in the Trojan war time. He, after some years, hearing the overthrow of Priam, for to make the treasure his own, murdereth the child. The body of the child is taken up by Hecuba. She, the same day, findeth a slight to be revenged most cruelly of the tyrant. Where now would one of our tragedy writers begin, but with the delivery of the child? Then should he sail over into Thrace, and so spend I know not how many years, and travel numbers of places. But where doth Euripides? Even with the finding of the body, leaving the rest to be told by the spirit of Polydorus. This needs no further to be enlarged; the dullest wit may conceive it.

But besides these gross absurdities, how all their plays be neither right tragedies nor right comedies, mingling kings and clowns, not because the matter so carrieth it, but thrust in the clown by head and shoulders to play a part in majestical matters, with neither decency nor discretion, so as neither the admiration and commiseration nor the right sportfulness is by their mongrel tragicomedy obtained. I know Apuleius did somewhat so, but that is a thing recounted with space of time, not represented in one moment: and I know the ancients have one or two examples of tragicomedies, as Plautus hath *Amphitryo*. But if we mark them well we shall find that they never, or very daintily, match hornpipes and funerals. So falleth it out that, having indeed no right comedy, in that comical part of our tragedy we have nothing but scurrility unworthy of any chaste ears, or some extreme show of doltishness, indeed fit to lift up a loud laughter, and nothing else; where the whole tract of a comedy should be full of delight, as the tragedy should be still maintained in a well-raised admiration.

But our comedians think there is no delight without laughter; which is very wrong, for though laughter may come with delight, yet cometh it not of delight, as though delight should be the cause of laughter; but well may one thing breed both together. Nay rather in themselves they have, as it were, a kind of contrariety; for delight we scarcely do but in things that have a conveniency to ourselves or to the general nature; laughter almost ever cometh of things most disproportioned to ourselves and nature. Delight hath a joy in it, either permanent or present. Laughter hath only a scornful tickling. For example, we are ravished with delight to see a fair woman, and yet are far from being moved to laughter. We laugh at deformed creatures, wherein certainly we cannot delight. We delight in good chances, we laugh at mischances; we delight to hear the happiness of our friends and country, at which he were worthy to be laughed at that would laugh. We shall, contrarily, laugh sometimes to find a matter quite mistaken and go down the hill against the bias, in the mouth of some such men as for the respect of them one shall be heartily sorry, yet he cannot choose but laugh; and so is rather pained than delighted with laughter. Yet deny I not but that they may go well together. For as in Alexander's picture well set out we delight without laughter, and in twenty mad antics we laugh without delight, so in Hercules, painted with his great beard and furious countenance, in woman's attire, spinning at Omphale's commandment, it breeds both delight and laughter. For the representing of so strange a power in love procures delight; and the scornfulness of the action stirreth laughter. But I speak to this purpose, that all the end of the comical part be not upon such scornful matters as stir laughter only, but mix with it that delightful teaching which is the end of poesy. And the great fault even in that point of laughter, and forbidden plainly by Aristotle, is that they stir laughter in sinful things, which are rather execrable than ridiculous; or in miserable, which are rather to be pitied than scorned. For what is it to make folks gape at a wretched beggar or a beggarly clown; or against law of hospitality to jest at strangers, because they speak not English so well as we do? What do we learn? since it is certain.

> *Nil habet infelix paupertas durius in se,*
> *Quam quod ridiculos homines facit.*

But rather a busy loving courtier, a heartless threatening Thraso, a self-wise-seeming schoolmaster, a wry transformed traveller—these if we saw walk in stage names, which we play naturally, therein were delightful laughter, and teaching delightfulness; as in the other, the tragedies of Buchanan do justly bring forth a divine admiration. But I have lavished out too many words of this play matter. I do it because, as they are excelling parts of poesy, so is there none so much used in England, and none can be more pitifully abused; which, like an unmannerly daughter showing a bad education, causeth her mother Poesy's honesty to be called in question.

VERSIFICATION

Now of versifying there are two sorts, the one ancient, the other modern: the ancient marked the quantity of each syllable and according to that framed his verse; the modern observing only number, with some regard of the accent, the chief life of it standeth in that like sounding of the words which we call rhyme. Whether of these be the more excellent would bear many speeches. The ancient no doubt more fit for music, both words and time observing quantity, and more fit lively to express divers passions by the low or lofty sound of the well-weighed syllable. The latter likewise with his rhyme striketh a certain music to the ear; and in fine since it doth delight, though by another way, it obtaineth the same purpose; there being in either sweetness, and wanting in neither majesty.

—c. 1583; published 1595.

PART V

The Literary-Dramatic Situation

THE STAGE: PRO AND CON

Con (1583)

Then, seeing that plays were first invented by the devil, practiced by the heathen gentiles, and dedicated to their false idols, gods, and goddesses, as the house, stage, and apparel to Venus, the music to Apollo, the penning to Minerva and the Muses, the action and pronunciation to Mercury and the rest, it is more than manifest that they are no fit exercises for a Christian man to follow. But if there were no evil in them save this; namely, that the arguments of tragedies is anger, wrath, immunity, cruelty, injury, incest, murder, and such like, the persons or actors are gods, goddesses, furies, fiends, hags, kings, queens, or potentates. Of comedies the matter and ground is love, bawdry, cosenage, flattery, whoredom, adultery; the persons, or agents, whores, queens, bawds, scullions, knaves, courtesans, lecherous old men, amorous young men, with such like of infinite variety. If, I say, there were nothing else but this, it were sufficient to withdraw a good Christian from the using of them; for so often as they go to those houses where players frequent, they go to Venus's palace and satan's synagogue to worship devils and betray Christ Jesus. . . .

There is no mischief which these plays maintain not. For do they not nourish idleness? And *otia dant vitia*, idleness is the mother of vice. Do they not draw the people from hearing the word of God, from godly lectures and sermons? For you shall have them flock thither, thick and threefold, when the church of God shall be bare and empty. . . . Do they not maintain bawdry, infinite foolery, and renew the remembrance of heathen idolatry? Do they not induce whoredom and uncleanness? Nay, are they not rather plain devourers of maidenly virginity and chastity? For proof whereof, but mark the flocking and running to Theaters and Curtains, daily and hourly, night and day, time and tide, to see plays and interludes; where such wanton gestures, such bawdy speeches, such laughing and fleering, such kissing and bussing, such clipping and culling, such winking and glancing of wanton eyes, and the like, is used, as is wonderful to behold. Then, these goodly pageants being done, every mate sorts to his mate, every one brings another homeward of their way very friendly, and in their secret conclaves (covertly) they play the sodomites, or worse. And these be the fruits of plays or interludes for the most part. And whereas you say there are good examples to be learned in them, truely so there are: if you will learn falsehood; if you will learn cosenage; if you will learn to deceive; if you will learn to play the hypocrite, to cog, lie, and falsify; if you will learne to jest, laugh, and fleer, to grin, to nod, and mow; if you will learn to play the vice, to swear, tear, and blaspheme both Heaven and Earth. If you will learn to become a bawd, unclean, and to devirginate maids, to deflower honest wives: if you will learn to murder, slay, kill, pick, steal, rob, and rove. If you will learn to rebel against princes, to commit treasons, to consume treasures, to practise idleness, to sing and talk of bawdy love and venery. If you will learn to deride, scoff, mock, and flout, to flatter and smooth. If you will learn to play the whoremaster, the glutton, drunkard, or incestuous person. If you will learn to become proud, haughty, and arrogant; and, finally, if you will learn to condemn God and all his laws, to care neither for heaven nor hell, and to commit all kind of sin and mischief, you need to go to no other school, for all these good examples may you see painted before your eyes in interludes and plays; wherefore that man who giveth money for the maintenance of them must needs incur the damage of *premunire*, that is, eternal damnation, except they repent. For the Apostle biddeth us beware lest we communicate with other men's sins, and this their doing is not only to communicate with other men's sins and maintain evil to the destruction of themselves and many others, but also a maintaining of a great sort of idle lubbers, and buzzing dronets, to suck up and devour the good honey whereupon the poor bees should live.

—Phillip Stubbes, *The Anatomie of Abuses.*

The Lord Mayor of London
to John Whitgift, Archbishop of Canterbury (1592)

Our most humble duties to Your Grace remembered. Whereas by the daily and disorderly exercise of a number of players and playing houses erected within this city, the youth thereof is greatly corrupted and their manners infected with many evil and ungodly qualities, by reason of the wanton and profane devices represented on the stages by the said players, the prentices and servants withdrawn from their works, and all sorts in general from the daily resort unto sermons and other Christian exercises, to the great hindrance of the trades and traders of this city and profanation of the good and the godly religion established amongst us. To which places also do usually resort great numbers of light and lewd disposed persons, as harlots, cutpurses, coseners, pilferers, and such like, and there, under the color of resort to those places to hear the plays, devise divers evil and ungodly matches, confederacies, and conspiracies, which by means of the opportunity of the place cannot be prevented nor discovered, as otherwise they might be. In consideration whereof, we most humbly beseech Your Grace for your godly care for the reforming of so great abuses tending to the offence of Almighty God, the profanation and slander of His true religion, and the corrupting of our youth, which are the seed of the church of God and the commonwealth among us, to vouchsafe us your good favor and help for the reforming and banishing of so great evil out of this city, which ourselves of long time, though to small purpose, have so earnestly desired and endeavored by all means that possibly we could. And because we understand that the Queen Majesty is and must be served at certain times by this sort of people, for which purpose she hath granted her letters patents to Mr. Tilney, Master of her Revels, by virtue whereof he being authorized to reform, exercise, or suppress all manner of players, plays, and playing houses whatsoever, did first license the said playing houses within this city for Her Majesty's said service, which before that time lay open to all the statutes for the punishing of these and such like disorders. We are most humbly and earnestly to beseech Your Grace to call unto you the said Master of Her Majesty's Revels, with whom also we have conferred of late to that purpose, and to treat with him, if by any means it may be devised that Her Majesty may be served with these recreations as hath been accustomed (which in our opinions may easily be done by the private exercise of Her Majesty's own players in convenient place) and the city freed from these continual disorders, which thereby do grow and increase daily among us. Whereby Your Grace shall not only benefit and bind unto you the politic state and government of this city, which by no one thing is so greatly annoyed and disquieted as by players and plays, and the disorders which follow thereupon, but also take away a great offence from the church of God and hinderance to His gospel, to the great contentment of all good Christians, specially the preachers and ministers of the word of God about this city, who have long time and yet do make their earnest continual complaint unto us for the redress hereof. And thus recommending our most humble duties and service to Your Grace, we commit the same to the grace of the Almighty. From London the 25th of February 1591.

Your Grace's most humble.

To the Right Reverend Father in God My Lord the Arch-bishop of Canterbury His Grace

Pro (1592)

To them that demand what fruits the poets of our time bring forth, or wherein they are able to prove themselves necessary to the state, thus I answer: first and foremost, they have cleansed our language from barbarism and made the vulgar sort here in London (which is the fountain whose rivers flow round about England) to aspire to a richer purity of speech than is communicated with the commonality of any nation under heaven. The virtuous by their praises they encourage to be more virtuous; to vicious men they are as infernal hags to haunt their ghosts with eternal infamy after death. The soldier, in hope to have his high deeds celebrated by their pens, despiseth a whole army of perils, and acteth wonders exceeding all human conjecture. Those that care neither for God nor the devil, by their quills are kept in awe.

That state of kingdom that is in league with all the world,

and hath no foreign sword to vex it, is not half so strong or confirmed to endure as that which lives every hour in fear of invasion. There is a certain waste of the people for whom there is no use but war; and these men must have some employment still to cut them off; *Nam si foras hostem non habent, domi invenient.* If they have no service abroad, they will make mutinies at home. Or if the affairs of the state be such as cannot exhale all these corrupt excrements, it is very expedient they have some light toys to busy their heads withal, cast before them as bones to gnaw upon, which may keep them from having leisure to intermeddle with higher matters.

To this effect, the policy of plays is very necessary, howsoever some shallow-brained censurers (not the deepest searches into the secrets of government) mightily oppugn them. For whereas the afternoon being idlest time of the day, wherein men that are their own masters (as gentlemen of the court, the Inns of the Court, and the number of captains and soldiers about London) do wholly bestow themselves upon pleasure, and that pleasure they divide (how virtuously, it skills not) either into gaming, following of harlots, drinking, or seeing a play; is it not then better (since of four extremes all the world cannot keep them but they will choose one) that they should betake them to the least, which is plays?

In plays, all cozenages, all cunning drifts overgilded with outward holiness, all strategems of war, all the cankerworms that breed on the rust of peace, are most lively anatomized; they show the ill success of treason, the fall of hasty climbers, the wretched end of usurpers, the misery of civil dissension, and how just God is evermore in punishing of murder. And to prove every one of these allegations could I propound the circumstances of this play and that play, if I meant to handle this theme otherwise than *obiter*.

—Thomas Nashe, *Peirce Penniless.*

"FAMOUSED FOR AN ARCH PLAYMAKING POET"
(1592)

The Life and Death of Robert Greene, Master of Arts

I need not make long discourse of my parents, who for their
gravity and honest life were well known and esteemed
amongst their neighbors; namely, in the city of Norwich,
where I was bred and born. But as out of one selfsame clod
of clay there sprouts both stinking weeds and delightful
flowers; so from honest parents often grow most dishonest
children; for my father had care to have me in my nonage
brought up at school, that I might through the study of good
letters grow to be a friend to myself, a profitable member to
the commonwealth, and a comfort to him in his age. But as
early pricks the tree that will prove a thorn; so even in my
first years I began to follow the filthiness of mine own
desires, and neither to listen to the wholesome advertisements
of my parents, nor be ruled by the careful correction of my
master. For being at the University of Cambridge, I light
amongst wags as lewd as myself, with whom I consumed the
flower of my youth, who drew me to travel into Italy and
Spain, in which places I saw and practiced such villainy as is
abominable to declare. Thus by their counsel I sought to
furnish myself with coin, which I procured by cunning
sleights from my father and my friends, and my mother
pampered me so long, and secretly helped me to the oil of
angels, that I grew thereby prone to all mischief; so that
being then conversant with notable braggarts, boon companions, and ordinary spendthrifts that practiced sundry superficial studies, I became as a scion grafted into the same stock,
whereby I did absolutely participate of their nature and
qualities.

At my return into England I ruffled out in my silks, in the
habit of malcontent, and seemed so discontent that no place
would please me to abide in, nor no vocation cause me to
stay myself in; but after I had by degrees proceeded Master
of Arts, I left the university and away to London, where

(after I had continued some short time, and driven myself out of credit with sundry of my friends) I became an author of plays, and a penner of love pamphlets, so that I soon grew famous in that quality, that who for that trade grown so ordinary about London as Robin Greene? Young yet in years, though old in wickedness, I began to resolve that there was nothing bad that was profitable; whereupon I grew so rooted in all mischief that I had as great a delight in wickedness as sundry hath in godliness; and as much felicity I took in villainy as other had in honesty. . . .

Yet let me confess a truth, that even once, and yet but once, I felt a fear and horror in my conscience, and then the terror of God's judgments did manifestly teach me that my life was bad, that by sin I deserved damnation, and that such was the greatness of my sin that I deserved no redemption. And this inward motion I received in Saint Andrew's church in the city of Norwich, at a lecture or sermon then preached by a godly learned man, whose doctrine, and the manner of whose teaching, I liked wonderful well; yea (in my conscience) such was his singleness of heart and zeal in his doctrine that he might have converted the most monster of the world.

Well, at that time, whosoever was worst, I knew myself as bad as he; for being new come from Italy (where I learned all the villainies under the heavens), I was drowned in pride, whoredom was my daily exercise, and gluttony with drunkenness was my only delight.

At this sermon the terror of God's judgments did manifestly teach me that my exercises were damnable, and that I should be wiped out of the book of life if I did not speedily repent my looseness of life and reform my misdemeanors.

At this sermon the said learned man (who doubtless was the child of God) did beat down sin in such pithy and persuasive manner that I began to call unto mind the danger of my soul, and the prejudice that at length would befall me for those gross sins which with greediness I daily committed; insomuch as sighing I said in myself, "Lord, have mercy upon me, and send me grace to amend and become a new man."

But this good motion lasted not long in me; for no sooner had I met with my copesmates, but seeing me in such a solemn humor they demanded the cause of my sadness; to whom when I had discovered that I sorrowed for my wickedness of life, and that the preacher's words had taken a deep impression in my conscience, they fell upon me in jesting manner, calling me puritan and precisian, and wished I might have a pulpit, with such other scoffing terms, that by their foolish persuasion the good and wholesome lesson I had learned went quite out of my remembrance; so that I fell again with the dog to my old vomit, and put my wicked life in practice, and that so thoroughly as ever I did before.

Thus although God sent his holy spirit to call me, and though I heard him, yet I regarded it no longer than the present time, when suddenly forsaking it, I went forward obstinately in my miss. Nevertheless, soon after, I married a gentleman's daughter of good account, with whom I lived for a while; but forasmuch as she would persuade me from my willful wickedness, after I had a child by her, I cast her off, having spent up the marriage money which I obtained by her.

Then left I her at six or seven, who went into Lincolnshire, and I to London; where in short space I fell into favor with such as were of honorable and good calling. But here note that though I knew how to get a friend, yet I had not the gift or reason how to keep a friend; for he that was my dearest friend, I would be sure so to behave myself towards him that he should ever after profess to be my utter enemy, or else vow never after to come in my company.

Thus my misdemeanors (too many to be recited) caused the most part of those so much to despise me that in the end I became friendless, except it were in a few alehouses, who commonly for my inordinate expenses would make much of me, until I were on the score far more than ever I meant to pay by twenty nobles thick. After I had wholly betaken me to the penning of plays (which was my continual exercise) I was so far from calling upon God that I seldom thought on God but took such delight in swearing and blaspheming the name of God that none could think otherwise of me than that I was the child of perdition.

These vanities and other trifling pamphlets I penned of love and vain fantasies was my chiefest stay of living, and for those my vain discourses I was beloved of the more vainer sort of people, who being my continual companions, came still to my lodging, and there would continue quaffing, carousing, and surfeiting with me all the day long.

But I thank God that he put it in my head to lay open the most horrible cozenages of the common cony-catchers, cozeners, and cross-biters, which I have indifferently handled in those my several discourses already imprinted. And my trust is that those discourses will do great good, and be very beneficial to the commonwealth of England.

But oh, my dear wife, whose company and sight I have refrained these six years: I ask God and thee forgiveness for so greatly wronging thee, of whom I seldom or never thought until now. Pardon me, I pray thee, wheresoever thou art, and God forgive me all my offenses.

The Manner of the Death and Last End of Robert Greene, Master of Arts

After that he had penned the former discourse, then lying sore sick of a surfeit which he had taken with drinking, he continued most patient and penitent; yea, he did with tears forsake the world, renounced swearing, and desired forgiveness of God and the world for all his offenses; so that during all the time of his sickness, which was about a month's space, he was never heard to swear, rave, or blaspheme the name of God, as he was accustomed to do before that time—which greatly comforted his well-willers, to see how mightily the grace of God did work in him.

He confessed himself that he was never heartsick but said that all his pain was in his belly. And although he continually scoured, yet still his belly swelled, and never left swelling upward until it swelled him at the heart and in his face.

During the whole time of his sickness he continually called upon God and recited these sentences following: "Oh Lord, forgive my manifold offenses. Oh Lord, have mercy upon me. Oh Lord, forgive me my secret sins, and in thy mercy, Lord, pardon them all. Thy mercy, Lord, is above thy works." And with such-like godly sentences he passed the time, even till he gave up the ghost.

And this is to be noted, that his sickness did not so greatly weaken him but that he walked to his chair and back again the night before he departed; and then, being feeble, laying him down on his bed about nine of the clock at night, a friend of his told him that his wife had sent him commendations, and that she was in good health; whereat he greatly rejoiced, confessed that he had mightily wronged her, and wished that he might see her before he departed; whereupon, feeling his time was but short, he took pen and ink and wrote her a letter to this effect:

Sweet wife, as ever there was any good will or friendship between thee and me, see this bearer (my host) satisfied of his debt; I owe him ten pound, and but for him I had perished in the streets. Forget and forgive my wrongs done unto thee, and Almighty God have mercy on my soul. Farewell till we meet in heaven, for on earth thou shalt never see me more. This is 2 of September 1592.

Written by thy dying husband,
ROBERT GREENE

THE NEW STYLE AND PROSODY

1 Tamburlaine the Great

THE PROLOGUE

From jigging veins of rhyming mother wits,
And such conceits as clownage keeps in pay,
We'll lead you to the stately tent of war,
Where you shall hear the Scythian Tamburlaine
Threat'ning the world with high astounding terms,
And scourging kingdoms with his conquering sword.
View but his picture in this tragic glass,
And then applaud his fortunes as you please.

—Christopher Marlowe.

To the Gentlemen Students of Both Universities (1589)

I am not ignorant how eloquent our gowned age is grown of late; so that every mechanical mate abhors the English he was born to, and plucks, with a solemn periphrasis, his *ut vales* from the inkhorn: which I impute not so much to the perfection of arts, as to the servile imitation of vainglorious tragedians, who contend not so seriously to excel in action as to embowel the clouds in a speech of comparison, thinking themselves more than initiated in poets' immortality if they but once get Boreas by the beard and the heavenly Bull by the dewlap. But herein I cannot so fully bequeath them to folly as their idiot artmasters, that intrude themselves to our ears as the alchemists of eloquence, who (mounted on the stage of arrogance) think to outbrave better pens with the swelling bombast of a bragging blank verse. Indeed it may be the ingrafted overflow of some kilcow conceit, that overcloyeth their imagination with a more than drunken resolution, being not extemporal in the invention of any other means to vent their manhood, commits the disgestion of their choleric incumbrances to the spacious volubility of a drumming decasyllabon. Mongst this kind of men that repose eternity in the mouth of a player, I can but engross some deep-read grammarians who, having no more learning in their skull than will serve to take up a commodity, nor art in their brain than was nourished in a serving man's idleness, will take upon them to be the ironical censors of all, when God and Poetry doth know they are the simplest of all.

It is a common practice nowadays amongst a sort of shifting companions, that run through every art and thrive by none, to leave the trade of *Noverint*, whereto they were born, and busy themselves with the endeavors of art, that could scarcely latinize their neck-verse if they should have need; yet English Seneca read by candlelight yields many good sentences, as "Blood is a beggar," and so forth; and if you entreat him fair in a frosty morning, he will afford you whole *Hamlets*, I should say handfuls, of tragical speeches. But O grief! *tempus edax rerum*, what's that will last always? The sea exhaled by drops will in continuance be dry, and Seneca, let blood line by line and page by page, at length must needs die to our stage; which makes his famished followers to imitate the Kyd in Aesop, who enamored with the Fox's new fangles, forsook all hopes of life to leap into a new occupation; and these men renouncing all possibilities of credit or estimation to intermeddle with Italian translations. Wherein how poorly they have plodded (as those that are neither provenzal men, nor are able to distinguish of articles), let all indifferent gentlemen that have travailed in that tongue discern by their two-penny pamphlets. And no marvel though their home-born mediocrity be such in this matter; for what can be hoped of those that thrust Elisium into hell, and have not learned, so long as they have lived in the spheres, the just measure of the horizon without an hexameter. Sufficeth them to bodge up a blank verse with ifs and ands; and other while for recreation after their candle stuff, having starched their beards most curiously, to make a peripatetical path into the inner parts of the city, and spend two or three hours in turning over French *Doudie*, where they attract more infection in one minute than they can do eloquence all days of their life by conversing with any authors of like argument.

—Thomas Nashe.

"Those Antics Garnished in Our Colors" of Rhetoric (1592)

TO THOSE GENTLEMEN HIS QUONDAM ACQUAINTANCE, THAT SPEND THEIR WITS IN MAKING PLAYS, R. G. WISHETH A BETTER EXERCISE, AND WISDOM TO PREVENT HIS EXTREMITIES.

Base-minded men all three of you, if by my misery ye be not warned; for unto none of you, like me, sought those burrs to cleave; those puppets, I mean, that speak from our mouths, those antics garnished in our colors. Is it not strange that I, to whom they all have been beholding; is it not like that you, to whom they all have been beholding, shall, were ye in that case that I am now, be both at once of them forsaken? Yes, trust them not; for there is an upstart crow, beautified with our feathers, that with his *tiger's heart wrapped in a player's hide*[7] supposes he is as well able to bombast out a blank verse as the best of you; and being an absolute *Johannes fac totum*, is in his own conceit the only Shake-scene in a country. Oh that I might entreat your rare wits to be employed in more profitable courses; and let those apes imitate your past excellence, and never more acquaint them with your admired inventions.

—Robert Greene, *A Groatsworth of Wit.*

AN APOLOGY (1592)

About three months since died Mr. Robert Greene, leaving many papers in sundry booksellers' hands, among other his *Groatsworth of Wit*, in which a letter written to divers play-makers is offensively by one or two of them taken, and because on the dead they cannot be avenged, they wilfully forge in their conceits a living author. . . . With neither of them that take offence was I acquainted, and with one of them I care not if I never be. The other, whom at that time I did not so much spare as since I wish I had, for that, as I have moderated the heat of living writers and might have used my own discretion (especially in such a case, the author being dead), that I did not I am as sorry as if the original fault had been my fault, because myself have seen his demeanor no less civil than he excellent in the quality he professes. Besides, divers of worship have reported his uprightness of dealing, which argues his honesty, and his facetious grace in writing that approves his art.

—Henry Chettle.

---

[7] "O tiger's heart wrapped in a woman's hide!" Shakespeare, *3 Henry VI*, 1. 4. 137.

ON *THE SPANISH TRAGEDY (JERONIMO)* (1598)

BOBADILLA. What new book have you there? What? *Go by Jeronimo.*

MATHEO. Ay, did you ever see it acted? is't not well penned?

BOBADILLA. Well penned: I would fain see all the poets of our time pen such another play as that was; they'll prate and swagger, and keep a stir of art and devices, when (by God's so) they are the most shallow, pitiful fellows that live upon the face of the earth again.

MATHEO. Indeed, here are a number of fine speeches in this book: *Oh eyes, no eyes, but fountains fraught with tears;* there's a conceit: Fountains fraught with tears. *Oh life, no life, but lively form of death*: is't not excellent? *Oh world, no world, but mass of public wrongs*; O God's me: *confused and filled with murder and misdeeds.* Is't not simply the best that ever you heard?
Ha, how do you like it?

BOBADILLA. 'Tis good.

—Ben Jonson, *Every Man in His Humour* 1. 3.

THE NEW REALISM (1598)

Every Man in His Humour

PROLOGUE

Though need make many poets, and some such
As art and nature have not better'd much,
Yet ours for want hath not so lov'd the stage
As he dare serve th'ill customs of the age,
Or purchase your delight at such a rate
As, for it, he himself must justly hate:
To make a child, now swaddled, to proceed
Man, and then shoot up, in one beard and weed,
Past threescore years; or, with three rusty swords,
And help of some few foot-and-half-foot words,
Fight over York and Lancaster's long jars,
And in the tiring-house bring wounds to scars.
He rather prays you will be pleas'd to see
One such to-day, as other plays should be;
Where neither chorus wafts you o'er the seas,
Nor creaking throne comes down the boys to please,
Nor nimble squib is seen to make afeard
The gentlewomen, nor roll'd bullet heard
To say it thunders, nor tempestuous drum
Rumbles to tell you when the storm doth come;
But deeds and language such as men do use,
And persons such as comedy would choose
When she would show an image of the times,
And sport with human follies, not with crimes;
Except we make 'em such, by loving still
Our popular errors, when we know th'are ill.
I mean such errors as you'll all confess,
By laughing at them, they deserve no less:
Which when you heartily do, there's hope left, then,
You, that have so grac'd monsters, may like men.

—Ben Jonson. Published 1616

A Woman Killed With Kindness (1603)

THE PROLOGUE

I come but as a harbinger, being sent
To tell you what these preparations mean.
Look for no glorious state: our Muse is bent
Upon a barren subject, a bare scene.

—Thomas Heywood

The Fashion of Playmaking (1611)

The fashion of playmaking I can properly compare to
nothing so naturally as the alteration in apparel; for in the
time of the great crop-doublet your huge bombastic plays,
quilted with mighty words to lean purpose, was only then in
fashion; and as the doublet fell, neater inventions began to
set up. Now, in the time of spruceness, our plays follow the
niceness of our garments: single plots, quaint conceits, lecherous jests, dressed up in hanging sleeves—and those are fit
for the times.

—Thomas Middleton, *The Roaring Girl*

THE CITIZEN AND THE PLAYERS

The Knight of the Burning Pestle (1607)

INDUCTION

Enter Speaker of the Prologue.

SPEAKER OF PROL. "From all that's near the court, from all that's great,

 Within the compass of the city-walls,

 We now have brought our scene——"

         [CITIZEN *leaps on the Stage.*]

CIT. Hold your peace, goodman boy!

S. OF PROL. What do you mean, sir?

CIT. That you have no good meaning: this seven years there hath been plays at this house, I have observed it, you have still girds at citizens; and now you call your play *The London Merchant.* Down with your title, boy! down with your title!

S. OF PROL. Are you a member of the noble city?

CIT. I am.

S. OF PROL. And a freeman?

CIT. Yea, and a grocer.

S. OF PROL. So, grocer, then, by your sweet favour, we intend no abuse to the city.

CIT. No, sir! yes sir: if you were not resolved to play the Jacks, what need you study for new subjects, purposely to abuse your betters? why could not you be contented, as well as others, with *The Legend of Whittington,* or *The Life and*

Death of Sir Thomas Gresham, with the Building of the Royal Exchange, or *The Story of Queen Eleanor, with the Rearing of London Bridge upon Woolsacks?*

S. OF PROL. You seem to be an understanding man: what would you have us do, sir?

CIT. Why, present something notably in honour of the commons of the city.

S. OF PROL. Why, what do you say to *The Life and Death of Fat Drake, or the Repairing of Fleet-privies?*

CIT. I do not like that; but I will have a citizen, and he shall be of my own trade.

S. OF PROL. Oh, you should have told us your mind a month since; our play is ready to begin now.

CIT. 'Tis all one for that; I will have a grocer, and he shall do admirable things.

S. OF PROL.   What will you have him do?

CIT. Marry, I will have him—

WIFE. [*below.*] Husband, husband!

RALPH.   [*below.*] Peace, mistress.

WIFE [*below.*]   Hold thy peace, Ralph; I know what I do, I warrant ye.—Husband, husband!

CIT. What sayst thou, cony?

WIFE. [*below.*] Let him kill a lion with a pestle, husband! let him kill a lion with a pestle!

CIT.   So he shall.—I'll have him kill a lion with a pestle.

WIFE. [*below.*] Husband! shall I come up, husband?

CIT. Ay, cony.—Ralph, help your mistress this way.— Pray, gentlemen, make her a little room.—I pray you, sir, lend me your hand to help up my wife: I thank you, sir.—So.

[WIFE *comes on the Stage.*]

WIFE. By your leave, gentlemen all; I'm something troublesome: I'm a stranger here; I was ne'er at one of these plays, as they say, before; but I should have seen *Jane Shore* once; and my husband hath promised me, any time this twelvemonth, to carry me to *The Bold Beauchamps,* but in truth he did not. I pray you, bear with me.

CIT. Boy, let my wife and I have a couple of stools and then begin; and let the grocer do rare things.

[*Stools are brought.*]

S. OF PROL. But, sir, we have never a boy to play him: every one hath a part already.

WIFE. Husband, husband, for God's sake, let Ralph play him! beshrew me, if I do not think he will go beyond them all.

CIT. Well remembered, wife.—Come up, Ralph.—I'll tell you, gentlemen; let them but lend him a suit of reparel and necessaries, and, by gad, if any of them all blow wind in the tail on him, I'll be hanged.

[RALPH *comes on the Stage.*]

WIFE. I pray you, youth, let him have a suit of reparel!— I'll be sworn, gentlemen, my husband tells you true: he will act you sometimes at our house, that all the neighbours cry out on him; he will fetch you up a couraging part so in the garret, that we are all as feared, I warrant you, that we quake again: we'll fear our children with him; if they be never so unruly, do but cry, "Ralph comes, Ralph comes!" to them, and they'll be as quiet as lambs.—Hold up thy head, Ralph; show the gentlemen what thou canst do; speak a huffing part; I warrant you, the gentlemen will accept of it.

CIT. Do, Ralph, do.

RALPH. "By Heaven, methinks, it were an easy leap
To pluck bright honour from the pale-faced moon;
Or dive into the bottom of the sea,
Where never fathom line touched any ground,
And pluck up drowned honour from the lake of hell."

CIT. How say you, gentlemen, is it not as I told you?

WIFE. Nay, gentlemen, he hath played before, my husband says, Mucedorus, before the wardens of our company.

CIT. Ay, and he should have played Jeronimo with a shoemaker for a wager.

S. OF PROL. He shall have a suit of apparel, if he will go in.

CIT. In, Ralph, in, Ralph; and set out the grocery in their kind, if thou lovest me.   [Exit RALPH.]

WIFE. I warrant, our Ralph will look finely when he's dressed.

S. OF PROL. But what will you have it called?

CIT. *The Grocer's Honour*.

S. OF PROL. Methinks *The Knight of the Burning Pestle* were better.

WIFE. I'll be sworn, husband, that's as good a name as can be.

CIT. Let it be so.—Begin, begin; my wife and I will sit down.

S. OF PROL. I pray you, do.

—Francis Beaumont.

CAMBRIDGE GRADUATES, POETS, PRINTERS, AND PLAYERS (1601)

JUDICIO

Here is a book, Ingenioso; why, to condemn it to Cloaca, the usual Tyburn of all misliving papers, were too fair a death for so foul an offender.

INGENIOSO

What's the name of it, I pray thee, Judicio?

JUDICIO

Look, it's here: *Belvedere.*

INGENIOSO

What, a bell-wether in Paul's Churchyard! so called because it keeps a bleating, or because it hath the tinkling bell of so many poets about the neck of it? What is the rest of the title?

JUDICIO

The Garden of the Muses.

INGENIOSO

What have we here, the poet garish, gaily bedecked, like fore-horse of the parish? What follows?

JUDICIO

Quem referent musæ, vivet, dum robora tellus,
Dum cælum stellas, dum vehit amnis aquas.
Who blurs fair paper with foul bastard rhymes,
Shall live full many an age in latter times:
Who makes a ballad for an alehouse door,

Shall live in latter times for evermore:
Then, Bodenham, thy muse shall live so long,
  As drafty ballads to thy praise are sung.
But what's his device? Parnassus with the sun and the laurel?
I wonder this owl dares look on the sun; and I marvel this
goose flies not the laurel: his device might have been better,
a fool going into the market-place to be seen, with this
motto: *Scribimus indocti*; or, a poor beggar gleaning of ears
in the end of harvest, with this word: *Sua cuique gloria*.

JUDICIO

Turn over the leaf, Ingenioso, and thou shalt see the pains
of this worthy gentleman: *Sentences, gathered out of all kind
of poets, referred to certain methodical heads, profitable for
the use of these times, to rhyme upon any occasion at a little
warning.* Read the names.

INGENIOSO

So I will, if thou wilt help me to censure them.

Edmund Spenser.	*Thomas Watson.*
Henry Constable.	*Michael Drayton.*
Thomas Lodge.	*John Davis.*
Samuel Daniel.	*John Marston.*

Kit Marlowe.

Good men and true; stand together; hear your censure.
What's thy judgment of Spenser?

JUDICIO

A sweeter swan than ever sung in Po,
A shriller nightingale than ever bless'd
The prouder groves of self-admiring Rome.
Blithe was each valley, and each shepherd proud,
While he did chant his rural minstrelsy:
Attentive was full many a dainty ear,
Nay, hearers hung upon his melting tongue,
While sweetly of his *Fairy* Queen he sung;
While to the waters' fall he tun'd her fame,
And in each bark engrav'd Eliza's name:

And yet for all, this unregarding soil
Unlac'd the line of his desired life,
Denying maintenance for his dear relief;
Careless care to prevent his exequy,
Scarce deigning to shut up his dying eye.

INGENIOSO

Pity it is that gentler wits should breed,
Where thickskin chuffs laugh at a scholar's need.
But softly may our Homer's ashes rest,
That lie by merry Chaucer's noble chest.
But, I pray thee, proceed briefly in thy censure, that I may
be proud of myself; as in the first, so in the last, my censure
may jump with thine.—Henry Constable, Samuel Daniel,
Thomas Lodge, Thomas Watson.

JUDICIO

Sweet Constable doth take the wond'ring ear,
And lays it up in willing prisonment:
Sweet honey-dropping Daniel doth wage
War with the proudest big Italian,
That melts his heart in sugar'd sonneting;
Only let him more sparingly make use
Of others' wit, and use his own the more,
That well may scorn base imitation.
For Lodge and Watson, men of some desert,
Yet subject to a critic's marginal;
Lodge for his oar in ev'ry paper boat,
He, that turns over Galen ev'ry day,
To sit and simper *Euphues'* Legacy.

INGENIOSO

Michael Drayton?

JUDICIO

Drayton's sweet muse is like a sanguine dye,
Able to ravish the rash gazer's eye.

INGENIOSO

However, he wants one true note of a poet of our times,

and that is this: he cannot swagger it well in a tavern, nor domineer in a hothouse. John Davies?

JUDICIO

Acute John Davies, I affect thy rhymes,
That jerk in hidden charms these looser times;
Thy plainer verse, thy unaffected vein,
Is graced with a fair and sweeping train.

INGENIOSO

Lock and Hudson?

JUDICIO

Lock and Hudson, sleep, you quiet shavers, among the shavings of the press, and let your books lie in some old nooks amongst old boots and shoes; so you may avoid my censure.

INGENIOSO

Why, then, clap a lock on their feet, and turn them to commons. John Marston?

JUDICIO

What, Monsieur Kinsayder, lifting up your leg, and pissing against the world? put up, man, put up, for shame!

INGENIOSO

Methinks he is a ruffian in his style,
Withouten bands or garters' ornament:
He quaffs a cup of Frenchman's Helicon;
Then roister doister in his oily terms,
Cuts, thrusts, and foins, at whomsoever he meets,
And strews about Ram-Alley meditations.
Tut, what cares he for modest close-couch'd terms,
Cleanly to gird our looser libertines?
Give him plain naked words, stripp'd from their
    shirts,
That might beseem plain-dealing Aretine.

JUDICIO

Ay, there is one, that backs a paper steed,
And manageth a penknife gallantly,
Strikes his poinardo at a button's breadth,
Brings the great battering-ram of terms to town;
And, at first volley of his cannon-shot,
Batters the walls of the old fusty world.

INGENIOSO

Christopher Marlowe?

JUDICIO

Marlowe was happy in his buskin'd muse;
Alas! unhappy in his life and end:
Pity it is that wit so ill should dwell,
Wit lent from heav'n, but vices sent from hell.

INGENIOSO

Our theatre hath lost, Pluto hath got,
A tragic penman for a dreary plot.
Benjamin Jonson?

JUDICIO

The wittiest fellow of a bricklayer in England.

INGENIOSO

A mere empiric, one that gets what he hath by observation, and makes only nature privy to what he indites; so slow
an inventor, that he were better betake himself to his old
trade of bricklaying; a bold whoreson, as confident now in
making of a book, as he was in times past in laying of a
brick. William Shakespeare?

JUDICIO

Who loves not Adon's love or Lucrece' rape,
His sweeter verse contains heart-robbing lines

Could but a graver subject him content,
Without love's foolish, lazy languishment.

INGENIOSO

Churchyard?
Hath not Shore's wife, although a light-skirts she,
Giv'n him a chaste, long-lasting memory?

JUDICIO

No; all light pamphlets one day I finden shall
A churchyard and a grave to bury all!
Thomas Nashe.

INGENIOSO

Ay, here is a fellow, Judicio, that carried the deadly stock
in his pen, whose muse was armed with a gagtooth, and his
pen possessed with Hercules' furies.

JUDICIO

Let all his faults sleep with his mournful chest,
And then for ever with his ashes rest:
His style was witty, though he had some gall,
Something he might have mended; so may all:
Yet this I say that, for a mother-wit,
Few men have ever seen the like of it.

INGENIOSO *reads the rest of the names.*

JUDICIO

As for these, they have some of them been the old hedge-
stakes of the press; and some of them are, at this instant, the
bots and glanders of the printing-house: fellows that stand
only upon terms to serve the term, with their blotted papers,
write, as men go to stool, for needs; and when they write,
they write as a bear pisses, now and then drop a pamphlet.

INGENIOSO

Durum telum necessitas. Good faith, they do, as I do—

exchange words for money. I have some traffic this day with Danter about a little book which I have made; the name of it is, *A Catalogue of Cambridge Cuckolds*. But this Belvedere, this methodical ass, hath made me almost forget my time; I'll now to Paul's Churchyard; meet me an hour hence at the sign of the Pegasus in Cheapside, and I'll moist thy temples with a cup of claret, as hard as the world goes. [*Exit* JUDICIO]

Enter DANTER *the Printer.*

INGENIOSO

Danter, thou art deceived, wit is dearer than thou takest it to be: I tell thee, this libel of Cambridge has much salt and pepper in the nose; it will sell sheerly underhand, when all these books of exhortations and catechisms lie moulding on thy shopboard.

DANTER

It's true: but, good faith, Master Ingenioso, I lost by your last book; and, you know, there is many a one that pays me largely for the printing of their inventions: but, for all this, you shall have forty shillings and an odd bottle of wine.

INGENIOSO

Forty shillings! A fit reward for one of your rheumatic poets, that beslavers all the paper he comes by, and furnishes all the chandlers with waste-papers to wrap candles in; but as for me, I'll be paid dear even for the dregs of my wit: little knows the world what belongs to the keeping of a good wit in waters, diets, drinks, tobacco, &c. It is a dainty and a costly creature; and therefore I must be paid sweetly. Furnish me with money, that I may put myself in a new suit of clothes, and I'll suit thy shop with a new suit of terms. It's the gallantest child my invention was ever delivered of: the title is, *A Chronicle of Cambridge Cuckolds*. Here a man may see what day of the month such a man's commons were enclosed, and when thrown open; and when any entailed some odd crowns upon the heirs of their bodies unlawfully begotten. Speak quickly: else I am gone.

DANTER

O, this will sell gallantly; I'll have it, whatsoever it cost: will you walk on, Master Ingenioso? We'll sit over a cup of wine, and agree on it.

INGENIOSO

A cup of wine is as good a constable as can be to take up the quarrel betwixt us.   [*Exeunt.*]

Enter BURBAGE *and* KEMP

BURBAGE

Now, Will Kemp, if we can entertain these scholars at a low rate, it will be well; they have oftentimes a good conceit in a part.

KEMP

It's true, indeed, honest Dick, but the slaves are somewhat proud; and besides, it's a good sport in a part to see them never speak in their walk, but at the end of the stage; just as though, in walking with a fellow, we should never speak but at a stile, a gate, or a ditch, where a man can go no further. I was once at a comedy in Cambridge, and there I saw a parasite make faces and mouths of all sorts on this fashion.

BURBAGE

A little teaching will mend these faults; and it may be, besides, they will be able to pen a part.

KEMP

Few of the university pen play well; they smell too much of that writer Ovid and that writer Metamorphosis, and talk too much of Proserpina and Jupiter. Why, here's our fellow Shakespeare puts them all down—ay, and Ben Jonson too. O, that Ben Jonson is a pestilent fellow; he brought up Horace, giving the poets a pill; but our fellow Shakespeare hath given him a purge that made him bewray his credit.

BURBAGE

It's a shrewd fellow, indeed. I wonder these scholars stay so long; they appointed to be here presently, that we might try them. O, here they come.

[*Enter* STUDIOSO *and* PHILOMUSUS]

STUDIOSO

Take heart, these lets our clouded thoughts refine;
The sun shines brightest when it 'gins decline.

BURBAGE

Mr. Philomusus and Mr. Studioso, God save you.

KEMP

Mr. Philomusus and Mr. Otioso, well-met.

PHILOMUSUS

The same to you, good Mr. Burbage. What, Mr. Kemp, how doth the emperor of Germany?

STUDIOSO

God save you, Mr. Kemp; welcome, Mr. Kemp, from dancing the morris over the Alps.

KEMP

Well, you merry knaves, you may come to the honour of it one day. Is it not better to make a fool of the world as I have done, than to be fooled of the world, as you scholars are? But be merry, my lads; you have happened upon the most excellent vocation in the world for money. They come north and south to bring it to our playhouse; and for honours, who of more report than Dick Burbage and Will Kemp? He is not counted a gentleman that knows not Dick Burbage and Will Kemp. There's not a country wench that can dance Sellenger's round, but can talk of Dick Burbage and Will Kemp.

PHILOMUSUS

Indeed, Mr. Kemp, you are very famous; but that is as well for works in print, as your part in cue.

KEMP

You are at Cambridge still with size cue, and be lusty humorous poets. You must untruss; I rode this my last circuit purposely, because I would be judge of your actions.

BURBAGE

Mr. Studioso, I pray you, take some part in this book, and act it, that I may see what will fit you best. I think your voice would serve for Hieronimo; observe how I act it, and then imitate me.   [He recites.]

STUDIOSO

Who calls Jeronimo from his naked bed?
And, &c.

BURBAGE

You will do well—after a while.

KEMP

Now for you. Methinks you should belong to my tuition; and your face, methinks, would be good for a foolish mayor or a foolish justice of peace. Mark me:—

Forasmuch as there be two states of a commonwealth, the one of peace, the other of tranquillity; two states of war, the one of discord, the other of dissension; two states of an incorporation, the one of the aldermen, the other of the brethern; two states of magistrates, the one of governing, the other of bearing rule. Now, as I said even now—for a good thing cannot be said too often. Virtue is the shoeing-horn of justice; that is, virtue is the shoeing-horn of doing well; that is, virtue is the shoeing-horn of doing justly; it behoveth me, and is my part to commend this shoeing-horn unto you. I hope this word shoeing-horn doth not offend any of you, my worshipful brethern; for you, being the worshipful headsmen of the town, know well what the horn meaneth. Now therefore I am determined not only to teach, but also to instruct, not only the ignorant, but also the simple; not only what is their duty towards their betters, but also what is their duty towards their superiors.

Come, let me see how you can do; sit down in the chair.

PHILOMUSUS

Forasmuch as there be, &c.

KEMP

Thou wilt do well in time, if thou wilt be ruled by thy betters, that is, by myself, and such grave aldermen of the playhouse as I am.

BURBAGE

I like your face, and the proportion of your body for Richard the Third. I pray, Mr. Philomusus, let me see you act a little of it.

PHILOMUSUS

Now is the winter of our discontent
Made glorious summer by the sun of York.

BURBAGE

Very well, I assure you. Well, Mr. Philomusus and Mr. Studioso, we see what ability you are of; I pray, walk with us to our fellows, and we'll agree presently.

PHILOMUSUS

We will follow you straight, Mr. Burbage.

KEMP

It's good manners to follow us, Mr. Philomusus and Mr. Otioso.

PHILOMUSUS

And must the basest trade yield us relief?
Must we be practis'd to those leaden spouts,
That nought down vent but what they do receive?
Some fatal fire hath scorch'd our fortune's wing,
And still we fall, as we do upward spring?
As we strive upward on the vaulted sky,
We fall, and feel our hateful destiny.

> —*The Return from Parnassus,* part two, "publicly acted by
> the students in St. John's College in Cambridge," Christmas
> season 1601-1602.

JOHN DONNE TO HENRY WOTTON (1597–98)

Believe me, sir, in my youth's giddiest days,
When to be like the Court was a play's praise,
Plays were not so like Courts as Courts are like plays.

AS YOU LIKE IT, WHAT YOU WILL, OR A WINTER'S TALE (1591)

PROLOGUE TO ENDYMION

Most high and happy Princess, we must tell you a tale of
the Man in the Moon, which, if it seem ridiculous for the
method, or superfluous for the matter, or for the means
incredible, for three faults we can make but one excuse: it is
a tale of the Man in the Moon.

It was forbidden in old time to dispute of Chimæra
because it was a fiction; we hope in our times none will apply

pastimes, because they are fancies; for there liveth none under the sun that knows what to make of the Man in the Moon. We present neither comedy, nor tragedy, nor story [history], nor anything but that whosoever heareth may say this: Why, here is a tale of the Man in the Moon.

—John Lyly.

HISTORY (1592)

Nay, what if I prove plays to be no extreme, but a rare exercise of virtue? First, for the subject of them, (for the most part) it is borrowed out of our English chronicles, wherein our forefathers' valiant acts (that have lain long buried in rusty brass and worm-eaten books) are revived, and they themselves raised from the grave of oblivion, and brought to plead their aged honors in open presence; than which, what can be a sharper reproof to these degenerate effeminate days of ours?

—Thomas Nashe, *Peirce Penniless.*

HISTORY, TRAGEDY, COMEDY (1599)

A Warning for Fair Women

THE INDUCTION

Enter at one door HISTORY *with Drum and Ensigne:* TRAGEDY *at another, in her one hand a whip, in the other hand a knife.*

TRAG. Whither away so fast? Peace with that drum!
Down with that ensign, which disturbs our stage!

Out with this luggage, with this foppery!
This brawling sheepskin is intolerable.

    HIST. Indeed, no marvel though we should give place
Unto a common executioner!
Room room! for God's sake let us stand away.
Oh, we shall have some doughty stuff to day.

Enter COMEDY *at the other end.*

    TRAG. What, yet more cats guts? oh, this filthy sound
Stifles mine ears. More cartwheels creaking yet?
A plague upon 't. I'll cut your fiddle strings
If you stand scraping thus to anger me!

    COM. Gup, mistress buskins, with a whirligig! are you so
      touchy?
Madam Melpomene, whose mare is dead,
That you are going to take off her skin?

    TRAG. A plague upon these filthy fiddling tricks,
Able to poison any noble wit.
Avoid the stage, or I will whip you hence!

    COM. Indeed thou may'st, for thou art murder's Beadle;
The common hangman unto Tyranny.
But History! what, all three met at once?
What wonder 's towards, that we are got together?

    HIST. My meaning was to have been here to-day,
But meeting with my lady Tragedy
She scolds me off:
And, Comedy, except thou canst prevail
I think she means to banish us the stage.

    COM. Tut, tut, she cannot; she may for a day
Or two, perhaps, be had in some request,
But once a week if we do not appear,
She shall find few that will attend her here.

    TRAG. I must confess you have some sparks of wit,
Some odd ends of old jests scrap'd up together,
To tickle shallow unjudicial ears:
Perhaps some puling passion of a lover,
But slight and childish. What is this to me?

I must have passions that must move the soul;
Make the heart heavy and throb within the bosom,
Extorting tears out of the strictest eyes—
To rack a thought, and strain it to his form,
Until I rap the senses from their course.
This is my office.

COM. How some damn'd tyrant to obtain a crown
Stabs, hangs, impoisons, smothers, cutteth throats:
And then a Chorus, too, comes howling in
And tells us of the worrying of a cat:
Then, too, a filthy whining ghost,
Lapt in some foul sheet, or a leather pilch,
Comes screaming like a pig half stick'd,
And cries, *Vindicta!*—Revenge, Revenge!
With that a little rosin flasheth forth,
Like smoke out of a tobacco pipe, or a boy's squib.
Then comes in two or three [more] like to drovers,
With tailors' bodkins, stabbing one another—
Is not this trim? Is not here goodly things,
That you should be so much accounted of?
I would not else—

HIST. Now, before God, thou'lt make her mad anon;
Thy jests are like a whisp unto a scold.

COM. Why, say I could, what care I, History?
Then shall we have a Tragedy indeed;
Pure purple buskin, blood and murder right.

TRAG. Thus, with your loose and idle similies,
You have abused me; but I'll whip you hence: [*she whips
        them.*]
I'll scourge and lash you both from off the stage.
'Tis you have kept the theatres so long,
Painted in play-bills upon every post,
That I am scorned of the multitude,
My name profan'd. But now I'll reign as Queen.
In great Apollo's name, and all the Muses,
By virtue of whose Godhead I am sent,
I charge you to begone and leave this place!

HIST. Look, Comedy, I mark'd it not till now,
The stage is hung with black, and I perceive
The auditors prepar'd for Tragedy.

COM. Nay, then, I see she shall be entertain'd.
These ornaments beseem not thee and me.
Then Tragedy kill them to-day with sorrow,
We'll make them laugh with mirthful jests tomorrow.

HIST. And, Tragedy, although to-day thou reign,
Tomorrow here I'll domineer again. [*Exeunt.*]

TRAG. [*turning to the people.*]
Are you both gone so soon? Why then I see
All this fair circuit here is left to me.
All you spectators, turn your cheerful eye:
Give entertainment unto Tragedy.
My scene is London, native and your own.
I sigh to think my subject too well known.
I am not feigned. Many now in this Round
Once to behold me in sad tears were drown'd.
Yet what I am I will not let you know,
Until my next ensuing scene shall show.

—"As it hath been lately divers times acted by the Right
Honorable, the Lord Chamberlain's servants."

TRAGEDY (1612)

The White Devil

"TO THE READER"

In publishing this tragedy I do but challenge to myself that
liberty which other men have ta'en before me; not that I
affect praise by it, for *nos haec novimus esse nihil*: only,
since it was acted in so dull a time of winter, presented in so
open and black a theater, that it wanted that which is the
only grace and setting out of a tragedy, a full and understanding auditory; and that since that time I have noted most
of the people that come to that playhouse resemble those
ignorant asses who, visiting stationers' shops, their use is not

to inquire for good books, but new books; I present it to the general view with this confidence:

Nec rhoncos metues maligniorum,
Nec scombris tunicas dabis molestas.

If it be objected this is no true dramatic poem, I shall easily confess it; *non potes in nugas dicere plura meas Ipse ego quam dixi*, willingly and not ignorantly in this kind have I faulted; for should a man present to such an auditory the most sententious tragedy that ever was written, observing all the critical laws, as height of style and gravity of person, enrich it with the sententious chorus, and as it were life and death in the passionate and weighty Nuntius; yet, after all this divine rapture, *O dura messorum ilia*, the breath that comes from the uncapable multitude is able to poison it; and ere it be acted let the author resolve to fix to every scene this of Horace: "*Haec hodie Porcis comedenda relinques.*"

To those who report I was a long time in finishing this tragedy, I confess I do not write with a goose quill, winged with two feathers; and if they will needs make it my fault, I must answer them with that of Euripides to Alcestides, a tragic writer: Alcestides objecting that Euripides had only in three days composed three verses, whereas himself had written three hundred, "Thou tell'st truth," quoth he, "but here's the difference: thine shall only be read for three days, whereas mine shall continue three ages."

Detraction is the sworn friend to ignorance; for mine own part I have ever truly cherish'd my good opinion of other men's worthy labors: especially of that full and height'ned style of Mr. Chapman; the labor'd and understanding works of Mr. Jonson; the no less worthy composures of the both worthily excellent Mr. Beaumont and Mr. Fletcher; and lastly, without wrong last to be named, the right happy and copious industry of Mr. Shakespeare, Mr. Dekker, and Mr. Heywood; wishing that I write may be read by their light: protesting that, in the strength of mine own judgment, I know them so worthy that, though I rest silent in my own work, yet to most of theirs I dare, without flattery, fix that of Martial: "*Non norunt haec monumenta mori.*"

—John Webster.

PASTORAL TRAGI-COMEDY (1609)

The Faithful Shepherdess

"TO THE READER"

If you be not reasonably assured of your knowledge in this
kind of poem, lay down the book, or read this, which I would
wish had been the prologue. It is a pastoral tragi-comedy,
which the people seeing when it was played, having ever had
a singular gift in defining, concluded to be a play of country
hired shepherds in gray cloaks, with curtailed dogs in strings,
sometimes laughing together, and sometimes killing one another; and, missing Whitsun-ales, cream, wassail, and morris
dances, began to be angry. In their error I would not have
you fall, lest you incur their censure. Understand, therefore,
a pastoral to be a representation of shepherds and shepherd-
esses with their actions and passions, which must be such as
may agree with their natures, at least not exceeding former
fictions and vulgar traditions; they are not to be adorned with
any art, but such improper ones as nature is said to bestow,
as singing and poetry; or such as experience may teach
them, as the virtues of herbs and fountains, the ordinary
course of the sun, moon, and stars, and such like. But you
are ever to remember shepherds to be such as all the ancient
poets, and modern of understanding, have received them;
that is, the owners of flocks, and not hirelings. A tragic-
comedy is not so called in respect of mirth and killing, but in
respect it wants deaths, which is enough to make it no
tragedy, yet brings some near it, which is enough to make it
no comedy, which must be a representation of familiar people, with such kind of trouble as no life be questioned; so
that a god is as lawful in this as in a tragedy, and mean
people as in a comedy. Thus much I hope will serve to justify
my poem, and make you understand it; to teach you more
for nothing, I do not know that I am in conscience bound.

—John Fletcher.

COMEDY (1600)

Every Man Out of His Humour

MITIS. I travail with another objection, signior, which I fear will be enforced against the author, ere I can be deliver'd of it.

CORDATUS. What's that, sir?

MITIS. That the argument of his comedy might have been of some other nature, as of a duke to be in love with a countess, and that countess to be in love with the duke's son, and the son to love the lady's waiting-maid; some such cross-wooing, with a clown to their servingman, better than to be thus near, and familiarly allied to the time.

CORDATUS. You say well, but I would fain hear one of these autumn-judgments define once, *Quid sit comœdia?* If he cannot, let him content himself with Cicero's definition, till he have strength to propose to himself a better, who would have a comedy to be *imitatio vitae, speculum consuetudinis, imago veritatis;* a thing throughout pleasant and ridiculous, and accommodated to the correction of manners. If the maker have fail'd in any particle of this, they may worthily tax him; but if not, why—be you, that are for them, silent, as I will be for him; and give way to the actors.

—Ben Jonson.

SET NOT TOO MUCH STORE ON ANTIQUITY

I know nothing can conduce more to letters than to examine the writings of the ancients, and not to rest in their sole authority, or take all upon trust from them; provided the plagues of judging and pronouncing against them, be away; such as are envy, bitterness, precipitation, impudence, and scurrile scoffing. For to all the observations of the ancients we have our own experience: which if we will use and apply, we have better means to pronounce. It is true they opened the gates and made the way, that went before us; but as guides, not commanders. Truth lies open to all; it is no man's several.

—Ben Jonson, *Timber, or Discoveries.*

PART VI

Show Business

LONDON PLAYHOUSES 1569–1629

In the year 1629 there was built a new fair playhouse near the Whitefriars. And this is the seventeenth stage, or common playhouse, which hath been new made within the space of threescore years within London and the suburbs, *viz.*, five inns, or common hostelries, turned to playhouses, one cockpit, St. Paul's singing school, one in the Blackfriars, and one in the Whitefriars, which was built last of all in the year 1629; all the rest not now named were erected only for common playhouses, besides the new built bear garden, which was built as well for plays and fencers' prizes as bull baiting, besides one in former time at Newington Butts. Before the space of threescore years above said, I neither knew, heard, nor read of any such theaters, set stages, or playhouses as have been purposely built within man's memory.

—EDMUND HOWES, *Stow's Annals* (1631).

THE OLD THEATER AND THE NEW

They acted nothing here but plays of the Holy Scripture or saints' lives; and that without any certain theaters or set companies till about the beginning of Queen Elizabeth's reign, they began here first to assemble into companies and set up theaters, first in the city (as in the inn yards of the Cross Keys and Bull in Grace and Bishopsgate Street at this day is to be seen), till that fanatic spirit which then began with the stage and after ended with the throne banished them thence into the suburbs, as after they did the kingdom in the beginning of our civil wars. In which time plays were so little incompatible with religion and the theater with the church as on weekdays after vespers both the Children of the Chapel and St. Paul's acted plays, the one in Whitefriars, the other behind the Convocation House in Paul's, till people growing more precise and plays more licentious, the theater of Paul's was quite suppressed and that of the Children of the Chapel converted to the use of the Children of Revels. . . .

It was the happiness of the actors of those times to have such poets as these to instruct them and write for them, and no less of those poets to have such docile and excellent actors to act their plays, as a Field and Burbage, of whom we may say that he was a delightful Proteus, so wholly transforming himself into his parts and putting off himself with his clothes as he never, not so much as in the tiring-house, assumed himself again until the play was done, there being as much difference between him and one of our common actors as between a ballad singer who only mouths it and an excellent singer who knows all his graces and can artfully vary and modulate his voice, even to know how much breath he is to give to every syllable. He had all the parts of an excellent orator, animating his words with speaking and speech with action, his auditors being never more delighted than when he spoke nor more sorry than when he held his peace, yet even then he was an excellent actor still, never falling in his part when he had done speaking but with his looks and gesture maintaining it still unto the height, he imagining *age quod agis* only spoke to him; so as those who call him a player do him wrong, no man being less idle than he, whose whole life is nothing else but action with only this difference from other men's, that as what is but a play to them is his business, so their business is but a play to him.

Now for the difference betwixt our theaters and those of former times: they were but plain and simple with no other scenes nor decorations of the stage but only old tapestry and the stage strewed with rushes (with their habits accordingly), whereas our now for cost and ornament are arrived at the height of magnificence. . . . for scenes and machines they are no new invention, our masques and some of our plays in former times, though not so ordinary, having had as good or rather better than any we have now.

—Richard Flecknoe, *A Short Discourse of the English Stage* (1664).

THE THEATER AND THE GLOBE

The father of us, Cuthbert and Richard Burbage, was the first builder of playhouses and was himself in his younger years a player. The Theater he built with many hundred pounds taken up at interest. The players that lived in those first times had only the profits arising from the doors, but now the players receive all the comings-in at the doors to themselves and half the galleries from the housekeepers. He [i.e., James Burbage, father of Cuthbert and Richard] built this house upon leased ground, by which means the landlord [i.e., Giles Alleyn] and he had a great suit in law and by his death the like troubles fell on us, his sons; we then bethought us of altering from thence and at like expense built the Globe with more sums of money taken up at interest, which lay heavy on us many years, and ourselves we joined those deserving men, Shakespeare, Heminges, Condell, Phillipps, and others, partners in the profits of that they call the house.

—Cuthbert Burbage, *testimony* (1635).

THE GLOBE, MODEL FOR THE FORTUNE (1600)

The frame of the said house to be set square and to contain fourscore foot of lawful assize every way square without and fifty-five foot of like assize square every way within, with a good sewer and strong foundation of piles, brick, lime, and sand, both without and within, to be wrought one foot of assize at the least above the ground. And the said frame to contain three stories in height, the first or lower story to contain twelve foot of lawful assize in height, the second story eleven foot of lawful assize in height, and the third or upper story to contain nine foot of lawful assize in height. All which stories shall contain twelve foot and a half of lawful assize in breadth throughout, besides a jutty forwards in either of the said two upper stories of ten inches of lawful assize, with four convenient divisions for gentlemen's rooms, and other sufficient and convenient divisions for two-penny rooms, with necessary seats to be placed and set as well in those rooms as throughout all the rest of the galleries of the said house, and with suchlike stairs, conveyances, and divisions without and within as are made and contrived in and to the late erected playhouse on the Bank in the said parish of St. Saviours called the Globe. With a stage and tiring-house to be made, erected, and set up within the said frame with a shadow or cover over the said stage, which stage shall be placed and set, as also the staircases of the said frame, in such sort as is prefigured in a plot thereof drawn, and which stage shall contain in length forty and three foot of lawful assize and in breadth to extend to the middle of the yard of the said house. The same stage to be paled in below with good, strong and sufficient new oaken boards, and likewise the lower story of the said frame withinside, and the same lower story to be also laid over and fenced with strong iron pikes. And the said stage to be in all other proportions contrived and fashioned like unto the stage of the said playhouse called the Globe. With convenient windows and lights glazed to the said tiring-house. And the said frame, stage, and staircases to be covered with tile and to have a sufficient gutter of lead to carry and convey the water from the covering of the said stage to fall backwards. And also all the said frame and the staircases thereof to be sufficiently enclosed without with lath, lime, and hair and the gentlemen's rooms and two-penny rooms to be sealed with lath, lime, and hair, and all the floors of the said galleries, stories, and stage to be boarded with good and sufficient new deal boards of the whole thickness where need shall be. And the said house and other things before mentioned to be made and done to be in all other contrivances, conveyances, fashions, thing, and things effected, finished, and done according to the manner and fashion of the said house called the Globe, saving only that all the principal and main posts of the said frame and stage forward shall be square and wrought plasterwise with carved proportions called satyrs to be placed and set on the top of every of the same posts, and saving also that the said Peter Sweet shall not be charged with any manner of painting in or about the said frame house or stage or any part thereof, nor rendering the walls within, nor sealing any more or other rooms then the gentlemen's rooms, two-penny rooms, and the stage before remembered.

—Contract with Peter Sweet, carpenter.

THEATERS AT SHAKESPEARE'S DEATH, AND LATER

TRUMAN. Before the wars there were in being all these playhouses at the same time. The Blackfriars and Globe on the Bankside. A winter and summer house belonging to the same company, called the King's Servants. The Cockpit or Phoenix in Drury Lane, called the Queen's Servants. The Private House in Salisbury Court, called the Prince's Servants. The Fortune near White Cross Street and the Red Bull at the upper end of St. John's Street. The two last were mostly frequented by citizens and the meaner sort of people. All these companies got money and lived in reputation, especially those of the Blackfriars, who were men of grave and sober behavior.

LOVEWIT. Which I much admire at. That the town, much less than at present, could then maintain five companies and yet now two can hardly subsist.

TRUMAN. Do not wonder but consider! That though the town was then, perhaps, not much more than half so populous as now, yet then the prices were small, there being no scenes, and better order kept among the company that came, which made very good people think a play an innocent diversion for an idle hour or two, the plays being then, for the most part, more instructive and moral.

—James Wright, *Historia Histrionica* (1699).

PROVINCIAL ACTORS
IN SHAKESPEARE'S BOYHOOD

In the city of Gloucester the manner is (as I think it is in other like corporations) that when players of interludes come to town, they first attend the mayor to inform him what nobleman's servants they are and so to get licence for their public playing; and if the mayor like the actors, or would show respect to their lord and master, he appoints them to play their first play before himself and the aldermen and common council of the city, and that is called the mayor's play, where everyone that will comes in without money, the mayor giving the players a reward as he thinks fit to show respect unto them. At such a play my father took me with him and made me stand between his legs as he sat upon one of the benches, where we saw and heard very well. The play was called *The Cradle of Security*, wherein was personated a king or some great prince with his courtiers of several kinds, amongst which three ladies were in special grace with him; and they keeping him in delights and pleasures drew him from his graver counselors, hearing of sermons, and listening to good counsel and admonitions, that in the end they got him to lie down in a cradle upon the stage, where these three ladies joining in a sweet song rocked him asleep, that he snorted again, and in the meantime closely conveyed under the cloths wherewithal he was covered a vizard like a swine's snout upon his face with three wire chains fastened thereunto, the other end whereof being holden severally by those three ladies, who fall to singing again and then discovered his face that the spectators might see how they had transformed him, going on with their singing. Whilst all this was acting there came forth of another door at the farthest end of the stage two old men, the one in blue like a sergeant at arms with his mace on his shoulder, the other in red with a drawn sword in his hand and leaning with the other hand upon the other's shoulder; and so they two went along in a soft pace round about the skirt of the stage till at last they came to the cradle, when all the court was in greatest jollity; and then the foremost old man with his mace stroke a fearful blow upon the cradle, whereat all the courtiers with the three ladies and

206

the vizard all vanished; and the desolate prince, starting up bare-faced and finding himself thus sent for to judgment, made a lamentable complaint of his miserable case and so was carried away by wicked spirits. This prince did personate in the moral the wicked of the world; the three ladies, pride, covetousness, and luxury; the two old men, the end of the world and the last judgment.

This sight took such impression in me that when I came towards man's estate it was as fresh in my memory as if I had seen it newly acted. From whence I observe out of mine own experience what great care should be had in the education of children to keep them from seeing of spectacles of ill examples and hearing of lascivious or scurrilous words, for that their young memories are like fair writing-tables, wherein if the fair sentences or lessons of grace be written, they may, by God's blessing, keep them from many vicious blots of life, wherewithal they may otherwise be tainted. ... And withal we may observe how far unlike the plays and harmless morals of former times are to those which have succeeded, many of which, by report of others, may be termed schoolmasters of vice and provocations to corruptions.

—R. Willis, *Mount Tabor* (1639).

THE PLAYERS' RELATIONSHIP TO THEIR PATRON

To the Right Honorable Earl of Leicester, their good lord and master. May it please Your Honor to understand that forasmuch as there is a certain proclamation out for reviving of a statute as touching retainers, as Your Lordship knoweth better than we can inform you thereof, we therefore, your humble servants and daily orators, your players, for avoiding all inconvenients that may grow by reason of the said statute, are bold to trouble Your Lordship with this our suit, humbly desiring Your Honor that (as you have been always our good lord and master) you will now vouchsafe to retain us at this present as your household servants and daily waiters, not that we mean to crave any further stipend or benefit at Your Lordship's hands but our liveries as we have had and also Your Honor's license to certify that we are your household servants when we shall have occasion to travel amongst our friends, as we do usually once a year and as other noblemen's players do and have done in time past, whereby we may enjoy our faculty in Your Lordship's name as we have done heretofore. Thus being bound and ready to be always at Your Lordship's commandment, we commit Your Honor to the tuition of the Almighty.

Long may your Lordship live in peace,
   A peer of noblest peers,
In health, wealth and prosperity
   Redoubling Nestor's years.

Your Lordship's servants most bounden,
     James Burbage
     John Perkin
     John Laneham
     William Johnson
     Robert Wilson
     Thomas Clarke

—Leicester's Men (1572).

THE DUTTONS SWITCH LORDS (1580)

The Duttons and their fellow players, forsaking the earl of Warwick, their master, became followers of the earl of Oxford and wrote themselves his comedians, which certain gentlemen altered and made chameleons. The Duttons, angry with that, compared themselves to any gentleman; therefore these arms were devised for them.

The field, a fart dirty, a gibbet cross-corded,
A dancing Dame Flirty of all men abhorred,
A lither lad scampant, a rogue in his rags,
A whore that is rampant, astride with her legs. . . .

THE QUEEN'S MEN

Comedians and stage players of former time were very poor
and ignorant in respect of these of this time, but being now
grown very skillful and exquisite actors for all matters, they
were entertained into the service of divers great lords, out of
which companies there were twelve of the best chosen, and
at the request of Sir Francis Walsingham they were sworn
the Queen's servants and were allowed wages and liveries as
grooms of the chamber; and until this year, 1583, the Queen
had no players. Among these twelve players were two rare
men, *viz.*, Thomas Wilson for a quick, delicate, refined,
extemporal wit and Richard Tarlton for a wondrous, plenti-
ful, pleasant, extemporal wit, he was the wonder of his time.
He lieth buried in Shoreditch Church. [In a note] He was so
beloved that men use his picture for their signs.

—Edmund Howes, *Stow's Annals* (1615).

THE LONDON STAGE (1585)

Comedies are given daily. It is particularly mirthful to behold
when the Queen's comedians act but annoying to a foreigner
who does not know the language, that he understands noth-

ing. There are some peculiar houses which are so made as to have about three galleries over one another, inasmuch as a great number of people always enters to see such an entertainment. It may well be that they take as much as from fifty to sixty dollars at once, especially when they act anything new which has not been given before and double prices are charged. This goes on nearly every day in the week; even though performances are forbidden on Friday and Saturday, it is not observed.

—Samuel Kiechel.

THE CHILDREN'S COMPANIES

SIR EDWARD FORTUNE. I saw the Children of Paul's last night,
  And troth they pleased me pretty, pretty well,
  The apes in time will do it handsomely.
PLANET. In faith, I like the audience that frequenteth there
  With much applause; a man shall not be choked
  With the stench of garlic nor be pasted
  To the barmy jacket of a beer-brewer.
BRABANT JUNIOR. 'Tis a good, gentle audience and I hope the boys
  Will come one day into the Court of requests.
BRABANT SENIOR. Aye, an they had good plays. But they produce
  Such musty fopperies of antiquity
  And do not suit the humorous age's backs
  With clothes in fashion.

—John Marston, *Jack Drum's Entertainment* (1601).

THE CHILDREN'S COMPANIES

A Note to the Master of Children of Paul's

Memorandum, that if any of the fine and foremost of these pastorals and comedies contained in this volume shall but overreach in length (the children not to begin before four, after prayers, and the gates of Paul's shutting at six, the time of supper) that then in time and place convenient, you do let pass some of the songs and make the consort shorter, for I suppose these plays be somewhat too long for that place. Howsoever, on your own experience and at your best direction, be it. Farewell to you all.

—William Percy (c. 1603).

PLAYS AT COURT (1604)

The first holy days we had every night a public play in the great hall, at which the King was ever present and liked or disliked as he saw cause, but it seems he takes no extraordinary pleasure in them. The Queen and Prince were more the players' friends, for on other nights they had them privately and hath since taken them to their protection.

—Carleton to Chamberlain.

LICENSE TO TRAVEL DURING THE PLAGUE
(1593)

Whereas it was thought meet that during the time of the
infection and continuance of the sickness in the city of
London there should no plays or interludes be used for the
avoiding of the assemblies and concourse of people in any
usual place appointed near the said city, and though the
bearers hereof, Edward Alleyn, servant to the Right Honorable the Lord High Admiral, William Kemp, Thomas Pope,
John Heminges, Augustine Phillips, and George Bryan, being
all one company, servants to our very good Lord the
Lord Strange, are restrained their exercise of playing within
the said city and liberties thereof, yet it is not thereby meant
but that they shall and may, in regard of the service by them
done and to be done at the Court, exercise their quality of
playing comedies, tragedies, and such like in any other cities,
towns, and corporations where the infection is not, so it be
not within seven miles of London or of the Court, that they
may be in the better readiness hereafter for Her Majesty's
service whensoever they shall be thereunto called. This therefore shall be to will and require you that they may without
their let or contradiction use their said exercise at their most
convenient times and places, the accustomed times of divine
prayers excepted.

GOVERNMENT RELIEF DURING PLAGUE (1604)

Amount: £30. Warrant: 8 Feb. Payee: Richard Burbage, one
of His Majesty's comedians ... for the maintenance and
relief of himself and the rest of his company, being prohib-
ited to present any plays publicly in or near London by
reason of great peril that might grow through the extraordinary concourse and assemble of people to a new increase of
the plague, till it shall please God to settle the city in a more
perfect health, by way of His Majesty's free gift.

THE TRAVELING PLAYERS AND THE
HIGHWAYMAN

Gamaliel Ratsey and his company, traveling up and down the country as they had oftentimes done before, *per varios casus et tot discrimina rerum,* still hazarding their several haps as they had several hopes, came by chance into an inn where that night there harbored a company of players, and Ratsey, framing himself to an humor of merriment, caused one or two of the chiefest of them to be sent for up into his chamber, where he demanded whose men they were and they answered they served such an honorable personage. I pray you, quoth Ratsey, let me hear your music, for I have often gone to plays more for music sake than for action, for some of you not content to do well but striving to overdo and go beyond yourselves, oftentimes, by St. George, mar all; yet your poets take great pains to make your parts fit for your mouths, though you gape never so wide. Other-some, I must needs confess, are very well deserving both for true action and fair delivery of speech, and yet, I warrant you, the very best have sometimes been content to go home at night with fifteen pence share apiece. Others there are whom fortune hath so well favored that, what by penny-sparing and long practice of playing, are grown so wealthy that they have expected to be knighted, or at least to be conjunct in authority and to sit with men of great worship on the bench of justice. But if there were none wiser than I am, there should more cats build colleges and more whores turn honest women than one before the world should be filled with such a wonder.

Well, music was played and that night passed over with such singing, dancing, and reveling as if my Lord Prodigal had been there in his ruins of excess and superfluity. In the morning Ratsey made the players taste of his bounty and so departed. But every day he had new inventions to obtain his purposes, and as often as fashions alter so often did he alter his stratagems, studying as much how to compass a poor man's purse as players do to win a full audience.

About a week after, he met with the same players, although he had so disguised himself with a false head of hair and beard that they could take no notice of him, and lying, as they did before, in one inn together, he was desirous they should play a private play before him, which they did not in the name of the former nobleman's servants, for like chameleons they had changed that color, but in the name of another whose indeed they were, although afterwards when he heard of their abuse, he discharged them and took away his warrant. For being far off, for their more countenance they would pretend to be protected by such an honorable man, denying their lord and master, and coming within ten or twenty miles of him again, they would shroud themselves under their own lord's favor.

Ratsey heard their play and seemed to like that, though he disliked the rest, and very liberally out with his purse and gave them forty shillings, with which they held themselves very richly satisfied, for they scarce had twenty shillings audience at any time for a play in the country. But Ratsey thought they should not enjoy it long, although he let them bear it about them till the next day in their purses, for the morning being come and they, having packed away their luggage and some part of their company before in a waggon, discharged the house and followed them presently.

Ratsey intended not to be long after but, having learned which way they travailed, he, being very well horsed and mounted upon his black gelding, soon overtook them; and when they saw it was the gentleman that had been so liberal with them the night before, they began to do him much courtesy and to greet his late kindness with many thanks. But that was not the matter which he aimed at. Therefore he roundly told them they were deceived in him, he was not the man they took him for. I am a soldier, sayeth he, and one that for means hath ventured my fortunes abroad and now for money am driven to hazard them at home; I am not to be played upon by players; therefore be short, deliver me your money; I will turn usurer now, my forty shillings again will not serve without interest.

They began to make many faces and to cap and knee but all would not serve their turn. He bade them leave off their cringing and compliments and their apish tricks and dispatch, which they did for fear of the worst, seeing to beg was bootless; and having made a desperate tender of their stock into Ratsey's hands, he bade them play for more, for, says he, it is an idle profession that brings in much profit, and every night where you come your playing bears your charges and somewhat into purse. Besides, you have fiddlers' fare, meat, drink, and money. If the worst be, it is but pawning your apparel, for as good actors and stalkers as you are have done it, though now they scorn it, but in any case hereafter be not counterfeits, abuse not honorable personages in using their names and countenance without their consent and privity, and because you are now destitute of a master, I will give you leave to play under my protection for a sennight's space, and I charge you do it lest when I meet you again I cut you shorter by the hams and share with you in a sharper manner than I have done at this time.

And for you, sirrah, says he to the chiefest of them, thou hast a good presence upon a stage; methinks thou darkenst thy merit by playing in the country. Get thee to London, for if one man were dead, they will have much need of such a one as thou art. There would be none in my opinion fitter than thyself to play his parts. My conceit is such of thee that I durst venture all the money in my purse on thy head to play Hamlet with him for a wager. There thou shalt learn to be frugal, for players were never so thrifty as they are now about London, and to feed upon all men, to let none feed upon thee; to make thy hand a stranger to thy pocket, thy heart slow to perform thy tongue's promise; and when thou feelest thy purse well lined, buy thee some place or lordship in the country, that, growing weary of playing, thy money may there bring thee to dignity and reputation, then thou needest care for no man nor not for them that before made thee proud with speaking their words upon the stage.

Sir, I thank you, quoth the player, for this good counsel; I promise you I will make use of it, for I have heard, indeed, of some that have gone to London very meanly and have come in time to be exceeding wealthy.

And in this presage and prophetical humor of mine, says Ratsey, kneel down. Rise up, Sir Simon Two-Shares and-a-Half, thou art now one of my knights and the first knight that ever was player in England. The next time I meet thee I must share with thee again for playing under my warrant, and so for this time adieu.

How ill he brooked this new knighthood, which he durst not but accept of, or like his late counsel, which he lost his coin for, is easy to be imagined, but whether he met with them again after the sennight's space that he charged them to play in his name, I have not heard it reported.

—Ratsey's Ghost (1605).

ENGLISH ACTORS ABROAD (1592)

Germany hath some few wandering comedians more deserving of pity then praise, for the serious parts are dully penned and worse acted, and the mirth they make is ridiculous and nothing less than witty, as I formerly have showed. So as I remember that when some of our cast despised stage players came out of England into Germany and played at Frankfort in the time of the mart, having neither a complete number of actors nor any good apparel nor any ornament of the stage, yet the Germans, not understanding a word they said, both men and women, flocked wonderfully to see their gesture and action rather than hear them speaking English, which they understood not, and pronouncing pieces and patches of English plays, which myself and some Englishmen there present could not hear without great wearisomeness. Yea, myself coming from Frankfort in the company of some chief merchants, Dutch and Flemish, heard them often brag of the good market they had made, only condoling that they had not the leisure to hear the English players.

—Fynes Moryson.

PLAY LICENSING: THE OFFICE OF THE REVELS

The Office of the Revels is noted to be one of the King's Majesty's standing offices, as are the Jewel House, the Wardrobe, the Ordnance, the Armory, and the Tents with the like allowances every ways that any of them have.

Which Office of the Revels consisteth of a wardrobe and other several rooms for artificers to work in, *viz.*, tailors, embroiderers, property makers, painters, wiredrawers, and carpenters, together with a convenient place for the rehearsals and setting forth of plays and other shows for those services.

In which Office the Master of the Office hath ever had a dwelling house for himself and his family, and the other officers are to have either dwelling houses assigned unto them by the master, for so goeth the words of their patents, or else a rent for the same as they had before they came unto St. John's.

—Tilney (1607).

THE MASTER OF REVELS ON THE MANUSCRIPT OF *SIR THOMAS MORE*

Leave out the insurrection wholly and the cause thereof and begin with Sir Thomas More at the mayor's sessions, with a report afterwards of his good service done, being Shrieve of London, upon a mutiny against the Lombards, only by a short report and not otherwise, at your perils.

CURRENT EVENTS STAGED (1599)

Two days ago the overthrow of Turnhout was acted upon a stage and all your names used that were at it, especially Sir Francis Vere, and he that played that part got a beard resembling his and a watchet [light blue] satin doublet with hose trimmed with silver lace. You was also introduced killing, slaying, and overthrowing the Spaniards, and honorable mention made of your service in seconding Sir Francis Vere, being engaged.

—Rowland Whyte.

"SPEAK THE SPEECH I PRAY YOU, AS I PRONOUNCED IT TO YOU"

As for the actors, they, as I have noted in England, are instructed daily as though at school; even the most prominent actors must permit themselves to be instructed in their parts by the poets, and this is what endows a well-written comedy with life and grace. Thus it is no wonder that the English comedians (I speak of the practiced ones) are more excellent than others.

—Rhenanus (1613)

FROM A THEATRICAL ACCOUNT BOOK

Item paid for carpenters' work and making the throne in the heavens the 4 of June 1595. £ 7 2s.

Lent unto Frances Henslow the 8 of May 1593 to lay down for his share to the Queen's players when they broke and went into the country to play the sum of 15 pounds to be paid unto me at his return out of the country I say lent. £15.

In the name of God Amen beginning at Newington my Lord Admiral men and my Lord Chamberlain men as followeth 1594

3 of June 1594	Received at *Hester and Ahasuerus*	8s.
4 of June 1594	Received at *The Jew of Malta*	10s.
5 of June 1594	Received at *Andronicus*	12s.
6 of June 1594	Received at *Cutlack*	11s.
8 of June 1594 new.	Received at *Bellendon*	17s.
9 of June 1594	Received at *Hamlet*	8s.
10 of June 1594	Received at *Hester*	5s.

218

11 of June 1594	Received at *The Taming of a Shrew* .... 9s.
12 of June 1594	Received at *Andronicus* .... 7s.
13 of June 1594	Received at *The Jew* .... 4s.
15 of June 1594	Received at *Bellendon* ....£3 4s.
17 of June 1594	Received at *Cutlack* ....35s.
18 of June 1594	Received at the *Ranger's Comedy* ......22s.
19 of June 1594	Received at the *Guise* ....54s.
20 of June 1594	Received at *Bellendon* ....30s.
22 of June 1594	Received at the *Ranger's Comedy* ......59s.
23 of June 1594	Received at *The Jew* ....23s.
24 of June 1594	Received at *Cutlack* ....25s.
25 of June 1594	Received at *The Massacre* ....36s.
26 of June 1594 new.	Received at *Galiaso* ....£3 4s.
27 of June 1594	Received at *Cutlack* ....36s.
30 of June 1594	Received at *The Jew of Malta* ....41s.

Received for two weeks' pay which was due unto the Master of Revels from the 12 of April 1596 unto the 26 of the same month 22s. I say received. 20s.

Lent unto Benjamin Jonson the 3 of December 1597 upon a book which he was to write for us before Christmas next after the date hereof, which he showed the plot unto the company I say lent in ready money unto him the sum of 20s.

Laid out for two jigs for the company to two young men the 12 of December 1597 the sum of 6s. 8d.

Lent unto Drayton and Chettle the 13 of March 1598 in part of payment of a book wherein is a part of a Welshman written which they have promised to deliver by the 22 day next following I say lent ready money. 40s.

Lent unto the company to pay Drayton and Dekker and Chettle their full payment for the book called *The Famous Wars of Henry I and the Prince of Wales* the sum of £4 5s.

Lent at that time unto the company for to spend at the reading of that book at The Sun in New Fish Street: 5s.

Lent unto Robert Shaw and Juby the 23 of October 1598 to lend unto Mr. Chapman on his playbook and two acts of a tragedy of Benjamin's plot the sum of £ 3.

Lent unto Thomas Dekker at the appointment of Robert Shaw the 31 of November 1599, which I borrowed of Mr. Griffin, for the altering of the book of *The Whole History of Fortunatus*, the sum of 20s.

Lent unto Mr. Alleyn the 25 of September 1601 to lend unto Benjamin Jonson upon his writing of his additions in *Jeronimo*, the sum of 40s.

Lent unto Thomas Downton the 14 of December 1602 to pay unto Mr. Middleton for a prologue and an epilogue for the play of Bacon for the Court, the sum of 5s.

Memorandum that the 6 of August 1597 I bound Richard Jones by an assumpsit of 2d. to continue and play with the company of my Lord Admiral's Players from Michaelmas next after the day above written until the end and term of three years immediately following and to play in my house only known by the name of the Rose and in no other house about London public, and if restraint be granted, then to go for the time into the country and after to return again to London, if he break this assumpsit then to forfeit unto me for the same a hundred marks of lawful money of England. Witness to this E. Alleyn and John Middleton.

—Philip Henslowe, *Diary*.

The Inventory of the Clown's suits and Hermit's suits
with diverse other suits as followeth,
1598, the 10 of March

1 senator's gown, 1 hood, and 5 senators capes.
1 suit for Neptune, firedrakes suits for Dobe.
4 Janisaries gowns, and 4 torchbearers' suits.
3 pair red strossers [tight hose], and 3 fairies' gowns of buckram.
4 Heralds' coats, and 3 soldiers coats, and 1 green gown for Marian.
6 green coats for Robin Hood, and 4 knaves' suits.
2 pair of green hose and Anderson's suit, 1 white shepen cloak.
2 russet coats, and 1 black freize coat, and 3 priests' coats.
2 white shepherds' coats, and 2 Danes' suits, and 1 pair of Danes' hose.
the Moor's limbs, and Hercules' limbs, and Will Summer's suit.

2 "Orlates" suits, hats, and gorgets, and 7 anticks coats.

"Cathemer" suit, 1 pair of cloth white stockings, 4 Turks' heads.

4 friars gowns, and 3 hoods to them, and 1 fool's coat, cap, and bauble, and Branholt's bodice, and Merlin's gown and cap.

2 black say gowns, and 2 cotton gowns, and 1 red say gown.

1 "mawe" gown of calico for the queen, 1 cardinal's hat.

1 red suit of cloth for Pyge, laid with white lace.

5 pair of hose for the clown, and 5 gerkins for them.

3 pair of canvas hose for "asane," 2 pair of black strossers.

1 yellow leather doublet for a clown, 1 Whittcom's doublet poke.

Eve's bodice, 1 pedant trusser, and 3 dons' hats.

1 pair of yellow cotton sleeves, 1 ghost's suit, and 1 ghost's bodice.

18 copes and hats, Verone's son's hose.

3 trumpets, and a drum, and a treble viol, a bass viol, a bandore, a cittern, an ancient, 1 white hat.

1 hat for Robin Hood, 1 hobby horse.

5 shirts, 1 surplice, 4 farthingales.

6 head tires, 1 fan, 4 rebatos, 2 jerkins trusses.

1 long sword.

—Philip Henslowe, *Papers.*

HOW A GALLANT SHOULD BEHAVE HIMSELF IN A PLAYHOUSE

The theater is your poets' Royal Exchange upon which their muses (that are now turned to merchants) meeting, barter away that light commodity of words for a lighter ware than words, plaudits and the breath of the great beast which, like the threatenings of two cowards, vanish all into air. Players are their factors who put away the stuff and make the best of it they possible can, as indeed 'tis their parts so to do. Your gallant, your courtier, and your captain had wont to be the soundest paymasters and I think are still the surest chapmen; and these by means that their heads are well stocked deal upon this comical freight by the gross when your groundling and gallery commoner buys his sport by the penny and like a haggler is glad to utter it again by retailing.

Sithence then the place is so free in entertainment, allowing a stool as well to the farmer's son as to your Templar, that your stinkard has the selfsame liberty to be there in his tobacco fumes which your sweet courtier hath, and that your carman and tinker claim as strong a voice in their suffrage and sit to give judgment on the play's life and death as well as the proudest Momus among the tribe of critic, it is fit that he whom the most tailors' bills do make room for when he comes should not be basely, like a viol, cased up in a corner.

Whether therefore the gatherers of the public or private playhouse stand to receive the afternoon's rent, let our gallant, having paid it, presently advance himself up to the throne of the stage. I mean not into the Lords' Room, which is now but the stage's suburbs. No, those boxes, by the iniquity of custom, conspiracy of waiting women and gentlemen ushers that there sweat together, and the covetousness of sharers, are contemptibly thrust into the rear and much new satin is there damned by being smothered to death in darkness. But on the very rushes where the comedy is to dance, yea and under the state of Cambyses himself must our feathered ostrich, like a piece of ordnance, be planted valiantly because impudently, beating down the mews and hisses of the opposed rascality.

For do but cast up a reckoning what large comings-in are pursed up by sitting on the stage. First, a conspicuous eminence is gotten, by which means the best and most essential parts of a gallant, good clothes, a proportionable leg, white hand, the Persian lock, and a tolerable beard, are perfectly revealed.

By sitting on the stage you have a signed patent to engross the whole commodity of censure, may lawfully presume to be a girder, and stand at the helm to steer the passage of scenes; yet no man shall once offer to hinder you from obtaining the title of an insolent overweening coxcomb.

By sitting on the stage you may, without traveling for it, at the very next door ask whose play it is and by that quest of enquiry the law warrants you to avoid much mistaking; if you know not the author, you may rail against him and peradventure so behave yourself that you may enforce the author to know you.

By sitting on the stage, if you be a knight, you may haply get you a mistress; if a mere Fleet Street gentleman, a wife; but assure yourself by continual residence you are the first and principal man in election to begin the number of "We three."

By spreading your body on the stage and by being a justice in examining of plays, you shall put yourself into such true scenical authority that some poet shall not dare to present his muse rudely upon your eyes without having first unmasked her, rifled her, and discovered all her bare and most mystical parts before you at a tavern, when you most knightly shall for his pains pay for both their suppers.

By sitting on the stage you may with small cost purchase the dear acquaintance of the boys, have a good stool for six-pence, at any time know what particular part any of the infants present, get your match lighted, examine the play suits' lace, and perhaps win wagers upon laying 'tis copper, etc. And to conclude, whether you be a fool or a Justice of Peace, a cuckold or a captain, a Lord Mayor's son or a dawcock, a knave or an under-sheriff, of what stamp soever you be, current or counterfeit, the stage, like time, will bring you to most perfect light and lay you open; neither are you to be hunted from thence though the scarecrows in the yard hoot at you, hiss at you, spit at you, yea, throw dirt even in your teeth; 'tis most gentlemanlike patience to endure all this and to laugh at the silly animals; but if the rabble with a full throat cry, "Away with the fool," you were worse than a madman to tarry by it, for the gentleman and the fool should never sit on the stage together.

Marry, let this observation go hand in hand with the rest, or rather, like a country servingman, some five yards before them: present not yourself on the stage, especially at a new play, until the quaking prologue hath by rubbing got color into his cheeks and is ready to give the trumpets their cue that he's upon point to enter; for then it is time, as though you were one of the properties or that you dropped out of the hangings, to creep from behind the arras with your tripos or three-footed stool in one hand and a teston mounted between a forefinger and a thumb in the other; for if you should bestow your person upon the vulgar when the belly of the house is but half full, your apparel is quite eaten up, the

fashion lost, and the proportion of your body in more danger
to be devoured than if it were served up in the counter
amongst the poultry; avoid that as you would the baston. It
shall crown you with rich commendation to laugh aloud in
the middest of the most serious and saddest scene of the
terriblest tragedy and to let that clapper, your tongue, be
tossed so high that all the house may ring of it; your lords
use it, your knights are apes to the lords and do so too, your
Inn of Court man is zany to the knights and (many very
scurvily) comes likewise limping after it; be thou a beagle to
them all and never lin [leave off] snuffing till you have
scented them, for by talking and laughing like a ploughman
in a morris you heap Pelion upon Ossa, glory upon glory. As,
first, all the eyes in the galleries will leave walking after the
players and only follow you; the simplest dolt in the house
snatches up your name and when he meets you in the streets
or that you fall into his hands in the middle of a watch, his
word shall be taken for you, he'll cry, "He's such a gallant,"
and you pass. Secondly, you publish your temperance to the
world, in that you seem not to resort thither to taste vain
pleasures with a hungry appetite but only as a gentleman to
spend a foolish hour or two because you can do nothing else.
Thirdly, you mightily disrelish the audience and disgrace the
author; marry, you take up (though it be at the worst hand)
a strong opinion of your own judgment and enforce the poet
to take pity of your weakness and by some dedicated sonnet
to bring you into a better paradise, only to stop your mouth.

If you can, either for love or money, provide yourself a
lodging by the waterside, for, above the conveniency it brings
to shun shoulder-clapping and to ship away your cockatrice
betimes in the morning, it adds a kind of state unto you to be
carried from thence to the stairs of your playhouse; hate a
sculler (remember that) worse than to be acquainted with
one o' th' scullery. No, your oars are your only sea crabs,
board them and take heed you never go twice together with
one pair; often shifting is a great credit to gentlemen, and
that dividing of your fare will make the poor watersnakes be
ready to pull you in pieces to enjoy your custom. No matter
whether upon landing you have money or no, you may swim
in twenty of their boats over the river upon ticket; marry,
when silver comes in, remember to pay treble their fare and
it will make your flounder-catchers to send more thanks after
you when you do not draw than when you do, for they know
it will be their own another day.

Before the play begins, fall to cards; you may win or lose as fencers do in a prize, and beat one another by confederacy, yet share the money when you meet at supper. Notwithstanding, to gull the ragamuffins that stand aloof gaping at you, throw the cards, having first torn four or five of them, round about the stage just upon the third sound as though you had lost; it skills not if the four knaves lie on their backs and outface the audience, there's none such fools as dare take exceptions at them because, ere the play go off, better knaves than they will fall into the company.

Now, sir, if the writer be a fellow that hath either epigrammed you or hath had a flirt at your mistress or hath brought either your feather or your red beard or your little legs, etc., on the stage, you shall disgrace him worse than by tossing him in a blanket or giving him the bastinado in a tavern if in the middle of his play, be it pastoral or comedy, moral or tragedy, you rise with a screwed and discontented face from your stool to be gone; no matter whether the scenes be good or no, the better they are, the worse do you distaste them; and being on your feet, sneak not away like a coward but salute all your gentle acquaintance that are spread either on the rushes or on stools about you and draw what troop you can from the stage after you; the mimics are beholden to you for allowing them elbow-room; their poet cries perhaps, "A pox go with you," but care not you for that, there's no music without frets.

Marry, if either the company or indisposition of the weather bind you to sit it out, my counsel is then that you turn plain ape, take up a rush and tickle the earnest ears of your fellow gallants to make other fools fall alaughing, mew at passionate speeches, blare at merry, find fault with the music, whew at the children's action, whistle at the songs, and above all curse the sharers that, whereas the same day you had bestowed forty shillings on an embroidered felt and feather, Scotch fashion, for your mistress in the Court or your punk in the city, within two hours after, you encounter with the very same block on the stage, when the haberdasher swore to you the impression was extant but that morning.

To conclude, hoard up the finest play-scraps you can get, upon which your lean wit may most savorly feed for want of other stuff when the Arcadian and Euphuized gentlewomen have their tongues sharpened to set upon you; that quality, next to your shuttlecock, is the only furniture to a courtier

that's but a new beginner and is but in his A-B-C of compli-
ment. The next places that are filled after the playhouses be
emptied are, or ought to be, taverns. Into a tavern then let us
next march, where the brains of one hogshead must be
beaten out to make up another.

—Thomas Dekker (1609).

PART VII

Sources

CHARACTER
RICHARD III

Richard, the third son, of whom we now intreat, was in wit and courage equal with either of them [Edward IV and George, Duke of Clarence], in body and prowess far under them both; little of stature, ill featured of limbs, crook-backed, his left shoulder much higher than his right, hard favored of visage, and such as is in states called warly, in other men otherwise; he was malicious, wrathful, envious, and from afore his birth ever froward. It is for truth reported that the duchess his mother had so much ado in her travail that she could not be delivered of him uncut; and that he came into the world with the feet forward, as men be born outward; and (as the fame runneth also) not un-toothed, whether men of hatred report above the truth, or else that nature changed her course in his beginning, which in the course of his life many things unnaturally committed. So that the full confluence of these qualities, with the defects of favor and amiable proportion, gave proof to this rule of physiognomy: *"Distortum vultum sequitur distorsio morum."*

None evil captain was he in the war, as to which his disposition was more meetly than for peace. Sundry victories had he, and sometimes overthrows, but never on default as for his own person, either of hardiness or politic order. Free was he called of dispense, and somewhat above his power liberal. With large gifts he got him unsteadfast friendship, for which he was fain to pill and spoil in other places, and got him steadfast hatred. He was close and secret, a deep dissembler, lowly of countenance, arrogant of heart, outwardly companiable where he inwardly hated, not letting to kiss whom he thought to kill: despiteous and cruel, not for evil will always, but oftener for ambition, and either for the surety or increase of his estate. Friend and foe was much-what indifferent where his advantage grew; he spared no man's death whose life withstood his purpose.

—"Written by Mr. Thomas More . . . about the year of Our Lord 1513," incorporated into Raphael Holinshed, *The Chronicles of England, Scotland, and Ireland*, 1587.

CHARACTER AND REAL LIFE
MUCH ADO ABOUT NOTHING

As I came from London homeward in my coach I saw at every town's end the number of ten or twelve standing with long staves and until I came to Enfield I thought no other of them but that they had stayed for avoiding of the rain or to drink at some alehouses, for so they did stand under penthouses at alehouses; but at Enfield, finding a dozen in a plump [group] when there was no rain, I bethought myself that they were appointed as watchmen for the apprehending of such as are missing; and thereupon I called some of them to me apart and asked them wherefore they stood there, and one of them answered, to take three young men; and, demanding how they should know the persons, "Marry," said they, "one of the parties hath a hooked nose." "And have you," quoth I, "no other mark?" "No," said they. Surely, sir, these watchmen stand so openly in plumps as no suspected person will come near them, and if they be no better instructed but to find three persons by one of them having a hooked nose, they may miss thereof.

—Lord Burghley to Sir Francis Walsingham, 1586

MOTIVE AND INCIDENT
1 HENRY IV

Henry, Earl of Northumberland, with his brother Thomas, Earl of Worcester, and his son the Lord Henry Percy, surnamed Hotspur, which were to King Henry in the beginning of his reign both faithful friends and earnest aiders, began now to envy his wealth and felicity; and especially they were grieved because the King demanded of the earl and his son such Scottish prisoners as were taken at Holmedon and Nesbit. For of all the captives which were taken in the conflicts fought in those two places, there was delivered to the King's possession only Mordake, Earl of Fife, the duke of Albany's son, though the king did divers and sundry times require deliverance of the residue, and that with great threatenings. Wherewith the Percys being sore offended, for that they claimed them as their own proper prisoners and their peculiar prize, by the counsel of the Lord Thomas Percy, Earl of Worcester, whose study was ever (as some write) to procure malice and set things in a broil, came to the King unto Windsor (upon a purpose to prove him) and there required of him that either by ransom or otherwise, he would cause to be delivered out of prison Edmund Mortimer, Earl of March, their cousin german, whom (as they reported) Owen Glendower kept in filthy prison, shackled with irons, only for that he took his part and was to him faithful and true.

The King began not a little to muse at this request, and not without cause. For indeed it touched him somewhat near, since this Edmund was son to Roger, Earl of March, son to the Lady Philippa, daughter of Lionel, Duke of Clarence, the third son of King Edward III; which Edmund at King Richard's going into Ireland was proclaimed heir apparent to the crown and realm, whose aunt, called Elinor, the Lord Henry Percy had married; and therefore King Henry could not well hear that any man should be in earnest about the advancement of that lineage. The King when he had studied on the matter made answer that the earl of March was not taken prisoner for his cause, nor in his service, but willingly suffered himself to be taken because he would not withstand the attempts of Owen Glendower and his complices, and therefore he would neither ransom him nor relieve him.

The Percys with this answer and fraudulent excuse were not a little fumed, insomuch that Henry Hotspur said openly, "Behold, the heir of the realm is robbed of his right, and yet the robber with his own will not redeem him." So in this fury the Percys departed, minding nothing more than to dispose King Henry from the high type of his royalty, and to place in his seat their cousin Edmund, Earl of March, whom they did not only deliver out of captivity but also (to the high displeasure of King Henry) enter in league with the foresaid

Owen Glendower. Herewith, they by their deputies in the house of the archdeacon of Bangor, divided the realm amongst them, causing a tripartite indenture to be made and sealed with their seals, by the convenants whereof all England from Severn and Trent south and eastward was assigned to the earl of March: all Wales, and the lands beyond Severn westward, were appointed to Owen Glendower: and all the remnant from Trent northward, to the Lord Percy.

—Raphael Holinshed, *The Chronicles* (1587).

SPEECH AND INCIDENT
ANTONY AND CLEOPATRA

Cleopatra, . . . guessing by the former access and credit she had with Julius Caesar and C. Pompey (the son of Pompey the Great) only for her beauty, she began to have good hope that she might more easily win Antonius. For Caesar and Pompey knew her when she was but a young thing, and knew not then what the world meant: but now she went to Antonius at the age when a woman's beauty is at the prime, and she also of best judgment. So she furnished herself with a world of gifts, store of gold and silver, and of riches and other sumptuous ornaments, as is credible enough she might bring from so great a house and from so wealthy and rich a realm as Egypt was. But yet she carried nothing with her wherein she trusted more than in herself, and in the charms and enchantment of her surpassing beauty and grace. Therefore, when she was sent unto by divers letters, both from Antonius himself and also from his friends, she made so light of it and mocked Antonius so much that she disdained to set forward otherwise but to take her barge in the river of Cydnus; the poop whereof was of gold, the sails of purple, and the oars of silver, which kept stroke in rowing after the sound of the music of flutes, hautboys, citterns, viols, and such other instruments as they played upon in the barge. And now for the person of her self, she was laid under a pavilion of cloth of gold of tissue, appareled and attired like the goddess Venus, commonly drawn in picture: and hard by her, on either hand of her, pretty fair boys appareled as painters do set forth god Cupid, with little fans in their hands, with the which they fanned wind upon her. Her ladies and gentlewomen also, the fairest of them, were appareled like the nymphs Nereids (which are the mermaids of the waters) and like the Graces; some steering the helm, others tending the tackle and ropes of the barge, out of the which there came a wonderful surpassing sweet savor of perfumes that perfumed the wharf's side, pestered with innumerable multitudes of people. Some of them followed the barge all along the riverside: others also ran out of the city to see her coming in. So that in the end there ran such multitudes of people one after another to see her that Antonius was left posted alone in the marketplace in his imperial seat to give audience: and there went a rumor in the people's mouths that the goddess Venus was come to play with the god Bacchus for the general good of all Asia.

When Antonius saw that his men did forsake him, and yielded unto Caesar, and that his footmen were broken and overthrown, he then fled into the city, crying out that Cleopatra had betrayed him unto them with whom he had made war for her sake. Then she, being afraid of his fury, fled into the tomb which he had caused to be made, and there she locked the doors unto her, and shut all the springs of the locks with great bolts, and in the meantime sent unto Antonius to tell him that she was dead. Antonius, believing it said unto himself: "What doest thou look for further, Antonius, sith spiteful fortune hath taken from thee the only joy thou hadst, for whom thou yet reservedst thy life?" When he had said these words, he went into a chamber and unarmed himself, and being naked, said thus: "O Cleopatra, it grieveth me not that I have lost thy company, for I will not be long from thee: but I am sorry that, having been so great a captain and emperor, I am indeed condemned to be judged of less courage and noble mind than a woman." Now he had a man of his called Eros, whom he loved and trusted much, and whom he had long before caused to swear unto him that he should kill him when he did command him; and then he willed him to keep his promise. His man, drawing his sword, lifted it up as though he had meant to have stricken his

master; but turning his head at one side, he thrust his sword
into himself, and fell down dead at his master's foot. Then
said Antonius: "O noble Eros, I thank thee for this, and it is
valiantly done of thee, to shew me what I should do to
myself, which thou couldest not do for me." Therewithal he
took his sword and thrust it into his belly, and so fell down
upon a little bed. The wound he had killed him not presently,
for the blood stinted a little when he was laid: and when he
came somewhat to himself again, he prayed them that were
about him to dispatch him. But they all fled out of the
chamber, and left him crying out, tormenting himself: until
at last there came a secretary unto him (called Diomedes)
who was commanded to bring him into the tomb or monument where Cleopatra was. When he heard that she was
alive, he very earnestly prayed his men to carry his body
thither, and so he was carried in his men's arms into the
entry of the monument.

—Plutarch, *The Life of Marcus Antonius,* trans. by Sir
Thomas North (1579).

MAIN PLOT
MEASURE FOR MEASURE

The Right Excellent and Famous History of *Promos* and
Cassandra: Divided into two Comical Discourses. In the first
part is shown the unsufferable abuse of a lewd magistrate, the
virtuous behaviors of a chaste lady, the uncontrolled lewdness
of a favored courtesan, and the undeserved estimation of a
pernicious parasite.[8] In the second part is discoursed the
perfect magnanimity of a noble king in checking vice and
favoring virtue, wherein is shown the ruin and overthrow of
dishonest practices with the advancement of upright dealing.

---

[8] The courtesan and parasite figure in a subplot whose counterpart
in Shakespeare is the doings of Pompey, Mrs. Overdone, etc.

The work of George Whetstone's, Gentlemen, *Formae nulla fides*.

The Argument

In the city of Julio (sometimes under the dominion of Corvinus, King of Hungary and Bohemia) there was a law that what man so ever committed adultery should lose his head, and the woman offender should wear some disguised apparel during her life to make her infamously noted. This severe law, by the favor of some merciful magistrate, became little regarded, until the time of Lord Promos's authority; who, convicting a young gentleman named Andrugio of incontinency, condemned both him and his minion to the execution of this statute. Andrugio had a very virtuous and beautiful gentlewoman to his sister, named Cassandra. Cassandra, to enlarge her brother's life, submitted a humble petition to the Lord Promos. Promos, regarding her good behaviors and fantasying her great beauty, was much delighted with the sweet order of her talk and, doing good that evil might come thereof, for a time he reprieved her brother. But wicked man, turning his liking into unlawful lust, he set down the spoil of her honor, ransom for her brother's life. Chaste Cassandra, abhorring both him and his suit, by no persuasion would yield to this ransom. But, in fine, won with the importunity of her brother (pleading for life), upon these conditions she agreed to Promos: first that he should pardon her brother, and after marry her. Promos, as fearless in promise as careless in performance, with solemn vow signed her conditions. But worse than any infidel, his will satisfied, he performed neither the one nor the other. For to keep his authority unspotted with favor and to prevent Cassandra's clamors, he commanded the jailer secretly to present Cassandra with her brother's head. The jailer, with the outcries of Andrugio abhorring Promos's lewdness, by the providence of God, provided thus for his safety. He presented Cassandra with a felon's head newly executed, who (being mangled, knew it not from her brother's—by the jailer, who was set at liberty) was so aggrieved at this treachery that, at the point to kill herself, she spared that stroke to be avenged of Promos. And devising a way, she concluded to make her fortunes known unto the king. She (executing this resolution) was so highly favored of the king that forthwith he hasted to do justice on Promos, whose judgment was: to marry Cas-

sandra to repair her crazed honor; which done, for his
heinous offence he should lose his head. This marriage solemnized, Cassandra tied in the greatest bonds of affection to
her husband, became an earnest suitor for his life. The king
(tendering the general benefit of the commonwealth before
her special case, although he favored her much) would not
grant her suit. Andrugio (disguised among the company)
sorrowing the grief of his sister, betrayed his safety and
craved pardon. The king, to reknown the virtues of Cassandra, pardoned both him and Promos. The circumstances of
this rare history in action lively follows.

—George Whetstone, *Promos and Cassandra* (1578).

PLOT AND SUB-PLOT

KING LEAR

Leir [c. 749–694 B.C.], the son of Baldud, was admitted
ruler over the Britains in the year of the world 3105, at what
time Joas reigned in Judea. This Leir was a prince of right
noble demeanor, governing his land and subjects in great
wealth. He made the town of Caerlier, now called Leicester,
which stands upon the river of Soar. It is written that he had
by his wife three daughters, without other issue, whose names
were Gonorilla, Regan, and Cordeilla, which daughters he
greatly loved but specially Cordeilla, the youngest, far above
the two elder. When this Leir therefore was come to great
years and began to wax unwieldy through age, he thought to
understand the affections of his daughters towards him and
prefer her whom he best loved to the succession over the
kingdom. Whereupon he first asked Gonorilla, the eldest, how
well she loved him: who calling her gods to record protested
that she loved him more than her own life, which by right
and reason should be most dear unto her. With which answer
the father being well pleased, turned to the second and
demanded of her how well she loved him: who answered
(confirming her sayings with great oaths) that she loved him

more than tongue could express, and far above all other creatures of the world.

Then called he his youngest daughter Cordeilla before him, and asked of her what account she made of him, unto whom she made this answer as follows: "Knowing the great love and fatherly zeal that you have always borne toward me (for which I may not answer you otherwise than I think, and as my conscience leads me) I protest unto you that I have loved you ever and will continually (while I live) love you as my natural father. And if you would more understand of the love that I bear you, ascertain yourself that so much as you have, so much are you worth, and so much I love you, and no more." The father, being nothing content with this answer, married his two eldest daughters, the one unto Henninus, the Duke of Cornwall, and the other unto Maglanus, the Duke of Albania, betwixt whom he willed and ordained that his land should be divided after his death, and the one half thereof immediately should be assigned to them in hand. But for the third daughter, Cordeilla, he reserved nothing.

Nevertheless it fortuned that one of the princes of Gallia (which now is called France) whose name was Aganippus, hearing of the beauty, womanhood, and good conditions of the said Cordeilla, desired to have her in marriage, and sent over to her father requiring that he might have her to wife. To whom answer was made that he might have his daughter, but as for any dowry he could have none, for all was promised and assured to her other sisters already. Aganippus, notwithstanding this answer of denial to receive anything by way of dowry with Cordeilla, took her to wife, only moved thereto (I say) for respect of her person and amiable virtues. This Aganippus was one of the twelve knights that ruled Gallia in those days, as in the British history it is recorded. But to proceed.

After that Leir was fallen into age, the two dukes that had married his two eldest daughters, thinking it long ere the government of the land did come to their hands, arose against him in armor and reft from him the governance of the land, upon conditions to be continued for term of life: by the which he was put to his portion, that is, to live after a rate assigned to him for the maintenance of his estate, which in process of time was diminished as well by Maglanus as by Henninus. But the greatest grief that Leir took was to see the unkindness of his daughters, which seemed to think that all was too much which their father had, the same being never so little: insomuch that going from the one to the other he was brought to that misery that scarcely they would allow him one servant to wait upon him.

In the end, such was the unkindness, or (as I may say) the unnaturalness which he found in his two daughters, notwithstanding their fair and pleasant words uttered in time past, that being constrained of necessity he fled the land and sailed into Gallia, there to seek some comfort of his youngest daughter, Cordeilla, whom before time he hated. The Lady Cordeilla hearing that he was arrived in poor state, she first sent to him privily a certain sum of money to apparel himself withal, and to retain a certain number of servants that might attend upon him in honorable wise, as appertained to the estate which he had borne. And then so accompanied, she appointed him to come to the court; which he did and was so joyfully, honorably, and lovingly received, both by his son-in-law Aganippus and also by his daughter Cordeilla, that his heart was greatly comforted: for he was no less honored than if he had been king of the whole country himself.

Now when he had informed his son-in-law and his daughter in what sort he had been used by his other daughters, Aganippus caused a mighty army to be put in a readiness, and likewise a great navy of ships to be rigged to pass over into Britain with Leir, his father-in-law, to see him again restored to his kingdom. It was accorded that Cordeilla should also go with him to take possession of the land, the which he promised to leave unto her as the rightful inheritor after his decease, notwithstanding any former grant made to her sisters or to their husbands in any manner of wise.

Hereupon, when this army and navy of ships were ready, Leir and his daughter Cordeilla with her husband took the sea, and arriving in Britain fought with their enemies and discomfited them in battle, in the which Maglanus and Henninus were slain. And then was Leir restored to his kingdom, which he ruled after this by the space of two years, and then died, forty years after he first begun to reign. His body was buried at Leicester in a vault under the channel of the river of Soar beneath the town.

Cordeilla, the youngest daughter of Leir, was admitted queen and supreme governess of Britain in the year of the world 3155, before the building of Rome 54, Uzziah then reigning in Judea and Jeroboam over Israel. This Cordeilla after her father's decease ruled the land of Britain right worthily during the space of five years, in which meantime her husband died. And then about the end of those five years her two nephews, Margan and Cunedag, sons to her aforesaid sisters, disdaining to be under the government of a woman, levied war against her and destroyed a great part of the land, and finally took her prisoner and laid her fast in ward; wherewith she took such a grief, being a woman of a manly courage, and despairing to recover liberty, there she slew herself when she had reigned (as before is mentioned) the term of five years.

—Raphael Holinshed, *The Chronicles* (1587).

Next him king Leyr in happie peace long raynd,
But had no issue male him to succeed,
But three faire daughters, which were well uptraind
In all that seemed fitt for kingly seed:
Mongst whom his realme he equally decreed
To have divided. Tho, when feeble age
Nigh to his utmost date he saw proceed,
He called his daughters, and with speeches sage
Inquyrd, which of them most did love her parentage.

The eldest, Gonorill, gan to protest
That she much more than her owne life him lov'd;
And Regan greater love to him profest
Then all the world, when ever it were proov'd;
But Cordeill said she lov'd him as behoov'd:
Whose simple answere, wanting colours fayre
To paint it forth, him to displeasaunce moov'd,
That in his crown he counted her no hayre,
But twixt the other twain his kingdom whole did shayre.

So wedded th' one to Maglan king of Scottes,
And thother to the king of Cambria,
And twixt them shayrd his realme by equal lottes;
But without dowre the wise Cordelia.
Was sent to Aggannip of Celtica.
Their aged Syre, thus eased of his crowne,
A private life ledd in Albania
With Gonorill, long had in great renowne,
That nought him griev'd to beene from rule deposed
    downe.

But true it is that, when the oyle is spent,
The light goes out, and weeke is throwne away:

So, when he had resignd his regiment,
His daughter gan despise his drouping day,
And wearie wax of his continuall stay.
Tho to his daughter Regan he repayrd,
Who him at first well used every way;
But when of his departure she despayrd,
Her bountie she abated, and his cheare empayrd.

The wretched man gan then avise too late,
That love is not where most it is profest;
Too truely tryde in his extremest state.
At last, resolv'd likewise to prove the rest,
He to Cordelia him selfe addrest,
Who with entyre affection him receav'd,
As for her Syre and king her seemed best;
And after all an army strong she leav'd,
To war on those which him had of his realme bereav'd.

So to his crowne she him restord againe;
In which he dyde, made ripe for death by eld,
And after wild it should to her remaine,
Who peaceably the same long time did weld,
And all mens harts in dew obedience held;
Till that her sisters children, woxen strong,
Through proud ambition against her rebeld,
And overcommen kept in prison long,
Till weary of that wretched life her selfe she hong.

—Edmund Spenser, *The Faerie Queene*, Book 2, Canto 10
(1590).

The Pitiful State and Story of the Paphlagonian Unkind King and His Kind Son, First Related by the Son, Then by the Blind Father

It was in the kingdom of Galacia, the season being (as in the depth of winter) very cold, and as then suddenly grown to so extreme and foul a storm, that never any winter (I think) brought forth a fouler child: so that the princes were even compelled by the hail, that the pride of the wind blew into their faces, to seek some shrouding place within a certain hollow rock offering it unto them, they made it their shield against the tempest's fury. And so staying there, till the violence thereof was passed, they heard the speech of a couple, who not perceiving them (being hid within that rude canopy) held a strange and pitiful disputation which made them step out; yet in such a sort as they might see unseen. There they perceived an aged man, and a young, scarcely come to the age of a man, both poorly arrayed, extremely weather-beaten: the old man blind, the young man leading him: and yet through all those miseries, in both these seemed to appear a kind of nobleness not suitable to that affliction. But the first words they heard were these of the old man.

"Well, Leonatus," said he, "since I cannot persuade thee to lead me to that which should end my grief, and thy trouble, let me now entreat thee to leave me; fear not, my misery cannot be greater than it is, and nothing does become me but misery: fear not the danger of my blind steps, I cannot fall worse than I am. And do not I pray thee, do not obstinately continue to infect thee with my wretchedness. But fly, fly from this region, only worthy of me."

"Dear father," answered he, "do not take away from me the only remnant of my happiness: while I have power to do you service, I am not wholly miserable."

"Ah my son," said he, and with that he groaned as if sorrow strove to break his heart, "how evil fits it me to have such a son, and how much doth thy kindness upbraid my wickedness?"

These doleful speeches, and some others to like purpose (well showing they had not been born to the fortune they were in) moved the princes to go out unto them and ask the younger what they were.

"Sirs," answered he, with a good grace, and made the more agreeable by a certain noble kind of piteousness, "I see well you are strangers, that know not our misery, so well here known that no man dare know but that we must be miserable. Indeed our state is such as though nothing is so needful unto us as pity, yet nothing is more dangerous unto us than to make ourselves so known as may stir pity. But your presence promiseth that cruelty shall not overrun hate. And if it did, in truth our state is sunk below the degrees of fear.

"This old man (whom I lead) was lately rightful prince of this country of Paphlagonia, by the hardhearted ungratefulness of a son of his deprived, not only of his kingdom (whereof no foreign forces were ever able to spoil him) but of his sight, the riches which Nature grants to the poorest creatures. Whereby, and by other his unnatural dealings, he hath been driven to such grief, as even now he would have had me to have led him to the top of this rock, thence to cast himself headlong to death, and so would have made me, who received my life of him, to be the worker of his destruction. But noble gentlemen," said he, "if either of you have a father, and feel what dutiful affection is engrafted in a son's heart, let me entreat you to convey this afflicted prince to some place of rest and security; amongst your worthy acts it shall be none of the least, that a king of such might and fame, and so unjustly oppressed, is in any sort by you relieved."

But before they could make him answer, his father began to speak. "Ah my son," said he, "how evil an historian are you, that leave out the chief knot of all the discourse? My wickedness, my wickedness. And if thou dost it to spare my cares (the only sense now left me proper for knowledge) assure thyself thou dost mistake me. And I take witness of that sun which you see" (with that he cast up his blind eyes, as if he would hunt for light) "and wish myself in worse case than I do wish myself, which is as evil as may be, if I speak untruly; that nothing is so welcome to my thoughts as the publishing of my shame. Therefore know you gentlemen (to whom from my heart I wish that it may not prove ominous foretoken of misfortune to have met with such a miser as I am) that whatsoever my son—O God, that truth binds me to reproach him with the name of my son—has said, is true. But besides those truths, this also is true, that having had in lawful marriage, of a mother fit to bear royal children, this son (such one as partly you see, and better shall know by my short declaration) and so enjoyed the expectations in the world of him till he was grown to justify their expectations (so as I needed envy no father for the chief comfort of mortality, to leave another one's self after me) I was carried by a bastard son of mine (if at least I be bound to believe the words of that base woman, my concubine, his mother) first to mislike, then to hate, lastly to destroy, to do my best to destroy, this son (I think you think) undeserving destruction. What ways he used to bring me to it, if I should tell you, I should tediously trouble you with as much poisonous hypocrisy, desperate fraud, smooth malice, hidden ambition, and smiling envy, as in any living person could be harbored:

but I list it not. No remembrance (no, of naughtiness) delights me but mine own; and methinks the accusing his trains might in some manner excuse my fault, which certainly I loathe to do. But the conclusion is that I gave order to some servants of mine, whom I thought as apt for such charities as myself, to lead him out into a forest and there to kill him.

"But those thieves (better natured to my son than myself) spared his life, letting him go, to learn to live poorly: which he did, giving himself to be a private soldier in a country hereby. But as he was ready to be greatly advanced for some noble pieces of service which he did, he heard news of me: who (drunk in my affection to that unlawful and unnatural son of mine) suffered myself so to be governed by him that all favors and punishments passed by him, all offices and places of importance distributed to his favorites; so that ere I was aware, I had left myself nothing but the name of a king: which he shortly weary of too, with many indignities (if anything may be called an indignity which was laid upon me) threw me out of my seat, and put out my eyes; and then (proud in his tyranny) let me go, neither imprisoning nor killing me: but rather delighting to make me feel my misery, misery indeed, if ever there were any; full of wretchedness, fuller of disgrace, and fullest of guiltiness. And as he came to the crown by so unjust means, as unjustly he kept it by force of stranger soldiers in citadels, the nests of tyranny and murderers of liberty; disarming all his own countrymen that no man durst show himself a well-willer of mine: to say the truth (I think) few of them being so (considering my cruel folly to my good son, and foolish kindness to my unkind bastard): but if there were any who fell to pity of so great a fall, and had yet any sparks of unstained duty left in them towards me, yet durst they not show it, scarcely with giving me alms at their doors; which yet was the only sustenance of my distressed life, nobody daring to show so much charity as to lend me a hand to guide my dark steps. Till this son of mine (God knows worthy of a more virtuous and more fortunate father) forgetting my abominable wrongs, not recking danger, and neglecting the present good way he was in doing himself good, came hither to do this kind office you see him perform towards me, to my unspeakable grief; not only because his kindness is a glass, even to my blind eyes, of my naughtiness, but that above all griefs it grieves me he should desperately adventure the loss of his soul-deserving life for mine, that yet owe more to fortune for my deserts, as if he would carry mud in a chest or crystal. For well I know, he that now reigneth, how much soever (and with good reason) he despises me, of all men despised; yet he will not let slip any advantage to make away him whose just title (ennobled by courage and goodness) may one day shake the seat of a never secure tyranny. And for this cause I craved of him to lead me to the top of this rock, indeed I must confess, with meaning to free him from so serpentine a companion as I am. But he, finding what I purposed, only therein since he was born showed himself disobedient unto me.

"And now, gentlemen, you have the true story, which I pray you publish to the world, that my mischievous proceedings may be the glory of his filial piety, the only reward now left for so great a merit. And if it may be, let me obtain that of you which my son denies me: for never was there more pity in saving any, than in ending me; both because therein my agonies shall end, and so shall you preserve this excellent young man who else willfully follows his own ruin."

The matter in itself lamentable, lamentably expressed by the old prince (which needed not take to himself the gestures of pity, since his face could not put off the marks thereof) greatly moved the two princes to compassion, which could not stay in such hearts as theirs without seeking remedy. But by and by the occasion was presented: for Plexirtus (so was the bastard called) came thither with forty horses only of purpose to murder this brother; of whose coming he had soon advertisement, and thought no eyes of sufficient credit in such a matter but his own; and therefore came himself to be actor and spectator. And as soon as he came, not regarding the weak (as he thought) guard of but two men, commanded some of his followers to set their hands to his in the killing of Leonatus. But the young prince (though not otherwise armed but with a sword) how falsely soever he was dealt with by others, would not betray himself, but bravely drawing it out, made the death of the first that assaulted him warn his fellows to come more warily after him. But then Pyrocles and Musidorus were quickly become parties (so just a defense deserving as much as old friendship) and so did behave them among that company (more injurious than valiant) that many of them lost their lives for their wicked master.

Yet perhaps had the number of them at last prevailed, if the king of Pontus (lately by them [Pyrocles and Musidorus] made so) had not come unlooked for to their succor. Who (having had a dream which had fixed his imagination vehemently upon some great danger presently to follow those two princes whom he most dearly loved) was come in all haste, following as well as he could their track with a hundred horses in that country which he thought (considering who then reigned) a fit place enough to make the stage of any tragedy.

But then the match had been so ill made for Plexirtus, that his ill-led life and worse gotten honor should have tumbled together to destruction had there not come in Tydeus and Telenor, with forty or fifty in their suit, to the defense of Plexirtus. These two were brothers, of the noblest house in that country, brought up from their infancy with Plexirtus: men of such prowess as not to know fear in themselves, and yet to teach it others that should deal with them: for they had often made their lives triumph over most terrible dangers; never dismayed, and ever fortunate; and truly no more settled in their valor than disposed to goodness and justice, if either they had lighted on a better friend, or could have learned to make friendship a child, and not the father, of virtue. But bringing up (rather than choice) having first knit their minds unto him (indeed crafty enough, either to hide his faults, or never to show them but when they might pay home) they willingly held out the course rather to satisfy him than all the world; and rather to be good friends than good men: so as, though they did not like the evil he did, yet they liked him that did the evil; and though not counselors of the offense, yet protectors of the offender. Now they, having heard of this sudden going out with so small a company in a country full of evil-wishing minds toward him (though they knew not the cause) followed him; till they found him in such case as they were to venture their lives, or else he to lose his: which they did with such force of mind and body that truly I may justly say Pyrocles and Musidorus had never till then found any that could make them so well repeat their hardest lesson in the feats of arms. And, briefly, so they [Tydeus and Telenor] did that if they overcame not yet were they not overcome, but carried away that ungrateful master of theirs to a place of security, howsoever the princes labored to the contrary. But this matter being thus far begun, it became not the constancy of the princes so to leave it; but in all haste making forces both in Pontus and Phrygia, they had in few days left him [Plexirtus] but only that one strong place where he was. For fear having been the only knot that had fastened his people unto him, that once untied by a greater force they all scattered from him, like so many birds whose cage had been broken.

In which season the blind king (having in the chief city of his realm set the crown upon his son Leonatus's head) with many tears (both of joy and sorrow) setting forth to the whole people his own fault and his son's virtue, after he had kissed him and forced his son to accept honor of him (as of his new become subject) even in a moment died, as it should seem: his heart broken with unkindness and affliction, stretched so far beyond his limits with this excess of comfort as it was able no longer to keep safe his royal spirits.

—Sir Philip Sidney, *Arcadia* (1590), 2. 10.

PART VIII

Shakespeare's Works in His Lifetime

1592. *1 Henry VI*

How would it have joyed brave Talbot, the terror of the French, to think that after he had lain two hundred years in his tomb he should triumph again on the stage and have his bones new embalmed with the tears of ten thousand spectators at least (at several times), who in the tragedian that represents his person imagine they behold him fresh bleeding!

—Thomas Nashe, *Pierce Penniless.*

1594. December 28. *The Comedy of Errors*

The next grand night was intended to be upon Innocents' Day at night, at which time there was a great presence of lords, ladies, and worshipful personages that did expect some notable performance at that time, which indeed had been effected if the multitude of beholders had not been so exceeding great that thereby there was no convenient room for those that were actors.

When the ambassador [from the Inner Temple] was placed as aforesaid and that there was something to be performed for the delight of the beholders, there arose such a disordered tumult and crowd upon the stage that there was no opportunity to effect that which was intended. There came so great a number of worshipful personages upon the stage that might not be displaced and gentlewomen, whose sex did privilege them from violence, that when the Prince and his officers had in vain a good while expected and endeavored a reformation, at length there was no hope of redress for that present. The Lord Ambassador and his train thought that they were not so kindly entertained as was before expected and thereupon would not stay any longer at that time, but, in a sort, discontented and displeased. After their departure the throngs and tumults did somewhat cease, although so much of them continued as was able to disorder and confound any good inventions whatsoever. In regard whereof, as also for that the sports intended were especially for the gracing of the Templarians, it was thought good not to offer anything of account saving dancing and reveling with gentlewomen; and after such sports a *Comedy of Errors* (like to Plautus his *Menechmus*) was played by the players. So that night was begun and continued to the end in nothing but confusion and errors, whereupon it was ever afterwards called "The Night of Errors."

—*Gesta Grayorum*

1597.   *Richard III*

The Tragedy of King Richard the Third. Containing his treacherous plots against his brother Clarence, the pitiful murder of his innocent nephews, his tyrannical usurpation, with the whole course of his detested life and most deserved death. As it hath been lately acted by the Right Honorable the Lord Chamberlain his Servants.

—Title page of the First Quarto.

1598.   *Love's Labour's Lost*

Love's Labour Lost: I once did see a play
    Ycleped so, so called to my pain,
Which I to hear to my small joy did stay,
    Giving attendance on my froward dame.
        My misgiving mind presaging to me ill,
        Yet was I drawn to see it 'gainst my will.
Each actor played in cunning wise his part,
    But chiefly those entrapped in Cupid's snare. . . .

—Robert Tofte, *The Month's Mind of a Melancholy Lover.*

1598.   Shakespeare, the Equal of the Ancients

As the Greek tongue is made famous and eloquent by Homer, Hesiod, Euripides, Aeschylus, Sophocles, Pindarus, Phocylides, and Aristophanes; and the Latin tongue by Vergil, Ovid, Horace, Silius Italicus, Lucanus, Lucretius, Ausonius, and Claudianus: so the English tongue is mightily enriched and gorgeously invested in rare ornaments and resplendent habiliments by Sir Philip Sidney, Spenser, Daniel, Drayton, Warner, Shakespeare, Marlowe, and Chapman. As the soul of Euphorbus was thought to live in Pythagoras: so the sweet witty soul of Ovid lives in mellifluous and honey-tongued Shakespeare, witness his *Venus and Adonis*, his *Lucrece*, his sugared sonnets among his private friends, etc.

As Plautus and Seneca are accounted the best for comedy and tragedy among the Latins, so Shakespeare among the English is the most excellent in both kinds for the stage. For comedy witness his *Gentlemen of Verona*, his *Errors*, his *Love's Labour's Lost*, his *Love's Labour's Won*, his *Midsum-*

mer's Night Dream, and his *Merchant of Venice;* for tragedy his *Richard II., Richard III., Henry IV, King John, Titus Andronicus,* and his *Romeo and Juliet.*

As Epius Stolo said that the muses would speak with Plautus' tongue if they would speak Latin, so I say that the muses would speak with Shakespeare's fine-filed phrase if they would speak English.

—Francis Meres, *Palladis Tamia.*

1598. *Venus and Adonis, The Rape of Lucrece*
And, Shakespeare, thou whose honey-flowing vein,
Pleasing the world, thy praises doth obtain,
Whose *Venus* and whose *Lucrece,* sweet and chaste,
Thy name in fame's immortal book have placed,
    Live ever you, at least in fame live ever:
    Well may the body die, but fame dies never.

—Richard Barnfield, *A Remembrance of Some English Poets.*

1598. *Romeo and Juliet*
Luscus, what's played today? Faith now I know
I set thy lips abroach from whence doth flow
Naught but pure Juliet and Romeo.
Say, who acts best, Drusus or Roscio?
Now I have him that ne'er of aught did speak
But when of plays or players he did treat.
H' hath made a commonplace book out of plays
And speaks in print; at least whate'er he says
Is warranted by Curtain plaudites.

—John Marston, *The Scourge of Villainy,* Satire X.

1598. *1 Henry IV*
The History of Henry the Fourth with the battle at Shrewsbury between the King and Lord Henry Percy, surnamed Henry Hotspur of the North. With the humorous conceits of Sir John Falstaff.

—Title page of the First Quarto.

1599 (?). *Venus and Adonis, The Rape of Lucrece,* and *Hamlet*
The younger sort takes much delight in Shakespeare's *Venus and Adonis,* but his *Lucrece* and his tragedy of *Ham-*

let, Prince of Denmark, have it in them to please the wiser sort.

—Gabriel Harvey; note in his copy of Speght's *Chaucer*.

1599. *Venus and Adonis, The Rape of Lucrece, Romeo and Juliet*, and *Richard II or III*

> Honey-tongued Shakespeare, when I saw thine issue
> I swore Apollo got them and none other;
> Their rosy-tainted features, clothed in tissue,
> Some heaven-born goddess said to be their mother:
> Rose-cheek'd Adonis with his amber tresses,
> Fair, fire-hot Venus charming him to love her,
> Chaste Lucretia virgin-like her dresses,
> Proud lust-stung Tarquin seeking still to prove her,
> Romeo, Richard, more whose names I know not,
> Their sugar'd tongues and pure attractive beauty
> Say they are saints, although that saints they show not,
> For thousands vow to them subjective duty.
>   They burn in love thy children. Shakespeare, let them:
>   Go, woo thy muse, more nymphish brood beget them.

—John Weever, sonnet "Ad Gulielmum Shakespeare" in *Epigrams in the Oldest Cut and Newest Fashion*.

1599. *Henry IV*: The Rival Play

> It is no pampered glutton we present,
> Nor aged counselor to youthful sin,
> But one whose virtue shone above the rest,
> A valiant martyr and a virtuous peer.
> . . . Let fair truth be graced,
> Since forged invention former time defaced.

—Prologue to *Sir John Oldcastle*.

1599. *Venus and Adonis* and *Romeo and Juliet*

GULL [IO]. Pardon, fair lady, though sick-thoughted Gullio makes amain unto thee and like a bold-faced suitor 'gins to woo thee.

INGEN [IOSO]. (We shall have nothing but pure Shakespeare and shreds of poetry that he hath gathered at the theaters!)

GULL. Pardon me, my mistress, as I am a gentleman, the

moon in comparison of thy bright hue a mere slut, Anthony's
Cleopatra a black browed milkmaid, Helen a dowdy.

INGEN. (Mark, *Romeo and Juliet*! O monstrous theft! I
think he will run through a whole book of Samuel Daniel's!)

GULL. Thrice fairer than myself (thus I began)
The gods' fair riches, sweet above compare,
Stain to all nymphs, [m]ore lovely the [n] a man,
More white and red than doves and roses are!
Nature that made thee with herself had [at] strife,
Saith that the world hath ending with thy life.

INGEN. Sweet Mr. Shakespeare!

INGEN. My pen is your bounden vassal to command. But
what vein would it please you to have them in?

GULL. Not in a vain vein (pretty, i' faith!): make me them
in two or three divers veins, in Chaucer's, Gower's, and
Spenser's and Mr. Shakespeare's. Marry, I think I shall entertain those verses which run like these:

Even as the sun with purple colored face
Had ta'en his last leave on the weeping morn, etc.

O sweet Mr. Shakespeare! I'll have his picture in my study
at the court.

GULL. Let me hear Mr. Shakespeare's vein.

INGEN. Fair Venus, queen of beauty and of love,
Thy red doth stain the blushing of the morn,
Thy snowy neck shameth the milkwhite dove,
Thy presence doth this naked world adorn,
Gazing on thee all other nymphs I scorn.
When e'er thou diest slow shine that Saturday,
Beauty and grace must sleep with thee for aye!

GULL. No more! I am one that can judge according to the
proverb, *bovem ex unguibus*. Ay, marry, sir, these have some
life in them! Let this duncified world esteem of Spenser and
Chaucer, I'll worship sweet Mr. Shakespeare and to honor
him will lay his *Venus and Adonis* under my pillow, as we

read of one (I do not well remember his name but I am sure
he was a king) slept with Homer under his bed's head.

—*The Return from Parnassus,* part one.

1600 (?)   *2 Henry IV* and *The Merry Wives of Windsor*

Mr. Carlington,

I am here so pestered with country business that I shall
not be able as yet to come to London. If I stay here long in
this fashion, at my return I think you will find me so dull
that I shall be taken for Justice Silence or Justice Shallow;
wherefore I am to entreat you that you will take pity of me,
and as occurrences shall serve to send me such news from
time to time as shall happen, the knowledge of which,
though perhaps they will not exempt me from the opinion of
a Justice Shallow at London, yet I assure you they will make
me pass for a very sufficient gentleman in Gloucestershire.
...

Your assured friend,
Charles Percy

Dumbleton in Gloucestershire
this 27 of December

—Letter from Sir Charles Percy to a London friend

1600.   *2 Henry IV*

The Second Part of Henry the Fourth, continuing to his
death and coronation of Henry V. With the humors of Sir
John Falstaff and swaggering Pistol. As it hath been sundry
times publicly acted by the Right Honorable the Lord Chamberlain his Servants. Written by William Shakespeare.

—Title page of the First Quarto.

1600.   *The Merchant of Venice*

The most excellent History of the Merchant of Venice.
With the extreme cruelty of Shylock the Jew towards the said
Merchant in cutting a just pound of his flesh, and the obtain-
ing of Portia by the choice of three chests. As it hath been
divers times acted by the Lord Chamberlain his Servants.
Written by William Shakespeare.

—Title page of the First Quarto.

1600.   *Henry V*

The Chronicle History of Henry the fifth with his battle
fought at Agincourt in France. Together with Ancient Pistol.

As it hath been sundry times played by the Right Honorable the Lord Chamberlain his Servants.

—Title page of the First Quarto.

1601. February 18.   *Richard II* and Essex

The examination of Augustine Phillips, servant unto the Lord Chamberlain and one of his players, taken the 18 of February 1600 upon his oath. He saith that upon Friday last was sennight, or Thursday, Sir Charles Percy, Sir Joscelin Percy, and the Lord Monteagle with some three more spake to some of the players in the presence of this examinate to have the play of the deposing and killing of King Richard II to be played the Saturday next, promising to get them forty shillings more than their ordinary to play it; where this examinate and his fellows were determined to have played some other play, holding that play of King Richard to be so old and so long out of use as that they should have small or no company at it. But at their request this examinate and his fellows were content to play it the Saturday and had their forty shillings more than their ordinary for it, and so played it accordingly.

—Testimony of Shakespeare's partner and friend, Augustine Phillips.

1601.   *Julius Caesar*

The many-headed multitude were drawn
By Brutus' speech that Caesar was ambitious.
When eloquent Mark Antony had shown
His virtues, who but Brutus then was vicious?

—John Weever, *The Mirror of Martyrs.*

1602. February 2.   *Twelfth Night*

At our feast we had a play called *Twelfth Night, or What You Will,* much like *The Comedy of Errors* or *Menaechmi* in Plautus, but most like and near to that in Italian called *Inganni.* A good practice in it to make the steward believe his lady widow was in love with him by counterfeiting a letter in general terms, telling him what she liked best in him and prescribing his gesture in smiling, his apparel, etc., and then when he came to practice, making him believe they took him to be mad.

—John Manningham, *Diary.*

1602. March 13.   *Richard III*

Upon a time when Burbage played Richard III there was a citizen grew so far in liking with him that before she went from the play she appointed him to come that night unto her by the name of Richard III. Shakespeare, overhearing their conclusion, went before, was entertained and at his game ere Burbage came. Then message being brought that Richard III was at the door, Shakespeare caused return to be made that William the Conqueror was before Richard III. Shakespeare's name William.

—John Manningham, *Diary.*

1602.   *The Merry Wives of Windsor*

A most pleasant and excellent conceited comedy of Sir John Falstaff and The merry wives of Windsor intermixed with sundry variable and pleasing humors of Sir Hugh the Welsh Knight, Justice Shallow, and his wise cousin M. Slender. With the swaggering vein of Ancient Pistol and Corporal Nym. By William Shakespeare. As it hath been divers times acted by the Right Honorable my Lord Chamberlain's Servants. Both before Her Majesty and elsewhere.

—Title page of the First Quarto.

1604.   *Hamlet*

It should be like the never-too-well-read *Arcadia* where the prose and verse (matter and words) are like his mistress's eyes, one still excelling another and without corrival; or to come home to the vulgar's element, like friendly Shakespeare's tragedies where the comedian rides when the tragedian stands on tiptoe: faith it should please all, like Prince Hamlet. But in sadness then it were to be feared he would run mad; in sooth I will not be moon-sick to please, nor out of my wits though I displeased all.

—Anthony Scoloker, *Epistle to Daiphantus, or the Passions of Love.*

1604/5.   *Love's Labour's Lost*

Sir,

I have sent and been all this morning hunting for players, jugglers, and such kind of creatures but find them hard to find; wherefore leaving notes for them to seek me, Burbage is come and says there is no new play that the Queen hath not

seen but they have revived an old one called *Love's Labour's
Lost*, which for wit and mirth he says will please her exceedingly. And this is appointed to be played tomorrow night at
my lord of Southampton's, unless you send a writ to remove
the *corpus cum causa* to your house in the Strand. Burbage
is my messenger, ready attending your pleasure.

Yours most humbly,
Walter Cope

—Letter of Sir Walter Cope to Lord Cranborne (Sir Robert
Cecil).

1605.   Whom Succeeding Ages May Justly Admire

These may suffice for some poetical descriptions of our
ancient poets; if I would come to our time, what a world
could I present to you out of Sir Philip Sidney, Edmund
Spenser, Samuel Daniel, Hugh Holland, Ben Jonson, Thomas
Campion, Michael Drayton, George Chapman, John Marston,
William Shakespeare, and other most pregnant wits of these
our times, whom succeeding ages may justly admire.

—William Camden, *Remains of a Greater Work concerning
Britain.*

1607. September 5.   *Hamlet*

I sent the interpreter according to his desire aboard the
Hector where he broke fast and after came aboard me where
we gave the tragedy of *Hamlet.*

1607. September 30.   *Richard II*

Captain Hawkins dined with me where my companions
acted *King Richard II.*

1608. March 31.   *Hamlet*

I invited Captain Hawkins to a fish dinner and had *Hamlet*
acted aboard me, which I permit to keep my people from
idleness and unlawful games or sleep.

—Notes of Captain William Keeling of the East India Company ship *Dragon* off Sierra Leone.

1608.   *King Lear*

M. William Shakespeare: his true chronicle history of the
life and death of King Lear and his three daughters. With
the unfortunate life of Edgar, son and heir to the Earl of
Gloucester, and his sullen and assumed humor of Tom of

Bedlam. As it was played before the King's Majesty at Whitehall upon St. Stephen's night in Christmas Holidays. By His Majesty's Servants playing usually at the Globe on the Bankside.

—Title page of the First Quarto.

1609. *Troilus and Cressida*
The Famous History of Troilus and Cressida. Excellently expressing the beginning of their loves, with the conceited wooing of Pandarus, Prince of Licia. Written by William Shakespeare.

—Title page of the First Quarto. (second issue)

1610. April 30. *Othello*
Monday, His Excellency went to the Globe, the usual place where comedies are played. There was represented the history of the Moor of Venice.

—Extract from the diary of Prince Lewis Frederick of Wurtemberg, kept by his secretary, W. H. Wurmsser, chronicling his visit to England in 1610.

1611. April 20. *Macbeth*
In *Macbeth* at the Globe, 1610 [1611], the 20 of April, Saturday, there was to be observed, first, how Macbeth and Banquo, two noblemen of Scotland, riding through a wood, there stood before them three women, fairies or nymphs, and saluted Macbeth, saying three times unto him, "Hail Macbeth, King of Cawdor, for thou shalt be a king but shalt beget no kings, etc." Then said Banquo, "What, all to Macbeth and nothing to me?" "Yes," said the nymphs, "hail to thee Banquo, thou shalt beget kings, yet be no king." And so they departed and came to the court of Scotland, to Duncan, King of Scots, and it was in the days of Edward the Confessor. And Duncan bade them both kindly welcome and made Macbeth forthwith Prince of Northumberland and sent him home to his own castle and appointed Macbeth to provide for him, for he would sup with him the next day at night and did so. And Macbeth contrived to kill Duncan, and through the persuasion of his wife did that night murder the king in his own castle, being his guest; and there were many prodigies seen that night and the day before. And when Macbeth had murdered the king, the blood on his hands could not be washed off by any means, nor from his wife's hands, which

handled the bloody daggers in hiding them, by which means they became both much amazed and affronted. The murder being known, Duncan's two sons fled, the one to England, the other to Wales, to save themselves. They being fled, they were supposed guilty of the murder of their father, which was nothing so. Then was Macbeth crowned king; and then—for fear of Banquo, his old companion, that he should beget kings but be no king himself—he contrived the death of Banquo, and caused him to be murdered on the way as he rode. The next night, being at supper with his noblemen whom he had bid to a feast, to the which also Banquo should have come, he began to speak of noble Banquo and to wish that he were there. And as he thus did, standing up to drink a carouse to him, the ghost of Banquo came and sat down in his chair behind him. And he, turning about to sit down again, saw the ghost of Banquo, which fronted him so that he fell into a great passion of fear and fury, uttering many words about his murder, by which, when they heard that Banquo was murdered, they suspected Macbeth. Then Macduff fled to England to the King's son and so they raised an army and came into Scotland and at Dunsinane overthrew Macbeth. In the meantime, while Macduff was in England, Macbeth slew Macduff's wife and children, and after in the battle Macduff slew Macbeth. Observe also how Macbeth's queen did rise in the night in her sleep and walk and talked and confessed all, and the doctor noted her words.

—Dr. Simon Forman, *Diary*.

1611. *Cymbeline*

Of Cymbeline, King of England. Remember also the story of Cymbeline, King of England in Lucius' time: how Lucius came from Octavius Caesar for tribute, and being denied, after sent Lucius with a great army of soldiers who landed at Milford Haven, and after were vanquished by Cymbeline and Lucius taken prisoner. And all by means of three outlaws, of the which two of them were the sons of Cymbeline, stolen from him when they were but two years old by an old man whom Cymbeline banished; and he kept them on as his own sons twenty years with him in a cave. And how one of them slew Cloten, that was the queen's son, going to Milford Haven to seek the love of Imogen, the king's daughter, whom he had banished also for loving his daughter. And how the Italian that came from her love conveyed himself into a chest and said it was a chest of plate sent from her love and others to be presented to the king; and in the deepest of the night, she being asleep, he opened the chest and came forth of it and viewed her in her bed and the marks of her body and took away her bracelet, and after accused her of adultery to her love, etc.; and in the end how he came with the Romans into England and was taken prisoner, and after revealed to Imogen, who had turned herself into man's apparel and fled to meet her love at Milford Haven and chanced to fall on the cave in the woods where her two brothers were. And how, by eating a sleeping dram, they thought she had been dead and laid her in the woods and the body of Cloten by her in her love's apparel that he left behind him; and how she was found by Lucius, etc.

—Dr. Simon Forman, *Diary.*

1611. May 15. *The Winter's Tale*

In *The Winter's Tale* at the Globe, 1611, the 15 of May, Wednesday, observe there how Leontes, the King of Sicilia, was overcome with jealousy of his wife with the king of Bohemia, his friend that came to see him, and how he contrived his death and would have had his cupbearer to have poisoned, who gave the king of Bohemia warning thereof and fled with him to Bohemia. Remember also how he sent to the oracle of Apollo and the answer of Apollo that she was guiltless and that the king was jealous, etc.; and how, except the child was found again that was lost, the king should die without issue, for the child was carried into Bohemia and there laid in a forest and brought up by a shepherd; and the king of Bohemia's son married that wench. And how they fled into Sicilia to Leontes, and the shepherd having showed the letter of the nobleman by whom Leontes sent that child and the jewels found about her, she was known to be Leontes' daughter and was then sixteen years old. Remember also the rogue that came in all tottered [tattered] like Coltpixie [a roguish sprite], and how he feigned him sick and to have been robbed of all that he had and how he cozened the poor man of all his money, and after came to the sheepshear with a pedlar's pack and there cozened them again of all their money, and how he changed apparel with the king of Bohemia's son, and then how he turned courtier, etc. Beware of trusting feigned beggars or fawning fellows.

—Dr. Simon Forman, *Diary.*

1613. June 29. *Henry VIII*

Now, to let matters of state sleep, I will entertain you at the present with what has happened this week at the Bankside. The King's players had a new play called *All is True*, representing some principal pieces of the reign of Henry VIII, which was set forth with many extraordinary circumstances of pomp and majesty, even to the matting of the stage; the knights of the Order with their Georges and Garters, the Guards with their embroidered coats, and the like, sufficient in truth within a while to make greatness very familiar if not ridiculous. Now, King Henry making a masque at the Cardinal Wolsey's house and certain chambers being shot off at his entry, some of the paper or other stuff wherewith one of them was stopped did light on the thatch where, being thought at first but an idle smoke and their eyes more attentive to the show, it kindled inwardly and ran round like a train, consuming within less than an hour the whole house to the very grounds. This was the fatal period of that virtuous fabric wherein yet nothing did perish but wood and straw and a few forsaken cloaks; only one man had his breeches set on fire, that would perhaps have broiled him if he had not by the benefit of a provident wit put it out with bottle ale.

—Letter of Sir Henry Wotton to Sir Edmund Bacon.

1615 (?) Beaumont to Jonson
     Here I would let slip
 (If I had any in me) scholarship,
And from all learning keep these lines as clear
As Shakespeare's best are, which our heirs shall hear
Preachers apt to their auditors to show
How far sometimes a mortal man may go
By the dim light of nature. . . .

—Francis Beaumont, *To Mr. B. J.*

Later Comment by Contemporaries

1619. Jonson's Conversations with Drummond

His censure of the English poets was this . . . that Shakespeare wanted art.

Shakespeare in a play brought in a number of men saying

they had suffered shipwreck in Bohemia, where there is no
sea near by some hundred miles.
    —Ben Jonson, *Conversations with William Drummond.*

1623.   Preface to Shakespeare's Collected Plays
    [Shakespeare] who, as he was a happy imitator of nature,
was a most gentle expresser of it. His mind and hand went
together, and what he thought he uttered with that easiness
that we have scarce received from him a blot in his papers.
—John Heminge and Henry Condell, *Epistle* to the readers of
the Folio.

1623.   To the Memory of My Beloved, the Author, Mr.
William Shakespeare, . . . And What He hath Left Us.
    To draw no envy, Shakespeare, on thy name,
    Am I thus ample to thy book and fame,
    While I confess thy writings to be such
    As neither man nor muse can praise too much.
    'Tis true, and all men's suffrage. But these ways
    Were not the paths I meant unto thy praise,
    For silliest ignorance on these may light,
    Which when it sounds at best but echoes right;
    Or blind affection, which doth ne'er advance
    The truth, but gropes and urgeth all by chance;
    Or crafty malice might pretend this praise,
    And think to ruin where it seemed to raise.
    These are as some infamous bawd or whore
    Should praise a matron, what could hurt her more?
    But thou art proof against them, and indeed
    Above th' ill fortune of them, or the need.

    I therefore will begin. Soul of the age!
    The applause, delight, the wonder of our stage!
    My Shakespeare, rise! I will not lodge thee by
    Chaucer or Spenser, or bid Beaumont lie
    A little further to make thee a room.
    Thou art a monument without a tomb,
    And art alive still while thy book doth live
    And we have wits to read and praise to give.
    That I not mix thee so my brain excuses—
    I mean with great but disproportioned muses—
    For if I thought my judgment were of years,
    I should commit thee surely with thy peers,

And tell how far thou didst our Lyly outshine,
Or sporting Kyd, or Marlowe's mighty line.
And though thou hadst small Latin and less Greek,
From thence to honor thee I would not seek
For names, but call forth thund'ring Aeschylus,
Euripides, and Sophocles to us,
Pacuvius, Accius, him of Cordova, dead
To life again, to hear thy buskin tread
And shake a stage; or, when thy socks were on,
Leave thee alone for the comparison
Of all that insolent Greece or haughty Rome
Sent forth, or since did from their ashes come.

Triumph, my Britain! Thou hast one to show
To whom all scenes of Europe homage owe.
He was not of an age, but for all time;
And all the muses still were in their prime
When, like Apollo, he came forth to warm
Our ears, or like a Mercury to charm.
Nature herself was proud of his designs
And joyed to wear the dressing of his lines,
Which were so richly spun and woven so fit
As, since, she will vouchsafe no other wit.
The merry Greek, tart Aristophanes,
Neat Terence, witty Plautus, now not please,
But antiquated and deserted lie
As they were not of nature's family.

Yet must I not give nature all; thy art,
My gentle Shakespeare, must enjoy a part;
For though the poet's matter nature be,
His art doth give the fashion; and that he
Who casts to write a living line, must sweat,
Such as thine are, and strike the second heat
Upon the muses' anvil, turn the same,
And himself with it, that he thinks to frame,
Or for the laurel he may gain a scorn,
For a good poet's made as well as born,
And such wert thou. Look, how the father's face
Lives in his issue, even so the race
Of Shakespeare's mind and manners brightly shines
In his well-turned and true-filed lines,
In each of which he seems to shake a lance,
As brandished at the eyes of ignorance.

Sweet swan of Avon! what a sight it were
To see thee in our waters yet appear,
And make those flights upon the banks of Thames
That so did take Eliza and our James!
But stay, I see thee in the hemisphere
Advanced and made a constellation there.
Shine forth, thou star of poets, and with rage
Or influence chide or cheer the drooping stage,
Which since thy flight fro hence hath mourned like night,
And despairs day but for thy volume's light.

—Ben Jonson

1623. To the Memory of the Deceased Author, Master W. Shakespeare.

Nor shall I e'er believe or think thee dead,
Though missed, until our bankrout [bankrupt] stage be
  sped
(Impossible!) with some new strain t' outdo
Passions of Juliet and her Romeo,
Or till I hear a scene more nobly take. . . .

—Leonard Digges

1627. Of Poets and Poesy

. . . And be it said of thee,
Shakespeare, thou hadst as smooth a comic vein,
Fitting the sock, and in thy natural brain
As strong conception and as clear a rage
As anyone that trafficked with the stage.

—Michael Drayton, from "To my most dearly loved friend, Henry Reynolds, Esquire"

Before 1637. "On Our Shakespeare"

I remember the players have often mentioned it as an honor to Shakespeare that in his writing, whatsoever he penned, he never blotted out line. My answer hath been, would he had blotted a thousand, which they thought a malevolent speech. I had not told posterity this but for their ignorance who choose that circumstance to commend their friend by wherein he most faulted and to justify mine own candor, for I loved the man and do honor his memory, on this side idolatry, as much as any. He was, indeed, honest and of an open and free nature, had an excellent fancy, brave notions, and gentle expressions, wherein he flowed with that facility that sometime it was necessary he should be stopped:

Sufflaminandus erat, as Augustus said of Haterius. His wit was in his own power; would the rule of it had been so too. Many times he fell into those things could not escape laughter, as when he said in the person of Caesar, one speaking to him, "Caesar, thou dost me wrong!" He replied, "Caesar did never wrong but with just cause," and such like, which were ridiculous. But he redeemed his vices with his virtues; there was ever more in him to be praised than to be pardoned.

—Ben Jonson, *Timber, or Discoveries*

PART IX

Shakespeare's Works in Aftertimes

JOHN DRYDEN ON SHAKESPEARE

JUDGMENT

To begin, then, with Shakspeare. He was the man who of all modern, and perhaps ancient poets, had the largest and most comprehensive soul. All the images of nature were still present to him, and he drew them, not laboriously, but luckily; when he describes anything, you more than see it, you feel it too. Those who accuse him to have wanted learning, give him the greater commendation: he was naturally learned; he needed not the spectacles of books to read nature; he looked inwards, and found her there. I cannot say he is everywhere alike; were he so, I should do him injury to compare him with the greatest of mankind. He is many times flat, insipid; his comic wit degenerating into clenches, his serious swelling into bombast. But he is always great when some great occasion is presented to him; no man can say he ever had a fit subject for his wit, and did not then raise himself as high above the rest of poets, " *Quantum lenta solent inter viburna cupressi.*" The consideration of this made Mr. Hales of Eton say, that there was no subject of which any poet ever writ, but he would produce it much better done in Shakspeare; and however others are now generally preferred before him, yet the age wherein he lived, which had contemporaries with him Fletcher and Jonson, never equalled them to him in their esteem: and in the last king's court, when Ben's reputation was at highest, Sir John Suckling, and with him the greater part of the courtiers, set our Shakspeare far above him.

(1668)

CALIBAN

To return once more to Shakspeare; no man ever drew so many characters, or generally distinguished them better from one another, excepting only Jonson. I will instance but in one to show the copiousness of his intention; it is that of Caliban, or the monster, in the *Tempest.* He seems there to have created a person which was not in nature, a boldness which, at first sight, would appear intolerable; for he makes him a species of himself, begotten by an incubus on a witch; but this, as I have elsewhere proved, is not wholly beyond the bounds of credibility, at least the vulgar still believe it. We have the separated notions of a spirit and of a witch (and spirits, according to Plato, are vested with a subtle body; according to some of his followers have different sexes); therefore, as from the distinct apprehensions of a horse and of a man imagination has formed a centaur, so from those of an incubus and a sorceress Shakspeare has produced his monster. Whether or no his generation can be defended I leave to philosophy; but of this I am certain, that the poet has most judiciously furnished him with a person, a language, and a character, which will suit him, both by father's and mother's side: he has all the discontents and malice of a witch and of a devil, besides a convenient proportion of the deadly sins; gluttony, sloth, and lust are manifest; the deject-edness of a slave is likewise given him, and the ignorance of one bred up in a desert island. His person is monstrous, and, he is the product of unnatural lust; and his language is as hobgoblin as his person; in all things he is distinguished from other mortals.

(1679)

BOMBAST

If Shakspeare be allowed, as I think he must, to have made his characters distinct, it will easily be inferred that he understood the nature of the passions: because it has been proved already that confused passions make undistinguishable characters: yet I cannot deny that he has his failings; but they are not so much in the passions themselves as in his manner of expression: he often obscures his meaning by his words, and sometimes makes it unintelligible. I will not say of so great a poet that he distinguished not the blown puffy style from true sublimity; but I may venture to maintain that the fury of his fancy often transported him beyond the bounds of judgment, either in coining of new words and phrases, or racking words which were in use into the violence of a catachresis. It is not that I would explode the use of meta-phors from passion, for Longinus thinks them necessary to raise it: but to use them at every word, to say nothing without a metaphor, a simile, an image, or description is, I doubt, to smell a little too strongly of the buskin. I must be

forced to give an example of expressing passion figuratively;
but that I may do it with respect to Shakspeare, it shall not
be taken from anything of his: 'tis an exclamation against
fortune, quoted in his *Hamlet* but written by some other
poet:

> Out, out, thou strumpet, Fortune! all you gods,
> In general synod, take away her power;
> Break all the spokes and felleys from her wheel,
> And bowl the round nave down the hill of Heav'n,
> As low as to the fiends.

And immediately after, speaking of Hecuba, when Priam was
killed before her eyes:

> The mobbled queen
> Threatening the flame, ran up and down
> With bisson rheum; a clout about that head
> Where late the diadem stood; and for a robe,
> About her lank and all o'er-teemed loins,
> A blanket in th' alarm of fear caught up.
> Who this had seen, with tongue in venom steep'd
> 'Gainst Fortune's state would treason have pronuounced;
> But if the gods themselves did see her then,
> When she saw Pyrrhus make malicious sport
> In mincing with his sword her husband's limbs,
> The instant burst of clamour that she made
> (Unless things mortal move them not at all)
> Would have made milk the burning eyes of heaven,
> And passion in the gods.

What a pudder is here kept in raising the expression of
trifling thoughts! Would not a man have thought that the
poet had been bound prentice to a wheelwright for his first
rant? and had followed a ragman for the clout and blanket in
second? Fortune is painted on a wheel, and therefore the
writer, in a rage, will have poetical justice done upon every
member of that engine: after this execution, he bowls the
nave downhill, from Heaven, to the fiends (an unreasonable
long mark, a man would think); 'tis well there are no solid
orbs to stop it in the way, or no element of fire to consume
it: but when it came to the earth it must be monstrous heavy
to break ground as low as the center. His making milk the

burning eyes of heaven was a pretty tolerable flight too: and I think no man ever drew milk out of eyes before him: yet, to make the wonder greater, these eyes were burning. Such a sight indeed were enough to have raised passion in the gods; but to excuse the effects of it, he tells you perhaps they did not see it. Wise men would be glad to find a little sense couched under all these pompous words; for bombast is commonly the delight of that audience which loves poetry but understands it not: and as commonly has been the practice of those writers who, not being able to infuse a natural passion into the mind, have made it their business to ply the ears, and to stun their judges by the noise. But Shakspeare does not often thus; for the passions in his scene between Brutus and Cassius are extremely natural, the thoughts are such as arise from the matter, the expression of them not viciously figurative.

I cannot leave this subject before I do justice to the divine poet by giving you one of his passionate descriptions: 'tis of Richard II when he was deposed and led in triumph through the streets of London by Henry of Bolingbroke: the painting of it is so lively, and the words so moving, that I have scarce read anything comparable to it in any other language. Suppose you have seen already the fortunate usurper passing through the crowd, and followed by the shouts and acclamations of the people; and now behold King Richard entering upon the scene: consider the wretchedness of his condition and his carriage in it; and refrain from pity if you can:

> As in a theatre, the eyes of men,
> After a well-graced actor leaves the stage,
> Are idly bent on him that enters next,
> Thinking his prattle to be tedious:
> Even so, or with much more contempt, men's eyes
> Did scowl on Richard: no man cried, God save him:
> No joyful tongue gave him his welcome home,
> But dust was thrown upon his sacred head,
> Which with such gentle sorrow he shook off,
> His face still combating with tears and smiles
> (The badges of his grief and patience),
> That had not God (for some strong purpose) steel'd
> The hearts of men, they must perforce have melted,
> And barbarism itself have pitied him.

To speak justly of this whole matter: 'tis neither height of thought that is discommended, nor pathetic vehemence, nor any nobleness of expression in its proper place: but 'tis a false measure of all these, something which is like them, and is not them; 'tis the Bristol-stone which appears like a diamond; 'tis an extravagant thought instead of a sublime one; 'tis roaring madness instead of vehemence; and a sound of words instead of sense. If Shakspeare were stripped of all the bombasts in his passions, and dressed in the most vulgar words, we should find the beauties of his thoughts remaining; if his embroideries were burnt down, there would still be silver at the bottom of the melting-pot: but I fear (at least let me fear it for myself) that we, who ape his sounding words, have nothing of his thought, but are all outside; there is not so much as a dwarf within our giant's clothes. Therefore, let not Shakspeare suffer for our sakes; 'tis our fault, who succeed him in an age which is more refined, if we imitate him so ill that we copy his failings only and make a virtue of that in our writings which in his was an imperfection.

(1679)

FROM THE PREFACE AND NOTES TO
THE PLAYS OF WILLIAM SHAKESPEARE (1765)

Samuel Johnson

That praises are without reason lavished on the dead, and that the honors due only to excellence are paid to antiquity, is a complaint likely to be always continued by those who, being able to add nothing to truth, hope for eminence from the heresies of paradox; or those who, being forced by disappointment upon consolatory expedients, are willing to hope from posterity what the present age refuses and flatter themselves that the regard which is yet denied by envy will be at last bestowed by time.

Antiquity, like every other quality that attracts the notice of mankind, has undoubtedly votaries that reverence it, not from reason, but from prejudice. Some seem to admire indiscriminately whatever has been long preserved, without considering that time has sometimes cooperated with chance; all perhaps are more willing to honor past than present excellence; and the mind contemplates genius through the shades of age, as the eye surveys the sun through artificial opacity. The great contention of criticism is to find the faults of the moderns and the beauties of the ancients. While an author is yet living, we estimate his powers by his worst performance; and when he is dead, we rate them by his best.

To works, however, of which the excellence is not absolute and definite, but gradual and comparative; to works not raised upon principles demonstrative and scientific, but appealing wholly to observation and experience, no other test can be applied than length of duration and continuance of esteem. What mankind have long possessed they have often examined and compared; and if they persist to value the possession, it is because frequent comparisons have confirmed opinion in its favor. As among the works of nature no man can properly call a river deep or a mountain high, without the knowledge of many mountains and many rivers; so, in the productions of genius, nothing can be styled excellent till it has been compared with other works of the same kind. Demonstration immediately displays its power and has nothing to hope or fear from the flux of years; but works tentative and experimental must be estimated by their proportion to the general and collective ability of man, as it is discovered in a long succession of endeavors. Of the first building that was raised, it might be with certainty determined that it was round or square, but whether it was spacious or lofty must have been referred to time. The Pythagorean scale of numbers was at once discovered to be perfect; but the poems of Homer we yet know not to transcend the common limits of human intelligence but by remarking that nation after nation, and century after century, has been able to do little more than transpose his incidents, new-name his characters, and paraphrase his sentiments.

The reverence due to writings that have long subsisted arises, therefore, not from any credulous confidence in the superior wisdom of past ages or gloomy persuasion of the degeneracy of mankind, but is the consequence of acknowledged and indubitable positions, that what has been longest known has been most considered, and what is most considered is best understood.

The poet of whose works I have undertaken the revision may now begin to assume the dignity of an ancient and claim the privilege of established fame and prescriptive veneration. He has long outlived his century, the term commonly fixed as the test of literary merit. Whatever advantages he might once derive from personal allusions, local customs, or temporary opinions have for many years been lost; and every topic of merriment or motive of sorrow which the modes of artificial life afforded him now only obscure the scenes which they once illuminated. The effects of favor and competition are at an end; the tradition of his friendships and his enmities have perished; his works support no opinion with arguments nor supply any faction with invectives; they can neither indulge vanity nor gratify malignity; but are read without any other reason than the desire of pleasure and are therefore praised only as pleasure is obtained; yet, thus unassisted by interest or passion, they have passed through variations of taste and changes of manners, and, as they devolved from one generation to another, have received new honors at every transmission.

But because human judgment, though it be gradually gaining upon certainty, never becomes infallible; and approbation, though long continued, may yet be only the approbation of prejudice or fashion; it is proper to inquire by what peculiarities of excellence Shakespeare has gained and kept the favor of his countrymen.

Nothing can please many, and please long, but just representations of general nature. Particular manners can be known to few, and therefore few only can judge how nearly they are copied. The irregular combinations of fanciful invention may delight awhile by that novelty of which the common satiety of life sends us all in quest; but the pleasures of sudden wonder are soon exhausted, and the mind can only repose on the stability of truth.

Shakespeare is, above all writers, at least above all modern writers, the poet of nature, the poet that holds up to his readers a faithful mirror of manners and of life. His characters are not modified by the customs of particular places, unpracticed by the rest of the world; by the peculiarities of studies or professions which can operate but upon small numbers; or by the accidents of transient fashions or temporary opinions: they are the genuine progeny of common humanity, such as the world will always supply, and observation will always find. His persons act and speak by the influence of those general passions and principles by which all minds are agitated and the whole system of life is continued in motion. In the writings of other poets a character is too often an individual; in those of Shakespeare it is commonly a species.

It is from this wide extension of design that so much instruction is derived. It is this which fills the plays of Shakespeare with practical axioms and domestic wisdom. It was said of Euripides that every verse was a precept; and it may be said of Shakespeare that from his works may be collected a system of civil and economical prudence. Yet his real power is not shown in the splendor of particular passages, but by the progress of his fable and the tenor of his dialogue; and he that tries to recommend him by select quotations will succeed like the pedant in Hierocles, who, when he offered his house to sale, carried a brick in his pocket as a specimen.

It will not easily be imagined how much Shapespeare excels in accommodating his sentiments to real life but by comparing him with other authors. It was observed of the ancient schools of declamation that the more diligently they were frequented, the more was the student disqualified for the world, because he found nothing there which he should ever meet in any other place. The same remark may be applied to every stage but that of Shakespeare. The theater, when it is under any other direction, is peopled by such characters as were never seen, conversing in a language which was never heard, upon topics which will never arise in the commerce of mankind. But the dialogue of this author is often so evidently determined by the incident which produces it, and is pursued with so much ease and simplicity, that it seems scarcely to claim the merit of fiction, but to have been gleaned by diligent selection out of common conversation and common occurrences.

Upon every other stage the universal agent is love, by whose power all good and evil is distributed and every action quickened or retarded. To bring a lover, a lady, and a rival into the fable; to entangle them in contradictory obligations, perplex them with oppositions of interest, and harass them with violence of desires inconsistent with each other; to make them meet in rapture and part in agony, to fill their mouths with hyperbolical joy and outrageous sorrow, to distress them as nothing human ever was distressed, to deliver them as nothing human ever was delivered, is the business of a modern dramatist. For this, probability is violated, life is misrepresented, and language is depraved. But love is only one of many passions; and as it has no great influence upon the sum of life, it has little operation in the dramas of a poet who caught his ideas from the living world and exhibited only what he saw before him. He knew that any other passion, as it was regular or exorbitant, was a cause of happiness or calamity.

Characters thus ample and general were not easily discriminated and preserved, yet perhaps no poet ever kept his personages more distinct from each other. I will not say with Pope that every speech may be assigned to the proper speaker, because many speeches there are which have nothing characteristical; but, perhaps, though some may be equally adapted to every person, it will be difficult to find any that can be properly transferred from the present possessor to another claimant. The choice is right, when there is reason for choice.

Other dramatists can only gain attention by hyperbolical or aggravated characters, by fabulous and unexampled excellence or depravity, as the writers of barbarous romances invigorated the reader by a giant and a dwarf; and he that should form his expectations of human affairs from the play, or from the tale, would be equally deceived. Shakespeare has no heroes; his scenes are occupied only by men, who act and speak as the reader thinks that he should himself have spoken or acted on the same occasion. Even where the agency is supernatural, the dialogue is level with life. Other writers disguise the most natural passions and most frequent incidents; so that he who contemplates them in the book will not know them in the world. Shakespeare approximates the remote and familiarizes the wonderful; the event which he represents will not happen, but, if it were possible, its effects would probably be such as he has assigned; and it may be said that he has not only shown human nature as it acts in real exigencies, but as it would be found in trials to which it cannot be exposed.

This, therefore, is the praise of Shakespeare, that his drama is the mirror of life; that he who has mazed his imagination in following the phantoms which other writers raise up before him, may here be cured of his delirious ecstasies by reading human sentiments in human language, by scenes from which a hermit may estimate the transactions of the world and a confessor predict the progress of the passions.

His adherence to general nature has exposed him to the censure of critics who form their judgments upon narrower principles. Dennis and Rymer think his Romans not sufficiently Roman; and Voltaire censures his kings as not completely royal. Dennis is offended that Menenius, a senator of Rome, should play the buffoon; and Voltaire perhaps thinks decency violated when the Danish usurper is represented as a drunkard. But Shakespeare always makes nature predominate over accident; and, if he preserves the essential character, is not very careful of distinctions superinduced and adventitious. His story requires Romans or kings, but he thinks only on men. He knew that Rome, like every other city, had men of all dispositions; and wanting a buffoon, he went into the senate house for that which the senate house would certainly have afforded him. He was inclined to show an usurper and a murderer not only odious, but despicable; he therefore added drunkenness to his other qualities, knowing that kings love wine like other men, and that wine exerts its natural power upon kings. These are the petty cavils of petty minds; a poet overlooks the casual distinction of country and condition, as a painter, satisfied with the figure, neglects the drapery.

The censure which he has incurred by mixing comic and tragic scenes, as it extends to all his works, deserves more consideration. Let the fact be first stated and then examined.

Shakespeare's plays are not in the rigorous and critical sense either tragedies or comedies, but compositions of a distinct kind; exhibiting the real state of sublunary nature, which partakes of good and evil, joy and sorrow, mingled with endless variety of proportion and innumerable modes of combination; and expressing the course of the world, in which the loss of one is the gain of another; in which, at the same time, the reveller is hasting to his wine, and the mourner burying his friend; in which the malignity of one is sometimes defeated by the frolic of another; and many mischiefs and many benefits are done and hindered without design.

Out of this chaos of mingled purposes and casualties the ancient poets, according to the laws which custom had prescribed, selected some the crimes of men, and some their absurdities; some the momentous vicissitudes of life, and some the lighter occurrences; some the terrors of distress, and some the gaieties of prosperity. Thus rose the two modes of imitation, known by the names of *tragedy* and *comedy,* compositions intended to promote different ends by contrary means, and considered as so little allied that I do not recollect among the Greeks or Romans a single writer who attempted both.

Shakespeare has united the powers of exciting laughter and sorrow not only in one mind but in one composition. Almost all his plays are divided between serious and ludicrous characters, and, in the successive evolutions of the design, sometimes produce seriousness and sorrow, and sometimes levity and laughter.

That this is a practice contrary to the rules of criticism will be readily allowed; but there is always an appeal open from criticism to nature. The end of writing is to instruct; the end of poetry is to instruct by pleasing. That the mingled drama may convey all the instruction of tragedy or comedy cannot be denied, because it includes both in its alternations of exhibition and approaches nearer than either to the appearance of life, by showing how great machinations and slender designs may promote or obviate one another, and the high and the low cooperate in the general system by unavoidable concatenation.

It is objected that by this change of scenes the passions are interrupted in their progression, and that the principal event, being not advanced by a due gradation of preparatory incidents, wants at least the power to move, which constitutes the perfection of dramatic poetry. This reasoning is so specious that it is received as true even by those who in daily experience feel it to be false. The interchanges of mingled scenes seldom fail to produce the intended vicissitudes of passion. Fiction cannot move so much but that the attention may be easily transferred; and though it must be allowed that pleasing melancholy be sometimes interrupted by unwelcome levity, yet let it be considered likewise that melancholy is often not pleasing, and that the disturbance of one man may be the relief of another; that different auditors have different habitudes; and that, upon the whole, all pleasure consists in variety.

The players, who in their edition divided our author's works into comedies, histories, and tragedies, seem not to have distinguished the three kinds by any very exact or definite ideas.

An action which ended happily to the principal persons, however serious or distressful through its intermediate incidents, in their opinion constituted a comedy. This idea of a comedy continued long amongst us; and plays were written which, by changing the catastrophe, were tragedies today and comedies tomorrow.

Tragedy was not in those times a poem of more general dignity or elevation than comedy; it required only a calamitous conclusion, with which the common criticism of the age was satisfied, whatever lighter pleasure it afforded in its progress.

History was a series of actions, with no other than chronological succession, independent on each other, and without any tendency to introduce or regulate the conclusion. It is not always very nicely distinguished from tragedy. There is not much nearer approach to unity of action in the tragedy of *Antony and Cleopatra* than in the history of *Richard II*. But a history might be continued through many plays; as it had no plan, it had no limits.

Through all these denominations of the drama, Shakespeare's mode of composition is the same: an interchange of seriousness and merriment, by which the mind is softened at one time and exhilarated at another. But whatever be his purpose, whether to gladden or depress, or to conduct the story, without vehemence or emotion, through tracts of easy and familiar dialogue, he never fails to attain his purpose; as he commands us, we laugh or mourn, or sit silent with quiet expectation, in tranquillity without indifference.

When Shakespeare's plan is understood, most of the criticisms of Rymer and Voltaire vanish away. The play of *Hamlet* is opened, without impropriety, by two sentinels; Iago bellows at Brabantio's window without injury to the scheme of the play, though in terms which a modern audience would not easily endure; the character of Polonius is seasonable and useful; and the gravediggers themselves may be heard with applause.

Shakespeare engaged in dramatic poetry with the world open before him; the rules of the ancients were yet known to few; the public judgment was unformed; he had no example of such fame as might force him upon imitation, nor critics of such authority as might restrain his extravagance; he therefore indulged his natural disposition; and his disposition, as Rymer has remarked, led him to comedy. In tragedy he often writes, with great appearance of toil and study, what is written at last with little felicity; but, in his comic scenes, he seems to produce, without labor, what no labor can improve. In tragedy he is always struggling after some occasion to be comic; but in comedy he seems to repose, or to luxuriate, as in a mode of thinking congenial to his nature. In his tragic scenes there is always something wanting, but his comedy often surpasses expectation or desire. His comedy pleases by the thoughts and the language, and his tragedy for the greater part by incident and action. His tragedy seems to be skill, his comedy to be instinct.

The force of his comic scenes has suffered little diminution, from the changes made by a century and a half, in manners or in words. As his personages act upon principles arising from genuine passion, very little modified by particular forms, their pleasures and vexations are communicable to all times and to all places; they are natural, and therefore durable. The adventitious peculiarities of personal habits are only superficial dyes, bright and pleasing for a little while, yet soon fading to a dim tinct, without any remains of former lustre; but the discriminations of true passion are the colors of nature; they pervade the whole mass and can only perish with the body that exhibits them. The accidental compositions of heterogeneous modes are dissolved by the chance which combined them; but the uniform simplicity of primitive qualities neither admits increase nor suffers decay. The sand heaped by one flood is scattered by another, but the rock always continues in its place. The stream of time, which is continually washing the dissoluble fabrics of other poets, passes without injury by the adamant of Shakespeare.

If there be, what I believe there is, in every nation a style which never becomes obsolete, a certain mode of phraseology so consonant and congenial to the analogy and principles of its respective language as to remain settled and unaltered; this style is probably to be sought in the common intercourse of life, among those who speak only to be understood, without ambition of elegance. The polite are always catching modish innovations, and the learned depart from established forms of speech in hope of finding or making better; those who wish for distinction forsake the vulgar, when the vulgar is right; but there is a conversation above grossness and below refinement, where propriety resides, and where this poet seems to have gathered his comic dialogue. He is therefore more agreeable to the ears of the present age than any other author equally remote and among his other excellencies deserves to be studied as one of the original masters of our language.

These observations are to be considered not as unexceptionably constant, but as containing general and predominant truth. Shakespeare's familiar dialogue is affirmed to be smooth and clear, yet not wholly without ruggedness or difficulty; as a country may be eminently fruitful, though it has spots unfit for cultivation; his characters are praised as natural, though their sentiments are sometimes forced and their actions improbable; as the earth upon the whole is spherical, though its surface is varied with protuberances and cavities.

Shakespeare with his excellencies has likewise faults, and faults sufficient to obscure and overwhelm any other merit. I shall show them in the proportion in which they appear to me, without envious malignity or superstitious veneration. No question can be more innocently discussed than a dead poet's pretensions to renown; and little regard is due to that bigotry which sets candor higher than truth.

His first defect is that to which may be imputed most of the evil in books or in men. He sacrifices virtue to convenience and is so much more careful to please than to instruct that he seems to write without any moral purpose. From his writings indeed a system of social duty may be selected, for he that thinks reasonably must think morally; but his precepts and axioms drop casually from him; he makes no just distribution of good or evil, nor is always careful to show in the virtuous a disapprobation of the wicked; he carries his persons indifferently through right and wrong and at the close dismisses them without further care and leaves their examples to operate by chance. This fault the barbarity of his age cannot extenuate; for it is always a writer's duty to make the world better, and justice is a virtue independent on time or place.

The plots are often so loosely formed that a very slight consideration may improve them, and so carelessly pursued that he seems not always fully to comprehend his own design. He omits opportunities of instructing or delighting which the train of his story seems to force upon him, and apparently rejects those exhibitions which would be more affecting, for the sake of those which are more easy.

It may be observed that in many of his plays the latter part is evidently neglected. When he found himself near the end of his work, and in view of his reward, he shortened the labor to snatch the profit. He therefore remits his efforts where he should most vigorously exert them, and his catastrophe is improbably produced or imperfectly represented.

He had no regard to distinction of time or place, but gives to one age or nation, without scruple, the customs, institutions, and opinions of another, at the expense not only of likelihood but of possibility. These faults Pope has endeavored, with more zeal than judgment, to transfer to his imagined interpolators. We need not wonder to find Hector quoting Aristotle, when we see the loves of Theseus and Hippolyta combined with the Gothic mythology of fairies. Shakespeare, indeed, was not the only violator of chronology, for in the same age Sidney, who wanted not the advantages of learning, has, in his *Arcadia*, confounded the pastoral with the feudal times, the days of innocence, quiet, and security, with those of turbulence, violence, and adventure.

In his comic scenes he is seldom very successful when he engages his characters in reciprocations of smartness and contests of sarcasm; their jests are commonly gross, and their pleasantry licentious; neither his gentlemen nor his ladies have much delicacy nor are sufficiently distinguished from his clowns by any appearance of refined manners. Whether he represented the real conversation of his time is not easy to determine. The reign of Elizabeth is commonly supposed to have been a time of stateliness, formality, and reserve; yet perhaps the relaxations of that severity were not very elegant. There must, however, have been always some modes of gaiety preferable to others, and a writer ought to choose the best.

In tragedy his performance seems constantly to be worse as his labor is more. The effusions of passion which exigence forces out are for the most part striking and energetic; but whenever he solicits his invention, or strains his faculties, the offspring of his throes is tumor, meanness, tediousness, and obscurity.

In narration he affects a disproportionate pomp of diction and a wearisome train of circumlocution and tells the incident imperfectly in many words which might have been more plainly delivered in few. Narration in dramatic poetry is naturally tedious, as it is unanimated and inactive and obstructs the progress of the action; it should therefore always be rapid and enlivened by frequent interruption. Shakespeare found it an incumbrance and, instead of lightening it by brevity, endeavored to recommend it by dignity and splendor.

His declamations or set speeches are commonly cold and weak, for his power was the power of nature; when he endeavored, like other tragic writers, to catch opportunities of amplification, and, instead of inquiring what the occasion demanded, to show how much his stores of knowledge could supply, he seldom escapes without the pity or resentment of his reader.

It is incident to him to be now and then entangled with an unwieldy sentiment, which he cannot well express and will not reject; he struggles with it awhile, and, if it continues stubborn, comprises it in words such as occur and leaves it to be disentangled and evolved by those who have more leisure to bestow upon it.

Not that always where the language is intricate the thought is subtle, or the image always great where the line is bulky; the equality of words to things is very often neglected, and trivial sentiments and vulgar ideas disappoint the attention to which they are recommended by sonorous epithets and swelling figures.

But the admirers of this great poet have most reason to complain when he approaches nearest to his highest excellence and seems fully resolved to sink them in dejection and mollify them with tender emotions by the fall of greatness, the danger of innocence, or the crosses of love. What he does best, he soon ceases to do. He is not long soft and pathetic without some idle conceit or contemptible equivocation. He no sooner begins to move than he counteracts himself; and terror and pity, as they are rising in the mind, are checked and blasted by sudden frigidity.

A quibble is to Shakespeare what luminous vapors are to the traveler; he follows it at all adventures; it is sure to lead him out of his way and sure to engulf him in the mire. It has some malignant power over his mind, and its fascinations are irresistible. Whatever be the dignity or profundity of his disquisition, whether he be enlarging knowledge or exalting affection, whether he be amusing attention with incidents or enchaining it in suspense, let but a quibble spring up before him, and he leaves his work unfinished. A quibble is the golden apple for which he will always turn aside from his career or stoop from his elevations. A quibble, poor and barren as it is, gave him such delight that he was content to purchase it by the sacrifice of reason, propriety, and truth. A quibble was to him the fatal Cleopatra for which he lost the world and was content to lose it.

AS YOU LIKE IT

Of this play the fable is wild and pleasing. I know not how the ladies will approve the facility with which both Rosalind and Celia give away their hearts. To Celia much may be forgiven for the heroism of her friendship. The character of Jaques is natural and well preserved. The comic dialogue is very sprightly, with less mixture of low buffoonery than in some other plays; and the graver part is elegant and harmonious. By hastening to the end of his work, Shakespeare suppressed the dialogue between the usurper and the hermit and lost an opportunity of exhibiting a moral lesson in which he might have found matter worthy of his highest powers.

TWELFTH NIGHT

This play is in the graver part elegant and easy, and in some of the lighter scenes exquisitely humorous. Aguecheek is drawn with great propriety, but his character is, in a great measure, that of a natural fatuity and is therefore not the proper prey of a satirist. The soliloquy of Malvolio is truly comic; he is betrayed to ridicule merely by his pride. The marriage of Olivia and the succeeding perplexity, though well enough contrived to divert on the stage, wants credibility and fails to produce the proper instruction required in the drama, as it exhibits no just picture of life.

1 HENRY IV

1. 2. 233. PRINCE HAL: "By so much shall I falsify men's hopes. . . ." This speech is very artfully introduced to keep the prince from appearing vile in the opinion of the audience; it prepares them for his future reformation; and, what is yet more valuable, exhibits a natural picture of a great mind offering excuses to itself and palliating those follies which it can neither justify nor forsake.

1. 3. 201. HOTSPUR: By heaven methinks it were an easy leap
To pluck bright honour from the pale-fac'd moon.

Though I am far from condemning this speech, with Gildon and Theobald, as absolute madness, yet I cannot find in it that profundity of reflection and beauty of allegory which the learned commentator Warburton has endeavored to display. This sally of Hotspur may be, I think, soberly and rationally vindicated as the violent eruption of a mind inflated with ambition and fired with resentment; as the boasted clamor of a man able to do much and eager to do more; as the hasty motion of turbulent desire; as the dark expression of indetermined thoughts.

2 HENRY IV

None of Shakespeare's plays are more read than the first and second parts of *Henry IV*. Perhaps no author has ever in two plays afforded so much delight. The great events are interesting, for the fate of kingdoms depends upon them; the slighter occurrences are diverting and, except one or two, sufficiently probable; the incidents are multiplied with wonderful fertility of invention, and the characters diversified with the utmost nicety of discernment and the profoundest skill in the nature of man.

The prince, who is the hero both of the comic and tragic part, is a young man of great abilities and violent passions, whose sentiments are right, though his actions are wrong; whose virtues are obscured by negligence, and whose understanding is dissipated by levity. In his idle hours he is rather loose than wicked; and when the occasion forces out his latent qualities, he is great without effort and brave without tumult. The trifler is roused into a hero, and the hero again reposes in the trifler. This character is great, original, and just.

Percy is a rugged soldier, choleric, and quarrelsome, and has only the soldier's virtues, generosity and courage.

But Falstaff, unimitated, unimitable Falstaff, how shall I describe thee? Thou compound of sense and vice; of sense which may be admired but not esteemed, of vice which may be despised but hardly detested. Falstaff is a character loaded with faults, and with those faults which naturally produce contempt. He is a thief and a glutton, a coward and a boaster, always ready to cheat the weak and prey upon the poor; to terrify the timorous and insult the defenseless. At once obsequious and malignant, he satirizes in their absence those whom he lives by flattering. He is familiar with the prince only as an agent of vice, but of this familiarity he is so proud as not only to be supercilious and haughty with common men but to think his interest of importance to the duke of Lancaster. Yet the man thus corrupt, thus despicable, makes himself necessary to the prince that despises him, by the most pleasing of all qualities, perpetual gaiety, by an unfailing power of exciting laughter, which is the more freely indulged as his wit is not of the splendid or ambitious kind but consists in easy escapes and sallies of levity, which make sport but raise no envy. It must be observed that he is stained with no enormous or sanguinary crimes, so that his licentiousness is not so offensive but that it may be borne for his mirth.

The moral to be drawn from this representation is that no man is more dangerous than he that, with a will to corrupt, hath the power to please; and that neither wit nor honesty ought to think themselves safe with such a companion when they see Henry seduced by Falstaff.

HENRY V

5. 1. 92. PISTOL: To England will I steal, and there I'll steal:

And patches will I get unto these cudgell'd scars,
And swear I got them in the Gallia wars.

[5. 1. 92]

The comic scenes of *The History of Henry IV* and *V* are now at an end, and all the comic personages are now dismissed. Falstaff and Mrs. Quickly are dead; Nym and Bardolph are hanged; Gadshill was lost immediately after the robbery; Poins and Peto have vanished since, one knows not how; and Pistol is now beaten into obscurity. I believe every reader regrets their departure.

HAMLET

Polonius is a man bred in courts, exercised in business, stored with observations, confident of his knowledge, proud of his eloquence, and declining into dotage. His mode of oratory is truly represented as designed to ridicule the practice of those times, of prefaces that made no introduction, and of method that embarrassed rather than explained. This part of his character is accidental, the rest is natural. Such a man is positive and confident, because he knows that his mind was once strong and knows not that it is become weak. Such a man excels in general principles but fails in the particular application. He is knowing in retrospect and ignorant in foresight. While he depends upon his memory and can draw from his repositories of knowledge, he utters weighty sentences and gives useful counsel; but as the mind in its enfeebled state cannot be kept long busy and intent, the old man is subject to sudden dereliction of his faculties, he loses the order of his ideas and entangles himself in his own thoughts, till he recovers the leading principle and falls again into his former train. This idea of dotage encroaching upon wisdom will solve all the phenomena of the character of Polonius.

If the dramas of Shakespeare were to be characterized each by the particular excellence which distinguishes it from the rest, we must allow to the tragedy of *Hamlet* the praise of variety. The incidents are so numerous that the argument of the play would make a long tale. The scenes are interchangeably diversified with merriment and solemnity; with merriment that includes judicious and instructive observations, and solemnity not strained by poetical violence above the natural sentiments of man. New characters appear from time to time in continual succession, exhibiting various forms of life and particular modes of conversation. The pretended madness of Hamlet causes much mirth, the mournful distraction of Ophelia fills the heart with tenderness, and every personage produces the effect intended, from the apparition that in the first act chills the blood with horror to the fop in the last that exposes affectation to just contempt.

The conduct is perhaps not wholly secure against objections. The action is indeed for the most part in continual progression, but there are some scenes which neither forward nor retard it. Of the feigned madness of Hamlet there appears no adequate cause, for he does nothing which he might not have done with the reputation of sanity. He plays the madman most when he treats Ophelia with so much rudeness, which seems to be useless and wanton cruelty.

Hamlet is, through the whole play, rather an instrument than an agent. After he has, by the stratagem of the play, convicted the king, he makes no attempt to punish him, and his death is at last effected by an incident which Hamlet has no part in producing.

The catastrophe is not very happily produced; the exchange of weapons is rather an expedient of necessity than a stroke of art. A scheme might easily have been formed to kill Hamlet with the dagger, and Laertes with the bowl.

The poet is accused of having shown little regard to poetical justice and may be charged with equal neglect of poetical probability. The apparition left the regions of the dead to little purpose; the revenge which he demands is not obtained but by the death of him that was required to take it; and the gratification which would arise from the destruction of an usurper and a murderer is abated by the untimely death of Ophelia, the young, the beautiful, the harmless, and the pious.

OTHELLO

The beauties of this play impress themselves so strongly upon the attention of the reader that they can draw no aid from critical illustration. The fiery openness of Othello, magnanimous, artless, and credulous, boundless in his confidence, ardent in his affection, inflexible in his resolution, and obdurate in his revenge; the cool malignity of Iago, silent in his resentment, subtle in his designs, and studious at once of his interest and his vengeance; the soft simplicity of Desdemona, confident of merit and conscious of innocence, her artless perseverance in her suit, and her slowness to suspect that she can be suspected, are such proofs of Shakespeare's skill in human nature as, I suppose, it is vain to seek in any modern writer. The gradual progress which Iago makes in the Moor's conviction and the circumstances which he employs to enflame him are so artfully natural that, though it will perhaps not be said of him, as he says of himself, that he is *a man not easily jealous,* yet we cannot but pity him when at last we find him *perplexed in the extreme.*

There is always danger lest wickedness, conjoined with abilities, should steal upon esteem, though it misses of approbation; but the character of Iago is so conducted that he is from the first scene to the last hated and despised.

Even the inferior characters of this play would be very conspicuous in any other piece, not only for their justness but their strength. Cassio is brave, benevolent, and honest, ruined only by his want of stubbornness to resist an insidious invitation. Roderigo's suspicious credulity and impatient submission to the cheats which he sees practiced upon him, and which by persuasion he suffers to be repeated, exhibit a strong picture of a weak mind betrayed by unlawful desires to a false friend; and the virtue of Emilia is such as we often find, worn loosely but not cast off, easy to commit small crimes but quickened and alarmed at atrocious villainies.

The scenes from the beginning to the end are busy, varied by happy interchanges, and regularly presenting the progression of the story; and the narrative in the end, though it tells but what is known already, yet is necessary to produce the death of Othello.

Had the scene opened in Cyprus, and the preceding incidents been occasionally related, there had been little wanting to a drama of the most exact and scrupulous regularity.

KING LEAR

The tragedy of Lear is deservedly celebrated among the dramas of Shakespeare. There is perhaps no play which keeps the attention so strongly fixed; which so much agitates our passions and interests our curiosity. The artful involutions of distinct interests, the striking opposition of contrary characters, the sudden changes of fortune, and the quick succession of events, fill the mind with a perpetual tumult of indignation, pity, and hope. There is no scene which does not contribute to the aggravation of the distress or conduct of the action, and scarce a line which does not conduce to the progress of the scene. So powerful is the current of the poet's imagination that the mind which once ventures within it is hurried irresistibly along.

On the seeming improbability of Lear's conduct it may be observed that he is represented according to the histories at that time vulgarly received as true. And perhaps if we turn our thoughts upon the barbarity and ignorance of the age to which this story is referred, it will appear not so unlikely as while we estimate Lear's manners by our own. Such preference of one daughter to another, or resignation of dominion on such conditions, would be yet credible if told of a petty prince of Guinea or Madagascar. Shakespeare, indeed, by the mention of his earls and dukes, has given us the idea of times more civilized and of life regulated by softer manners; and the truth is that though he so nicely discriminates and so minutely describes the characters of men, he commonly neglects and confounds the characters of ages, by mingling customs ancient and modern, English and foreign.

My learned friend Mr. Warton, who has in the *Adventurer* very minutely criticized this play, remarks that the instances of cruelty are too savage and shocking, and that the intervention of Edmund destroys the simplicity of the story. These objections may, I think, be answered by repeating that the cruelty of the daughters is an historical fact, to which the poet has added little, only having drawn it into a series by dialogue and action. But I am not able to apologize with equal plausibility for the extrusion of Gloucester's eyes, which seems an act too horrid to be endured in dramatic exhibition, and such as must always compel the mind to relieve its distress by incredulity. Yet let it be remembered that our author well knew what would please the audience for which he wrote.

The injury done by Edmund to the simplicity of the action is abundantly recompensed by the addition of variety, by the art with which he is made to cooperate with the chief design, and the opportunity which he gives the poet of combining perfidy with perfidy and connecting the wicked son with the wicked daughters, to impress this important moral, that villainy is never at a stop, that crimes lead to crimes and at last terminate in ruin.

But though this moral be incidentally enforced, Shakespeare has suffered the virtue of Cordelia to perish in a just cause, contrary to the natural ideas of justice, to the hope of the reader, and, what is yet more strange, to the faith of chronicles. Yet this conduct is justified by the Spectator, who blames Tate for giving Cordelia success and happiness in his alteration and declares that, in his opinion, *the tragedy has lost half its beauty.* Dennis has remarked, whether justly or not, that to secure the favorable reception of Cato, *the town was poisoned with most false and abominable criticism,* and that endeavors had been used to discredit and decry poetical justice. A play in which the wicked prosper and the virtuous miscarry may doubtless be good, because it is a just representation of the common events of human life; but since all reasonable beings naturally love justice, I cannot easily be persuaded that the observation of justice makes a play worse; or that, if other excellencies are equal, the audience will not always rise better pleased from the final triumph of persecuted virtue.

In the present case the public has decided. Cordelia, from the time of Tate, has always retired with victory and felicity. And, if my sensations could add anything to the general suffrage, I might relate, I was many years ago so shocked by Cordelia's death that I know not whether I ever endured to read again the last scenes of the play till I undertook to revise them as an editor.

There is another controversy among the critics concerning this play. It is disputed whether the predominant image in Lear's disordered mind be the loss of his kingdom or the cruelty of his daughters. Mr. Murphy, a very judicious critic, has evinced by induction of particular passages that the cruelty of his daughters is the primary source of his distress, and that the loss of royalty affects him only as a secondary and subordinate evil. He observes with great justness that Lear would move our compassion but little, did we not rather consider the injured father than the degraded king.

SAMUEL TAYLOR COLERIDGE ON SHAKESPEARE

Expectation in preference to surprise. "God said, let there be *light*, and there was *light*,"—not there *was* light. As the feeling with which we startle at a shooting star, compared with that of watching the sunrise at the pre-established moment, such and so low is surprise compared with expectation.

Independence of the interest on the plot. The plot interests us on account of the characters, not *vice versa*; it is the canvas only. Justification of the same strategem in Benedict and Beatrice—same vanity, etc. Take away from *Much Ado about Nothing* all that which is [not] indispensable to the plot, either as having little to do with it, or at best, like Dogberry and his comrades, forced into the service when any other less ingeniously absurd watchmen and night-constables would have answered; take away Benedict, Beatrice, Dogberry, and the reaction of the former on the character of Hero, and what will remain? In other writers the main agent of the plot is always the prominent character. In Shakespeare so or not so, as the character is in itself calculated or not calculated to form the plot. So Don John, the mainspring of the plot, is merely shown and withdrawn.

Independence of the interest on *the story* as the groundwork of the plot. Hence Shakespeare did not take the trouble of inventing stories. It was enough for him to select from those that had been invented or recorded such as had one or other, or both, of two recommendations, namely, suitableness to his purposes, and second, their being already parts of popular tradition—names we had often heard of, and of their fortunes, and we should like to see the *man* himself. It is the man himself that Shakespeare for the first time makes us acquainted with. Lear (omit the first scene, yet all remains). So Shylock.

Closely connected with this is that Shakespeare's characters are like those in life, to be *inferred* by the reader, not *told to him*. Of this excellence I know no other instance; and it has one mark of real life—that Shakespeare's characters have been as generally misunderstood and from precisely the same causes [as real persons]. If you take what his friends say, you may be deceived—still more so, if his enemies; and the character himself sees himself thro' the medium of his character, not exactly as it is. But the clown or the fool will suggest a shrewd hint; and take all together, and the impression is right, and all [the spectators] have it. And it may be given as the true Idea is given, and then all the speeches receive the light and attest by reflecting it.

HAMLET

Compare the easy language of common life in which this drama opens, with the wild wayward lyric of the opening of *Macbeth*. The language is familiar: no poetic descriptions of night, no elaborate information conveyed by one speaker to another of what both had before their immediate perceptions (such as the first distich in Addison's *Cato*, which is a translation into poetry of "Past four o'clock, and a damp morning")—yet nothing bordering on the comic on the one hand, and no striving of the intellect on the other. It is the language of *sensation* among men who feared no charge of effeminacy for feeling what they felt no want of resolution to bear. Yet the armor, the dead silence, the watchfulness that first interrupts it, the welcome relief of guard, the cold, the broken expressions as of a man's compelled attention to bodily feelings allowed no man—all excellently accord with and prepare for the after gradual rise into tragedy—but above all into a tragedy the interest of which is eminently *ad et apud intra*, as *Macbeth . . .* [?] is *ad extra*.

The preparation of *informative* of the audience [is] just as much as was precisely necessary: how gradual first, and with the uncertainty appertaining to a question: "What, has *this thing* appeared *again* to-night." Even the word "again" has its *credibilizing* effect. Then the representative of the ignorance of the audience, Horatio (not himself but [quoted by] Marcellus to Bernardo) anticipates the common solution, " ' tis but our phantasy." But Marcellus rises secondly into "[this] dreaded sight." Then this "thing" becomes at once an "apparition," and that too an intelligent spirit that is to be *spoken* to. "Tush, tush! 'twill not appear." Then the shivery feeling, at such a time, with two eyewitnesses, of sitting down to hear a story of a ghost, and this, too, a ghost that had appeared two nights before [at] about this very time. The effort of the

narrator to master his own imaginative terrors; the consequent elevation of the style, itself a continuation of this
effort; the turning off to an *outward* object, "yon same star."
O heaven! words are wasted to those that feel and to those
who do not feel the exquisite judgment of Shakespeare.

Hume himself could not but have faith in *this* Ghost
dramatically, let his anti-ghostism be as strong as Samson
against ghosts less powerfully raised.

THE CHARACTER OF HAMLET

Shakespeare's mode of conceiving characters out of his
own intellectual and moral faculties, by conceiving any one
intellectual or moral faculty in morbid excess and then placing himself, thus mutilated and diseased, under given circumstances. This we shall have repeated occasion to restate and
enforce. In Hamlet I conceive him to have wished to exem-
plify the moral necessity of a due balance between our
attention to outward objects and our meditation on inward
thoughts—a due balance between the real and the imaginary
world. In Hamlet this balance does not exist—his thoughts,
images, and fancy [being] far more vivid than his perceptions, and his very perceptions instantly passing thro' the
medium of his contemplations, and acquiring as they pass
form and color not naturally their own. Hence great, enormous, intellectual activity, and a consequent proportionate
aversion to real action, with all its symptoms and accompany-
ing qualities.

KING LEAR

Of all Shakespeare's plays, *Macbeth* is the most rapid,
Hamlet the slowest, in movement. *Lear* combines length with
rapidity,—like the hurricane and the whirlpool, absorbing
while it advances. It begins as a stormy day in summer, with
brightness; but that brightness is lurid, and anticipates the
tempest.

[I. i. 1-6.

KENT. I thought the king had more affected the duke of
Albany than Cornwall.

GLOU. It did always seem so to us: but now, in the division of the kingdom, it appears not which of the dukes he

values most; for equalities are so weighed that curiosity in neither can make choice of either's moiety.]

It was [not] without forethought, and it is not without its due significance, that the triple division is stated here as already determined and in all its particulars, previously to the trial of professions, as the relative rewards of which the daughters were to be made to consider their several portions. The strange, yet by no means unnatural, mixture of selfishness, sensibility, and habit of feeling derived from and fostered by the particular rank and usages of the individual; the intense desire to be intensely beloved, selfish, and yet characteristic of the selfishness of a loving and kindly nature—a feeble selfishness, self-supportless and leaning for all pleasure on another's breast; the selfish craving after a sympathy with a prodigal disinterestedness, contradicted by its own ostentation and the mode and nature of its claims; the anxiety, the distrust, the jealousy, which more or less accompany all selfish affections, and are among the surest contradistinctions of mere fondness from love, and which originate Lear's eager wish to enjoy his daughter's violent professions, while the inveterate habits of sovereignty convert the wish into claim and positive right, and the incompliance with it into crime and treason;—these facts, these passions, these moral verities, on which the whole tragedy is founded, are all prepared for, and will to the retrospect be found implied in, these first four or five lines of the play. They let us know that the trial is but a trick; and that the grossness of the old king's rage is in part the natural result of a silly trick suddenly and most unexpectedly baffled and disappointed. This having been provided in the fewest words, in a natural reply to as natural [a] question, which yet answers a secondary purpose of attracting our attention to the difference of diversity between the characters of Cornwall and Albany; the premises and data, as it were, having been thus afforded for our after-insight into the mind and mood of the person whose character, passions, and sufferings are the main *subject-matter* of the play;—from Lear, the *persona patiens* of his drama, Shakespeare passes without delay to the second in importance, to the main *agent* and prime mover—introduces Edmund to our acquaintance, and with the same felicity of judgement, in the same easy, natural way, prepares us for his character in the seemingly casual communication of its origin

and occasion. From the first drawing up of the curtain he has
stood before us in the united strength and beauty of earliest
manhood. Our eyes have been questioning him. Gifted thus
with high advantages of *person*, and further endowed by
nature with a powerful intellect and a strong energetic will,
even without any concurrence of circumstances and accident,
pride will be the sin that most easily besets him. But he is the
known and acknowledged son of the princely Gloster.
Edmund, therefore, has both the germ of pride and the
conditions best fitted to evolve and ripen it into a predominant feeling. Yet hitherto no reason appears why it should be
other than the not unusual pride of person, talent, and birth,
a pride auxiliary if not akin to many virtues, and the natural
ally of honorable [impulses?]. But alas! in his own presence
his own father takes shame to himself for the frank avowal
that he is his father—has "blushed so often to acknowledge
him that he is now braz'd to it." He hears his mother and the
circumstances of his birth spoken of with a most degrading
and licentious levity—described as a wanton by her own
paramour, and the remembrance of the animal sting, the low
criminal gratifications connected with her wantonness and
prostituted beauty assigned as the reason why "the whoreson
must be acknowledged." This, and the consciousness of its
notoriety—the gnawing conviction that every show of respect
is an effort of courtesy which recalls while it represses a
contrary feeling—this is the evertrickling flow of wormwood
and gall into the wounds of pride, the corrosive virus which
innoculates pride with a venom not its own, with envy,
hatred, a lust of that power which in its blaze of radiance
would hide the dark spots on his disk, [with] pangs of shame
personally undeserved and therefore felt as wrongs, and a
blind ferment of vindictive workings towards the occasions
and causes, especially towards a brother whose stainless birth
and lawful honors were the constant remembrancers of *his*
debasement, and were ever in the way to prevent all chance
of its being unknown or overlooked and forgotten. Add to
this that with excellent judgment and provident for the claims
of the moral sense, for that which relatively to the drama is
called poetic justice; and as the fittest means for reconciling
the feelings of the spectators to the horrors of Gloster's after
sufferings,—at least, of rendering them somewhat less unen-
durable (for I will not disguise my conviction that in this one
point the tragic has been urged beyond the outermost mark

and *ne plus ultra* of the dramatic)—Shakespeare has pre-
cluded all excuse and palliation of the guilt incurred by both
the parents of the base-born Edmund by Gloster's confession
that he was at the time a married man and already blest
with a lawful heir of his fortunes. The mournful alienation of
brotherly love occasioned by primogeniture in noble families,
or rather by the unnecessary distinctions engrafted thereon,
and this in children of the same stock, is still almost proverbi-
al on the continent—especially, as I know from my own
observation, in the south of Europe—and appears to have
been scarcely less common in our own island before the
Revolution of 1688, if we may judge from the characters and
sentiments so frequent in our elder comedies—the younger
brother, for instance, in Beaumont and Fletcher's *Scornful
Lady,* on one side and the Oliver in Shakespeare's own *As
You Like It,* on the other. Need it be said how heavy an
aggravation the stain of bastardy must have been, were it
only that the younger brother was liable to hear his own
dishonor and his mother's infamy related by his father with
an excusing shrug of the shoulders, and in a tone betwixt
waggery and shame.

By the circumstances here enumerated as so many predis-
posing causes, Edmund's character might well be deem'd
already sufficiently explained and prepared for. But in this
tragedy the story or fable constrained Shakespeare to introduce wickedness in an outrageous form, in Regan and Goneril. He had read nature too heedfully not to know that
courage, intellect, and strength of character were the most
impressive forms of power, and that to power in itself,
without reference to any moral end, an inevitable admiration
and complacency appertains, whether it be displayed in the
conquests of a Napoleon or Tamerlane, or in the foam and
thunder of a cataract. But in the display of such a character
it was of the highest importance to prevent the guilt from
passing into utter *monstrosity*—which again depends on the
presence or absence of causes and temptations sufficient to
account for the wickedness, without the necessity of recurring to a thorough fiendishness of nature for its origination.
For such are the appointed relations of intellectual power to
truth, and of truth to goodness, that it becomes both morally
and poetic[ally] unsafe to present what is admirable—what
our nature compels us to admire—in the mind, and what is
most detestable in the heart, as coexisting in the same individual without any apparent connection, or any modification

of the one by the other. That Shakespeare has in one instance, that of Iago, approached to this, and that he has done it successfully, is perhaps the most astonishing proof of his genius, and the opulence of its resources. But in the present tragedy, in which he [was] compelled to present a Goneril and Regan, it was most carefully to be avoided; and, therefore, the one only conceivable addition to the inauspicious influences on the preformation of Edmund's character is given in the information that all the kindly counteractions to the mischievous feelings of shame that might have been derived from co-domestication with Edgar and their common father, had been cut off by an absence from home and a foreign education from boyhood to the present time, and the prospect of its continuance, as if to preclude all risk of his interference with the father's views for the elder and legitimate son: "He hath been out nine years, and away he shall again."

It is well worthy notice, that *Lear* is the only serious performance of Shakespeare the interest and situations of which are derived from the assumption of a gross improbability; whereas Beaumont and Fletcher's tragedies are, almost all, founded on some out-of-the-way accident or exception to the general experience of mankind. But observe the matchless judgment of Shakespeare! First, improbable as the conduct of Lear is, in the first scene, yet it was an old story, rooted in the popular faith—a thing taken for granted already, and consequently without any of the *effects* of improbability. Secondly, it is merely the canvas to the characters and passions, a mere *occasion*—not (as in Beaumont and Fletcher) perpetually recurring, as the cause and *sine qua non* of the incidents and emotions. Let the first scene of *Lear* have been lost, and let it be only understood that a fond father had been duped by hypocritical professions of love and duty on the part of two daughters to disinherit a third, previously, and deservedly, more dear to him, and all the rest of the tragedy would retain its interest undiminished, and be perfectly intelligible. The *accidental* is nowhere the groundwork of the passions, but the καθολον, that which in all ages has been and ever will be close and native to the heart of man—parental anguish from filial ingratitude, the genuineness of worth, tho' coffered in bluntness, the vileness of smooth iniquity. Perhaps I ought to have added *The Merchant of Venice*; but here too the same remarks apply. It was an old tale; and substitute any other danger than that of the pound of flesh (the circumstance in which the improbability lies), yet all the situations and the emotions appertaining to them remain equally excellent and appropriate. Whereas take away from *The Mad Lover* the fantastic hypothesis of his engagement to cut out his own heart and have it presented to his mistress, and all the main scenes must go with it.

ANTONY AND CLEOPATRA AND ROMEO AND JULIET

This play should be perused in mental contrast with *Romeo and Juliet*;—as the love of passion and appetite opposed to the love of affection and instinct. But the art displayed in the character of Cleopatra is profound in this, especially, that the sense of criminality in her passion is lessened by our insight into its depth and energy, at the very moment that we cannot but perceive that the passion itself springs out of the habitual craving of a licentious nature, and that it is supported and reinforced by voluntary stimulus and sought-for associations, instead of blossoming out of spontaneous emotion.

MEASURE FOR MEASURE

This play, which is Shakespeare's throughout, is to me the most painful—say rather, the only painful—part of his genuine works. The comic and tragic parts equally border on the μισητόν, the one disgusting, the other horrible; and the pardon and marriage of Angelo not merely baffles the strong indignant claim of justice (for cruelty, with lust and damnable baseness, cannot be forgiven, because we cannot conceive them as being *morally* repented of) but it is likewise degrading to the character of woman.

ILLUSION

Still, however, there is a sort of improbability with which we are shocked in dramatic representation no less than in the narrative of real life. Consequently, there must be rules respecting it; and as rules are nothing but means to an end previously ascertained (the inattention to which simple truth has been the occasion of all the pedantry of the French school), we must first ascertain what the immediate end or object of the drama is. Here I find two extremes in critical decision: the French, which evidently presupposes that a perfect delusion is to be aimed at—an opinion which now needs no fresh confutation; the opposite, supported by Dr. Johnson, supposes the auditors throughout as in the full and positive reflective knowledge of the contrary. In evincing the impossibility of delusion, he makes no sufficient allowance for an intermediate state, which we distinguish by the term illusion.

In what this consists I cannot better explain than by referring you to the highest degree of it; namely, dreaming. It is laxly said that during sleep we take our dreams for realities, but this is irreconcilable with the nature of sleep, which consists in a suspension of the voluntary and, therefore, of the comparative power. The fact is that we pass no judgment either way: we simply do not judge them to be unreal, in consequence of which the images act on our minds, as far as they act at all, by their own force as images. Our state while we are dreaming differs from that in which we are in the perusal of a deeply interesting novel in the degree rather than in the kind, and from three causes: First, from the exclusion of all outward impressions on our senses the images in sleep become proportionally more vivid than they can be when the organs of sense are in their active state. Secondly, in sleep the sensations, and with these the emotions and passions which they counterfeit, are the causes of our dream-images, while in our waking hours our emotions are the effects of the images presented to us. (Apparitions [are] so *detectible*.) Lastly, in sleep we pass at once by a sudden collapse into this suspension of will and the comparative power: whereas in an interesting play, read or represented, we are brought up to this point, as far as it is requisite or desirable, gradually, by the art of the poet and the actors; and with the consent and positive aidance of our own will. We *choose* to be deceived. The rule, therefore, may be easily inferred. Whatever tends to prevent the mind from placing it [self] or from being gradually placed in this state in which the images have a negative reality must be a defect, and consequently anything that must force itself on the auditors' mind as improbable, not because it *is* improbable (for the whole play is foreknown to be) but because it cannot but *appear* as such.

But this again depends on the degree of excitement in which the mind is supposed to be. Many things would be intolerable in the first scene of a play that would not at all interrupt our enjoyment in the height of the interest. The narrow cockpit may hold:

> The vasty fields of France, or we may cram
> Within its wooden O the very casques
> That did affright the air at Agincourt.

And again, on the other hand, many obvious improbabilities will be endured as belonging to the groundwork of the story rather than to the drama, in the first scenes, which would disturb or disentrance us from all illusion in the acme of our excitement, as, for instance, Lear's division of his realm and banishment of Cordelia. But besides this dramatic probability, all the other excellencies of the drama, as unity of interest, with distinctness and subordination of the characters, appropriateness of style, nay, and the charm of language and sentiment for their own sakes, yet still as far as they tend to increase the inward excitement, are all means to this chief end, that of producing and supporting this willing illusion.

I have but one point more to add—namely, that tho' the excellencies above mentioned are means to this end, they do not therefore cease to be themselves *ends*, and as such carry their own justification with them as long as they do not contravene or interrupt the illusion. It is not even always or of necessity an objection to them, that they prevent it from rising to as great a height as it might otherwise have attained; it is enough, if they are compatible with as high a degree as is requisite.

(c. 1813)

THE ESSENTIALS OF SHAKESPEARE'S COMEDY

Edward Dowden

Perhaps it is impossible to include under any single general conception works which differ from each other as widely as *The Comedy of Errors, Measure for Measure,* and *The Tempest*; but if we cannot seize it as a whole, we may see from a little distance this side and that of comedy as understood by Shakespeare. Its vital center is not an idea, an abstraction, a doctrine, a moral thesis, but something concrete—persons involved in an action. When philosophical critics assure us that the theme of *The Merchant of Venice* is expressed by the words *Summum jus, summa injuria,* or that it exhibits "man in relation to money," we admire the motto they discovered in their nut, and prefer the kernel in our own. The persons and the actions are placed in some region, which is neither wholly one of fantasy nor yet one encumbered with the dross of actuality. Aery spirits, an earthborn Caliban, Robingoodfellow, the king and queen of Faery, may make their incursion into it, yet it is in the truest sense the haunt and home of "human mortals." The finer spirit of the poet's own age is forever present, but he makes no laborious effort to imitate life in the lower sense of reproducing contemporary manners. He turns away from his own country. Once—by command—Sir John Falstaff makes love to the laughing bourgeois wives of Windsor; but to comply with the necessity Shakespeare's comedy descends from verse to prose. Ben Jonson's invention is at home in Cob's Court and Picthatch, in the aisle of Paul's, or among the booths of Bartholomew Fair; having disguised the characters of his first important play under Italian names, he rightly christened them anew as Londoners. Shakespeare's imagination, throwing off the burden of the actual, disported itself in the Athenian moonlit wood and on the yellow sands of the enchanted island, under green boughs in Arden, in the garden at Belmont, in the palace of Illyria, at the shepherd's festival in Bohemia.

The action corresponds with the environment. In the great tragedies Shakespeare may on rare occasions demand certain

303

postulates at the outset. These having been granted, the plot evolves itself within the bounds of the credible. In *King Lear* the opening scene puts some strain upon our imaginative belief, but Shakespeare received the legend as it had been handed down to him, and all that follows the opening scene—though the action is vast and monstrous—obeys an order and logic which compel our acquiescence. It is not always so if we refuse its claims to fancy, in Shakespearean comedy. In a region which borders on the realm of fantasy we must be prepared to accept many happy surprises. Our desire for happiness inclines our hearts to a pleasant credulity; if chance at the right moment intervenes, it comes as our own embodied hope. When all and every one in Arden wood save Jaques, are on their way to wedlock, like couples coming to the ark, we are not disposed to question the reality of that old religious man upon the borders of the forest who suddenly converts the usurping duke, and turns back the mighty power which he had set on foot. We are grateful for such hermits and such convertites.

The characters again correspond in comedy with the environment and with the action. In tragedy character is either from the first fully formed and four-square, or, if it is developed by events, it develops in accordance with an internal law. Passion runs its inevitable course like a great wave driven of the wind, and breaks with thunder upon the shoal of death. The human actors disappear; only the general order of the world and the eternal moral law endure. But in comedy the individual must be preserved, and must at the close enter into possession of happy days; if he has erred through folly or vice, his error has not been mortal; he may in the last scene of the fifth act swiftly change his moral disposition as he would change his outward garb. The traitor Proteus is suddenly restored to his better mind, and Valentine is generous enough to resign to the repentant traitor all his rights in Silvia. Bertram, who almost to the last entangles himself in a network of dastardly lies, is rescued from his dishonesty and foolish pride by a successful trick, and becomes the loyal husband of Helena. The Duke Orsino transfers his amorous homage from his "fancy's queen" Olivia to his "fancy's queen" Viola with a most convenient facility. Angelo discovers his own baseness in the moment when he perceives it is discovered by the world, and is straightway virtuous enough to bring the happiness required by a fifth act to the wronged Mariana. Even Iachimo—the Iago of a comedy—makes sorrowful confession of his villainy, and restores the purloined bracelet and the ill-won ring. Such transformations as these indicate that even as regards character the law of comedy is a law of liberty. When it suits Shakespeare's purpose, the study of character can be profound and veracious; when occasion requires it, incident becomes all-important, and character yields to the requirements of the situation.

In truth, while it may be said that in Shakespearean tragedy character is fate, in Shakespearean comedy, among the contrasts and surprises which form so abundant a source of its vivacity, not the least effective contrast is that of character set over, as it were, against itself, not the least effective surprise is that of character entering upon new phases under the play of circumstance. The unity and logic of character may not in reality be impaired, but the unity is realized in and through diversity. In punning, a word is made to play a double part; it jostles its other self, and laughter ensues. What is so single and indivisible as personality? But if John is mistaken for Thomas, accident seems to triumph over law, and the incongruity arises of a doubled personal identity—the apparent and the real. Antipholus, of Syracuse, like the little woman of the nursery rhyme, whose sense of personality was dependent on the length of her petticoats, is almost persuaded that he is other than himself. If Viola disguises in doublet and hose, she secures by anticipation the victory of Sebastian over Olivia's heart, while in her own heart she endures a woman's hidden love for the Duke. One man in his brief time on Shakespeare's comic stage may play many parts. The ascetic scholars of Navarre are transformed into the most gallant of lovers and the most ingenious of sonneteers. Katherine the curst becomes more resolute in her wifely submission than she had been in her virgin *sauvagerie*. Signior Benedick, who challenged Cupid at the flight, in due time alters to Benedick, the married man; my dear Lady Disdain, in pity for him, and a little in pity for herself, has yielded upon great persuasion. If, as Montaigne teaches us, man is the most variable of animals, perhaps we learn as important a truth about human nature from Shakespeare's comedies as from his more profound study of the fatality of character and passion in the tragedies.

The essentials of Shakespearean comedy at its best are, after all simple and obvious enough—a delightful story, conducted, in some romantic region, by gracious and gallant persons, thwarted or aided by the mirthful god, Circumstance, and arriving at a fortunate issue. Such would not serve as a description of the comedies of Ben Jonson. He is pleased to keep us during the greater part of five laborious acts in the company of knaves and gulls, and at the close, poetic justice is satisfied with the detection of folly and a general retribution descending on evil-doers. Shakespeare, in comedy, is no such remorseless justicer. Don John, the bastard, is reserved for punishment, but it shall be upon the morrow, and the punishment shall be such as the mirthful Benedick may devise. Parolles escapes lightly with the laughter of Lafeu, and mockery, qualified by a supper, will not afflict him beyond endurance. Lucio is condemned to marry the mother of his child, which is so dire an evil that all other forfeits are remitted. Sir John Falstaff will join the rest by Mistress Page's country fire in jesting at his own discomfiture. Even Shylock is not wholly overwhelmed; he shall have godfathers and a godmother at his baptism, and remain in possession of half his worldly goods. Sebastian may live and discover that he is morally superior to Caliban, the thief, and Stephano, the drunkard. Iachimo kneels and receives the free forgiveness of Posthumus.

But if Shakespeare, in comedy, is niggard of punishment, he is liberal in rewards. And since almost all the stories he chooses for his comic stage are stories of love and lovers, what grand reward can be reserved for the fifth act so fitting as the reward of love? In the seventeenth-century masque amid all its mythological, fantastic, or humorous diversities, one point, or pivot, of the action remained fixed—the incidents must give occasion to a dance of the masquers. So in Shakespearian comedy we may, with almost equal certainty, reckon upon a marriage, or more marriages than one, in act, or in immediate prospect, before the curtain closes. Or, if not a marriage, for the lovers may be wedded lovers at the opening, then, after division, or separation of husband and wife, what we may call a remarriage, with misunderstandings cleared up and faults forgiven. When Shakespeare wrote his earlier plays he was himself young, and his gaze was fixed upon the future; exultant lovers begin their new life, and the song of joy is an epithalamium. When he wrote his latest plays, he was no longer young, and he thought of the blessedness of recovering the happy past, of knitting anew the strained or broken bonds of life, of connecting the former and the latter days in natural piety. Youth still must have its rapture; Florizel must win his royal shepherdess, queen of curds and cream; the nuptials of Ferdinand and Miranda, "these, our dear-beloved," must be duly solemnized at Naples; but Shakespeare's temper is no longer the temper of youth; he is of the company of Hermione and Prospero, and the music of the close is a grave and spiritual harmony.

Between the first scene and the last the path in comedy is beset with obstacles and dangers, past which love must find a way—"the course of true love never did run smooth." These may be either internal—some difficulty arising from character, or external—difference of blood or of rank, the choice of friends, slanderous tongues, rival passions, the spite of fortune. The resolution of the difficulty must be of a corresponding kind; temper, or rash determination, must yield to the predominance of love, or the external obstacles must be removed by well-directed effort, or by a happy turn of events. The young king of Navarre and his fellow-students are immured by their ascetic vow of culture; Isabella is all but ceremonially pledged to the life of religion; Olivia is secluded by her luxury of sentimental sorrow; Beatrice, born to be a lover, is at odds with love through her pride of independence and willful mirth; Bertram has the young colt's pleasure in freedom, refuses to be ranged, and suffers from the haughty blindness of youth, which cannot recognize its own chief need and highest gain. All such rebels against love will be subdued in good time. On the other hand, it is her father who has decreed that Hermia shall be parted from Lysander; both father and mother have rival designs for marring the destiny of sweet Nan Page; a false friend and fickle lover separates Valentine and Silvia; a malignant plotter, who would avenge on all happy creatures the wrong of his own base birth, strikes down Hero with the blow of slander as she stands before the altar. But love has on its side gallantry and resource, loyalty and valor, the good powers of nature and the magic of the moonlit faery wood; and so, over the mountains and over the waves, love at last finds out a way.

Love being the central theme of Shakespearean comedy, laughter cannot be its principal end, and cruel or harsh laughter is almost necessarily excluded. But the laughter of joy rings out in the earlier and middle comedies, and a smile, beautiful in its wisdom and serenity, illuminates the comedies of his closing period. If satire is present, it is only on rare occasions a satire of manners; it deals rather with something universal, a satire of the fatuity of self-lovers, of the power which the human heart has of self-deception, or it is a genial mockery of the ineptitude of brainless self-importance, or the little languid lover's amorous endeavours, or the lumbering pace of heavy-witted ignorance, which cannot catch a common meaning, even by the tail; at its average rate of progress the idea whisks too swiftly from the view of such slow gazers.

The dramatis personæ form a large and varied population, ranging in social rank from the king to the tinker and the bellows-mender. Princes, dukes, courtiers, pages, dissolute gallants, soldiers, sailors, shepherds, clowns, city mechanicals, the country justice, the constable and head-borough, the school-master, the parson, the faithful old servant, the lively waiting maid, roysterers, humorists, light-fingered rogues, foreign fantasticoes, middle-class English husbands and wives, Welshman, Frenchman, Spaniard, Italian, Jew, noble and gracious ladies, country wenches, courtesans, childhood, youth, manhood, old age, the maiden, the wife, the widow—all sorts and conditions of human mortals occupy the scene, while on this side enters Caliban, bearing his burden of pine-logs, and Ariel flies overhead upon the bat's back, on the other, the offended king of faery frowns upon Titania, and claims his pretty Eastern minion.

The characters are ordinarily ranged, with an excellent effect on dramatic perspective, in three groups or divisions. The lovers and their immediate friends or rivals occupy the middle plane. Above them are persons of influence or authority by virtue of age or rank, on whom in some measure the fortunes of the lovers depend. Below them are the humbler aiders and abettors of their designs, or subordinate figures lightly attached to the central action, yet sometimes playing into the hands of benevolent Chance, and always ready to diversify the scene, to enliven the stage, to afford a breathing-space between passages of high-wrought emotion, to fill an interval with glittering word-play or unconscious humor, to save romance from shrill intensity or too aerial ascension by the contact of reality. Shakespeare in comedy was hardly quite happy until he had found his Duke and his clown; then he had the space in which he could move at ease; love remains his central theme, but it is love which rises out of life; his principal figures are rendered more distinct, are seen more in the round, because they stand out from a rich and various background. (1903)

THE SUBSTANCE OF SHAKESPEAREAN TRAGEDY

A. C. Bradley

The question we are to consider in this lecture may be stated in a variety of ways. We may put it thus: What is the substance of a Shakespearean tragedy, taken in abstraction both from its form and from the differences in point of substance between one tragedy and another? Or thus: What is the nature of the tragic aspect of life as represented by Shakespeare? What is the general fact shown now in this tragedy and now in that? And we are putting the same question when we ask: What is Shakespeare's tragic conception, or conception of tragedy? ...

I

In approaching our subject it will be best, without attempting to shorten the path by referring to famous theories of the drama, to start directly from the facts, and to collect from them gradually an idea of Shakespearean tragedy. And first, to begin from the outside, such a tragedy brings before us a considerable number of persons (many more than the persons in a Greek play, unless the members of the chorus are reckoned among them); but it is pre-eminently the story of one person, the "hero," or at most of two, the "hero" and "heroine." Moreover, it is only in the love-tragedies, *Romeo and Juliet* and *Antony and Cleopatra*, that the heroine is as much the center of the action as the hero. The rest, including *Macbeth*, are single stars. So that, having noticed the peculiarity of these two dramas, we may henceforth, for the sake of brevity, ignore it, and may speak of the tragic story as being concerned primarily with one person.

The story, next, leads up to, and includes, the *death* of the hero. On the one hand (whatever may be true of tragedy elsewhere), no play at the end of which the hero remains alive is, in the full Shakespearean sense, a tragedy; and we no longer class *Troilus and Cressida* or *Cymbeline* as such, as did the editors of the Folio. On the other hand, the story depicts also the troubled part of the hero's life which precedes and leads up to his death; and an instantaneous death occurring by "accident" in the midst of prosperity would not suffice for it. It is, in fact, essentially a tale of suffering and calamity conducting to death.

The suffering and calamity are, moreover, exceptional. They befall a conspicuous person. They are themselves of some striking kind. They are also, as a rule, unexpected, and contrasted with previous happiness or glory. A tale, for example, of a man slowly worn to death by disease, poverty, little cares, sordid vices, petty persecutions, however piteous or dreadful it might be, would not be tragic in the Shakespearean sense.

Such exceptional suffering and calamity, then, affecting the hero, and—we must now add—generally extending far and wide beyond him, so as to make the whole scene a scene of woe, are an essential ingredient in tragedy, and a chief source of the tragic emotions, and especially of pity. But the proportions of this ingredient, and the direction taken by tragic pity, will naturally vary greatly. Pity, for example, has a much larger part in *King Lear* than in *Macbeth,* and is directed in the one case chiefly to the hero, in the other chiefly to minor characters.

Let us now pause for a moment on the ideas we have so far reached. They would more than suffice to describe the whole tragic fact as it presented itself to the medieval mind. To the medieval mind a tragedy meant a narrative rather than a play, and its notion of the matter of this narrative may readily be gathered from Dante or, still better, from Chaucer. Chaucer's *Monk's Tale* is a series of what he calls "tragedies"; and this means in fact a series of tales *De Casibus Illustrium Virorum*—stories of the Falls of Illustrious Men, such as Lucifer, Adam, Hecules and Nebuchadnezzar. And the Monk ends the tale of Croesus thus:

Anhanged was Cresus, the proudè kyng;
His roial tronè myghte hym not availle.
Tragédie is noon oother maner thyng,
Ne kan in syngyng criè ne biwaille
But for that Fortune alwey wole assaile
With unwar strook the regnès that been proude;
For whan men trusteth hire, thanne wol she faille,
And covere hire brighte facè with a clowde.

A total reverse of fortune, coming unawares upon a man

who "stood in high degree," happy and apparently secure,—such was the tragic fact to the medieval mind. It appealed strongly to the common human sympathy and pity; it startled also another feeling, that of fear. It frightened men and awed them. It made them feel that man is blind and helpless, the plaything of an inscrutable power, called by the name of Fortune or some other name,—a power which appears to smile on him for a little, and then on a sudden strikes him down in his pride.

Shakespeare's idea of the tragic fact is larger than this idea and goes beyond it; but it includes it, and it is worth while to observe the identity of the two in a certain point which is often ignored. Tragedy with Shakespeare is concerned always with persons of "high degree"; often with kings or princes; if not, with leaders in the state like Coriolanus, Brutus, Antony; at the least, as in *Romeo and Juliet*, with members of great houses, whose quarrels are of public moment. There is a decided difference here between *Othello* and our three other tragedies, but it is not a difference of kind. Othello himself is no mere private person; he is the general of the Republic. At the beginning we see him in the council-chamber of the Senate. The consciousness of his high position never leaves him. At the end, when he is determined to live no longer, he is as anxious as Hamlet not to be misjudged by the great world, and his last speech begins:

Soft you; a word or two before you go.
I have done the state some service, and they know it.

And this characteristic of Shakespeare's tragedies, though not the most vital, is neither external nor unimportant. The saying that every death bed is the scene of the fifth act of a tragedy has its meaning, but it would not be true if the word "tragedy" bore its dramatic sense. The pangs of despised love and the anguish of remorse, we say, are the same in a peasant and a prince; but, not to insist that they cannot be so when the prince is really a prince, the story of the prince, the triumvir, or the general, has a greatness and dignity of its own. His fate affects the welfare of a whole nation or empire; and when he falls suddenly from the height of earthly greatness to the dust, his fall produces a sense of contrast, of the powerlessness of man, and of the omnipotence—perhaps the caprice—of Fortune or Fate, which no tale of private life can possibly rival.

Such feelings are constantly evoked by Shakespeare's tragedies,—again in varying degrees. Perhaps they are the very strongest of the emotions awakened by the early tragedy of *Richard II*, where they receive a concentrated expression in Richard's famous speech about the antic Death, who sits in the hollow crown "That rounds the mortal temples of a king," grinning at his pomp, watching till his vanity and his fancied security have wholly encased him round, and then coming and boring with a little pin through his castle wall. And these feelings, though their predominance is subdued in the mightiest tragedies, remain powerful there. In the figure of the maddened Lear we see:

A sight most pitiful in the meanest wretch,
Past speaking of in a king:

and if we would realize the truth in this matter we cannot do better than compare with the effect of *King Lear* the effect of Turgenev's parallel and remarkable tale of peasant life, *A King Lear of the Steppes*.

II

A Shakespearean tragedy as so far considered may be called a story of exceptional calamity leading to the death of a man in high estate. But it is clearly much more than this, and we have now to regard it from another side. No amount of calamity which merely befell a man, descending from the clouds like lightning, or stealing from the darkness like pestilence, could alone provide the substance of its story. Job was the greatest of all the children of the east, and his afflictions were well-nigh more than he could bear; but even if we imagined them wearing him to death, that would not make his story tragic. Nor yet would it become so, in the Shakespearean sense, if the fire, and the great wind from the wilderness, and the torments of his flesh were conceived as sent by a supernatural power, whether just or malignant. The calamities of tragedy do not simply happen, nor are they sent; they proceed mainly from actions, and those the actions of men.

We see a number of human beings placed in certain circumstances; and we see, arising from the cooperation of their characters in these circumstances, certain actions. These actions beget others, and these others beget others again, until this series of interconnected deeds leads by an apparently inevitable sequence to a catastrophe. The effect of such a series on imagination is to make us regard the sufferings which accompany it, and the catastrophe in which it ends, not only or chiefly as something which happens to the persons concerned, but equally as something which is caused by them. This at least may be said of the principal persons, and, among them, of the hero, who always contributes in some measure to the disaster in which he perishes.

This second aspect of tragedy evidently differs greatly from the first. Men, from this point of view, appear to us primarily as agents, 'themselves the authors of their proper woe'; and our fear and pity, though they will not cease or diminish, will be modified accordingly. We are now to consider this second aspect, remembering that it too is only one aspect, and additional to the first, not a substitute for it.

The "story" or "action" of a Shakespearean tragedy does not consist, of course, solely of human actions or deeds; but the deeds are the pedominant factor. And these deeds are, for the most part, actions in the full sense of the word; not things done " 'tween asleep and wake," but acts or omissions thoroughly expressive of the doer,—characteristic deeds. The center of the tragedy, therefore, may be said with equal truth to lie in action issuing from character, or in character issuing in action.

Shakespeare's main interest lay here. To say that it lay in *mere* character, or was a psychological interest, would be a great mistake, for he was dramatic to the tips of his fingers. It is possible to find places where he has given a certain indulgence to his love of poetry, and even to his turn for general reflections; but it would be very difficult, and in his later tragedies perhaps impossible, to detect passages where he has allowed such freedom to the interest in character apart from action. But for the opposite extreme, for the abstraction of mere "plot" (which is a very different thing from the tragic "action"), for the kind of interest which predominates in a novel like *The Woman in White*, it is clear that he cared even less. I do not mean that this interest is absent from his dramas; but it is subordinate to others, and is so interwoven with them that we are rarely conscious of it apart, and rarely feel in any great strength the half-intellectual, half-nervous excitement of following an ingenious complication. What we do feel strongly, as a tragedy advances to its close, is that the calamities and catastrophe follow inevitably from the deeds of men, and that the main source of these deeds is character. The dictum that, with Shakespeare, "character is destiny" is no doubt an exaggeration, and one that may mislead (for many of his tragic personages, if they had not met with peculiar circumstances, would have escaped a tragic end, and might even have lived fairly untroubled lives); but it is the exaggeration of a vital truth.

This truth, with some of its qualifications, will appear more clearly if we now go on to ask what elements are to be found in the "story" or "action," occasionally or frequently, beside the characteristic deeds, and the sufferings and circumstances, of the persons. I will refer to three of these additional factors.

(a) Shakespeare, occasionally and for reasons which need not be discussed here, represents abnormal conditions of mind; insanity, for example, somnambulism, hallucinations. And deeds issuing from these are certainly not what we called deeds in the fullest sense, deeds expressive of character. No; but these abnormal conditions are never introduced as the origin of deeds of any dramatic moment. Lady Macbeth's sleepwalking has no influence whatever on the events that follow it. Macbeth did not murder Duncan because he saw a dagger in the air: he saw the dagger because he was about to murder Duncan. Lear's insanity is not the cause of a tragic conflict any more than Ophelia's; it is, like Ophelia's, the result of a conflict; and in both cases the effect is mainly pathetic. If Lear were really mad when he divided his kingdom, if Hamlet were really mad at any time in the story, they would cease to be tragic characters.

(b) Shakespeare also introduces the supernatural into some of his tragedies; he introduces ghosts, and witches who have supernatural knowledge. This supernatural element certainly cannot in most cases, if in any, be explained away as an illusion in the mind of one of the characters. And further, it does contribute to the action, and is in more than one instance an indispensable part of it: so that to describe human character, with circumstances, as always the sole motive force in this action would be a serious error. But the supernatural is always placed in the closest relation with character. It gives a confirmation and a distinct form to inward movements already present and exerting an influence; to the sense of failure in Brutus, to the stifled workings of conscience in Richard, to the half-formed thought or the horrified memory of guilt in Macbeth, to suspicion in Hamlet. Moreover, its influence is never of a compulsive kind. It forms no more than an element, however important, in the problem which the hero has to face; and we are never allowed to feel that it has removed his capacity or responsibility for dealing with this problem. So far indeed are we from feeling this, that many readers run to the opposite extreme, and openly or privately regard the supernatural as having nothing to do with the real interest of the play.

(c) Shakespeare, lastly, in most of his tragedies allows to "chance" or "accident" an appreciable influence at some point in the action. Chance or accident here will be found, I think, to mean any occurrence (not supernatural, of course) which enters the dramatic sequence neither from the agency of a character, nor from the obvious surrounding circumstances. It may be called an accident, in this sense, that Romeo never got the Friar's message about the potion, and that Juliet did not awake from her long sleep a minute sooner; an accident that Edgar arrived at the prison just too late to save Cordelia's life; an accident that Desdemona dropped her hankerchief at the most fatal of moments; an accident that the pirate ship attacked Hamlet's ship, so that he was able to return forthwith to Denmark. Now this operation of accident is a fact, and a prominent fact, of human life. To exclude it *wholly* from tragedy, therefore, would be, we may say, to fail in truth. And, besides, it is not merely a fact. That men may start a course of events but can neither calculate nor control it, is a *tragic* fact. The dramatist may use accident so as to make us feel this; and there are also other dramatic uses to which it may be put. Shakespeare accordingly admits it. On the other hand, any *large* admission of chance into the tragic sequence would certainly weaken, and might destroy, the sense of the casual connection of character, deed, and catastrophe. And Shakespeare really uses it very sparingly. We seldom find ourselves exclaiming, "What an unlucky accident!" I believe most readers would have to search painfully for instances. It is, further, frequently easy to see the dramatic intention of an accident; and some things which look like accidents have really a connection with character, and are therefore not in the full sense accidents. Finally, I believe it will be found that almost all the prominent accidents occur when the action is well advanced and the impression of the casual sequence is too firmly fixed to be impaired.

Thus it appears that these three elements in the "action" are subordinate, while the dominant factor consists in deeds which issue from character. So that, by way of summary, we may now alter our first statement, "A tragedy is a story of exceptional calamity leading to the death of a man in high estate," and we may say instead (what in its turn is one-sided, though less so), that the story is one of human actions producing exceptional calamity and ending in the death of such a man.

Before we leave the "action," however, there is another question that may usefully be asked. Can we define this "action" further by describing it as a conflict?

The frequent use of this idea in discussions on tragedy is ultimately due, I suppose, to the influence of Hegel's theory on the subject, certainly the most important theory since Aristotle's. But Hegel's view of the tragic conflict is not only unfamiliar to English readers and difficult to expound short-ly, but it had its origin in reflections on Greek tragedy and, as Hegel was well aware, applies only imperfectly to the works of Shakespeare. I shall, therefore, confine myself to the idea of conflict in its more general form. In this form it is obviously suitable to Shakespearean tragedy; but it is vague, and I will try to make it more precise by putting the ques-tion. Who are the combatants in this conflict?

Not seldom the conflict may quite naturally be conceived as lying between two persons, of whom the hero is one; or, more fully, as lying between two parties or groups, in one of which the hero is the leading figure. Or if we prefer to speak (as we may quite well do if we know what we are about) of the passions, tendencies, ideas, principles, forces, which ani-mate these persons or groups, we may say that two of such passions or ideas, regarded as animating two persons or groups, are the combatants. The love of Romeo and Juliet is in conflict with the hatred of their houses, represented by various other characters. The cause of Brutus and Cassius struggles with that of Julius, Octavius and Antony. In *Rich-ard II.* the King stands on one side, Bolingbroke and his party on the other. In *Macbeth* the hero and heroine are opposed to the representatives of Duncan. In all these cases the great majority of the *dramatis personae* fall without difficulty into antagonistic groups, and the conflict between these groups ends with the defeat of the hero.

Yet one cannot help feeling that in at least one of these

cases, *Macbeth*, there is something a little external in this way of looking at the action. And when we come to some other plays this feeling increases. No doubt most of the characters in *Hamlet, King Lear, Othello,* or *Antony and Cleopatra* can be arranged in opposed groups; and no doubt there is a conflict; and yet it seems misleading to describe this conflict as one *between these groups.* It cannot be simply this. For though Hamlet and the King are mortal foes, yet that which engrosses our interest and dwells in our memory at least as much as the conflict between them, is the conflict *within* one of them. And so it is, though not in the same degree, with *Antony and Cleopatra* and even with *Othello;* and, in fact, in a certain measure, it is so with nearly all the tragedies. There is an outward conflict of persons and groups, there is also a conflict of forces in the hero's soul; and even in *Julius Caesar* and *Macbeth* the interest of the former can hardly be said to exceed that of the latter.

The truth is that the type of tragedy in which the hero opposes to a hostile force an undivided soul is not the Shakespearean type. The souls of those who contend with the hero may be thus undivided; they generally are; but, as a rule, the hero, though he pursues his fated way, is, at least at some point in the action and sometimes at many, torn by an inward struggle; and it is frequently at such points that Shakespeare shows his most extraordinary power. If further we compare the earlier tragedies with the later, we find that it is in the latter, the maturest works, that this inward struggle is most emphasized. In the last of them, *Coriolanus,* its interest completely eclipses towards the close of the play that of the outward conflict. *Romeo and Juliet, Richard III. Richard II,* where the hero contends with an outward force, but comparatively little with himself, are all early plays.

If we are to include the outer and the inner struggle in a conception more definite than that of conflict in general, we must employ some such phrase as "spiritual force." This will mean whatever forces act in the human spirit, whether good or evil, whether personal passion or impersonal principle; doubts, desires, scruples, ideas—whatever can animate, shake, possess, and drive a man's soul. In a Shakespearean tragedy some such forces are shown in conflict. They are shown acting in men and generating strife between them. They are also shown, less universally, but quite as characteristically, generating disturbance and even conflict in the soul of the hero. Treasonous ambition in Macbeth collides with loyalty and patriotism in Macduff and Malcolm: here is the outward conflict. But these powers or principles equally collide in the soul of Macbeth himself: here is the inner. And neither by itself could make the tragedy.

We shall see later the importance of this idea. Here we need only observe that the notion of tragedy as a conflict emphasises the fact that action is the center of the story, while the concentration of interest, in the greater plays, on the inward struggle emphasises the fact that this action is essentially the expression of character.

III

Let us now turn from the "action" to the central figure in it; and, ignoring the characteristics which distinguish the heroes from one another, let us ask whether they have any common qualities which appear to be essential to the tragic effect.

One they certainly have. They are exceptional beings. We have seen already that the hero, with Shakespeare, is a person of high degree or of public importance, and that his actions or sufferings are of an unusual kind. But this is not all. His nature also is exceptional, and generally raises him in some respect much above the average level of humanity. This does not mean that he is an eccentric or a paragon. Shakespeare never drew monstrosities of virtue; some of his heroes are far from "good"; and if he drew eccentrics he gave them a subordinate position in the plot. His tragic characters are made of the stuff we find within ourselves and within the persons who surround them. But, by an intensification of the life which they share with others, they are raised above them; and the greatest are raised so far that, if we fully realize all that is implied in their words and actions, we become conscious that in real life we have known scarcely any one resembling them. Some, like Hamlet and Cleopatra, have genius. Others, like Othello, Lear, Macbeth, Coriolanus, are built on the grand scale; and desire, passion, or will attains in them a terrible force. In almost all we observe a marked one-sidedness, a predisposition in some particular direction; a total incapacity, in certain circumstances, of resisting the force which draws in this direction; a fatal tendency to identify the whole being with one interest, object, passion, or habit of mind. This, it would seem, is, for Shakespeare, the fundamental tragic trait. It is present in his early heroes, Romeo and Richard II, infatuated men, who otherwise rise comparatively little above the ordinary level. It is a fatal gift, but it carries with it a touch of greatness; and when there is joined to it nobility of mind, or genius, or immense force, we realise the full power and reach of the soul, and the conflict in which it engages acquires that magnitude which stirs not only sympathy and pity, but admiration, terror, and awe.

The easiest way to bring home to oneself the nature of the tragic character is to compare it with a character of another kind. Dramas like *Cymbeline* and the *Winter's Tale*, which might seem destined to end tragically, but actually end otherwise, owe their happy ending largely to the fact that the principal characters fail to reach tragic dimensions. And, conversely, if these persons were put in the place of the tragic heroes, the dramas in which they appeared would cease to be tragedies. Posthumus would never have acted as Othello did; Othello, on his side, would have met Iachimo's challenge with something more than words. If, like Posthumus, he had remained convinced of his wife's infidelity, he would not have repented her execution; if, like Leontes, he had come to believe that by an unjust accusation he had caused her death, he would never have lived on, like Leontes. In the same way the villain Iachimo has no touch of tragic greatness. But Iago comes nearer to it, and if Iago had slandered Imogen and had supposed his slanders to have led to her death, he certainly would not have turned melancholy and wished to die. One reason why the end of *The Merchant of Venice* fails to satisfy us is that Shylock is a tragic character, and that we cannot believe in his accepting his defeat and the conditions imposed on him. This was a case where Shakespeare's imagination ran away with him, so that he drew a figure with which the destined pleasant ending would not harmonize.

In the circumstances where we see the hero placed, his tragic trait, which is also his greatness, is fatal to him. To meet these circumstances something is required which a smaller man might have given, but which the hero cannot give. He errs, by action or omission; and his error, joining with other causes, brings on him ruin. This is always so with Shakespeare. As we have seen, the idea of the tragic hero as a being destroyed simply and solely by external forces is quite alien to him; and not less so is the idea of the hero as contributing to his destruction only by acts in which we see no flaw. But the fatal imperfection or error, which is never absent, is of different kinds and degrees. At one extreme stands the excess and precipitancy of Romeo, which scarcely, if at all, diminish our regard for him; at the other the murderous ambition of Richard III. In most cases the tragic error involves no conscious breach of right; in some (e.g. that of Brutus or Othello) it is accompanied by a full conviction of right. In Hamlet there is a painful consciousness that duty is being neglected; in Antony a clear knowledge that the worse of two courses is being pursued; but Richard and Macbeth are the only heroes who do what they themselves recognize to be villainous. It is important to observe that Shakespeare does admit such heroes, and also that he appears to feel, and exerts himself to meet, the difficulty that arises from their admission. The difficulty is that the spectator must desire their defeat and even their destruction; and yet this desire, and the satisfaction of it, are not tragic feelings. Shakespeare gives to Richard therefore a power which excites astonishment, and a courage which extorts admiration. He gives to Macbeth a similar, though less extraordinary, greatness, and adds to it a conscience so terrifying in its warnings and so maddening in its reproaches that the spectacle of inward torment compels a horrified sympathy and awe which balance, at the least, the desire for the hero's ruin.

The tragic hero with Shakespeare, then, need not be "good," though generally he is "good" and therefore at once wins sympathy in his error. But it is necessary that he should have so much of greatness that in his error and fall we may be vividly conscious of the possibilities of human nature. Hence, in the first place, a Shakespearean tragedy is never, like some miscalled tragedies, depressing. No one ever closes the book with the feeling that man is a poor mean creature. He may be wretched and he may be awful, but he is not small. His lot may be heart-rending and mysterious, but it is not contemptible. The most confirmed of cynics ceases to be a cynic while he reads these plays. And with this greatness of the tragic hero (which is not always confined to him) is connected, secondly, what I venture to describe as the center of the tragic impression. This central feeling is the impression of waste. With Shakespeare, at any rate, the pity and fear

which are stirred by the tragic story seem to unite with, and
even to merge in, a profound sense of sadness and mystery,
which is due to this impression of waste. "What a piece of
work is man," we cry; "so much more beautiful and so much
more terrible than we knew! Why should he be so if this
beauty and greatness only tortures itself and throws itself
away?" We seem to have before us a type of the mystery of
the whole world, the tragic fact which extends far beyond the
limits of tragedy. Everywhere, from the crushed rocks
beneath our feet to the soul of man, we see power, intelligence, life and glory, which astound us and seem to call for
our worship. And everywhere we see them perishing, devour-
ing one another and destroying themselves, often with dreadful
pain, as though they came into being for no other end.
Tragedy is the typical form of this mystery, because that
greatness of soul which it exhibits oppressed, conflicting and
destroyed, is the highest existence in our view. It forces
the mystery upon us, and it makes us realize so vividly the
worth of that which is wasted that we cannot possibly seek
comfort in the reflection that all is vanity.

IV

In this tragic world, then, where individuals, however great
they may be and however decisive their actions may appear,
are so evidently not the ultimate power, what is this power?
What account can we give of it which will correspond with
the imaginative impressions we receive? This will be our final
question.

The variety of the answers given to this question shows
how difficult it is. And the difficulty has many sources. Most
people, even among those who know Shakespeare well and
come into real contact with his mind, are inclined to isolate
and exaggerate some other aspect of the tragic fact. Some
are so much influenced by their own habitual beliefs that
they import them more or less into their interpretation of
every author who is "sympathetic" to them. And even where
neither of these causes of error appears to operate, another is
present from which it is probably impossible wholly to escape. What I mean is this. Any answer we give to the
question proposed ought to correspond with, or to represent
in terms of the understanding, our imaginative and emotional
experience in reading the tragedies. We have, of course, to
do our best by study and effort to make this experience true

to Shakespeare; but, that done to the best of our ability, the experience is the matter to be interpreted, and the test by which the interpretation must be tried. But it is extremely hard to make out exactly what this experience is because, in the very effort to make it out, our reflecting mind, full of everyday ideas, is always tending to transform it by the application of these ideas, and so to elicit a result which, instead of representing the fact, conventionalizes it. And the consequence is not only mistaken theories; it is that many a man will declare that he feels in reading a tragedy what he never really felt, while he fails to recognize what he actually did feel. It is not likely that we shall escape all these dangers in our effort to find an answer to the question regarding the tragic world and the ultimate power in it.

It will be agreed, however, first, that this question must not be answered in "religious" language. For although this or that *dramatis persona* may speak of gods or of God, of evil spirits or of Satan, of heaven and of hell, and although the poet may show us ghosts from another world, these ideas do not materially influence his representation of life, nor are they used to throw light on the mystery of its tragedy. The Elizabethan drama was almost wholly secular; and while Shakespeare was writing he practically confined his view to the world of nontheological observation and thought, so that he represents it substantially in one and the same way whether the period of the story is pre-Christian or Christian. He looked at this "secular" world most intently and seriously; and he painted it, we cannot but conclude, with entire fidelity, without the wish to enforce an opinion of his own, and, in essentials, without regard to anyone's hopes, fears, or beliefs. His greatness is largely due to this fidelity in a mind of extraordinary power; and if, as a private person, he had a religious faith, his tragic view can hardly have been in contradiction with this faith, but must have been included in it, and supplemented, not abolished, by additional ideas.

Two statements, next, may at once be made regarding the tragic fact as he represents it: one, that it is and remains to us something piteous, fearful and mysterious; the other, that the representation of it does not leave us crushed, rebellious or desperate. These statements will be accepted, I believe, by any reader who is in touch with Shakespeare's mind and can observe his own. Indeed such a reader is rather likely to complain that they are painfully obvious. But if they are true as well as obvious, something follows from them in regard to our present question.

From the first it follows that the ultimate power in the tragic world is not adequately described as a law or order which we can see to be just and benevolent,—as, in that sense, a "moral order": for in that case the spectacle of suffering and waste could not seem to us so fearful and mysterious as it does. And from the second it follows that this ultimate power is not adequately described as a fate, whether malicious and cruel, or blind and indifferent to human happiness and goodness: for in that case the spectacle would leave us desperate or rebellious. Yet one or other of these two ideas will be found to govern most accounts of Shakespeare's tragic view or world. These accounts isolate and exaggerate single aspects, either the aspect of action or that of suffering; either the close and unbroken connection of character, will, deed and catastrophe, which, taken alone, shows the individual simply as sinning against, or failing to conform to, the moral order and drawing his just doom on his own head; or else that pressure of outward forces, that sway of accident, and those blind and agonized struggles, which, taken alone, show him as the mere victim of some power which cares neither for his sins nor for his pain. Such views contradict one another, and no third view can unite them; but the several aspects from whose isolation and exaggeration they spring are both present in the fact, and a view which would be true to the fact and to the whole of our imaginative experience must in some way combine these aspects.

Let us begin, then, with the idea of fatality and glance at some of the impressions which give rise to it, without asking at present whether this idea is their natural or fitting expression. There can be no doubt that they do arise and that they ought to arise. If we do not feel at times that the hero is, in some sense, a doomed man; that he and others drift struggling to destruction like helpless creatures borne on an irrestible flood towards a cataract; that, faulty as they may be, their fault is far from being the sole or sufficient cause of all they suffer; and that the power from which they cannot escape is relentless and immovable, we have failed to receive an essential part of the full tragic effect.

The sources of these impressions are various, and I will refer only to a few. One of them is put into words by Shakespeare himself when he makes the player-king in *Ham-*

let say: "Our thoughts are ours, their ends none of our own"; "their ends" are the issues or outcomes of our thoughts, and these, says the speaker, are not our own. The tragic world is a world of action, and action is the translation of thought into reality. We see men and women confidently attempting it. They strike into the existing order of things in pursuance of their ideas. But what they achieve is not what they intended; it is terribly unlike it. They understand nothing, we say to ourselves, of the world on which they operate. They fight blindly in the dark, and the power that works through them makes them the instrument of a design which is not theirs. They act freely, and yet their action binds them hand and foot. And it makes no difference whether they meant well or ill. No one could mean better than Brutus, but he contrives misery for his country and death for himself. No one could mean worse than Iago, and he too is caught in the web he spins for others. Hamlet, recoiling from the rough duty of revenge, is pushed into blood-guiltiness he never dreamed of, and forced at last on the revenge he could not will. His adversary's murders, and no less his adversary's remorse, bring about the opposite of what they sought. Lear follows an old man's whim, half generous, half selfish; and in a moment it looses all the powers of darkness upon him. Othello agonises over an empty fiction, and, meaning to execute solemn justice, butchers innocence and strangles love. They understand themselves no better than the world about them. Coriolanus thinks that his heart is iron, and it melts like snow before a fire. Lady Macbeth, who thought she could dash out her own child's brains, finds herself hounded to death by the smell of a stranger's blood. Her husband thinks that to gain a crown he would jump the life to come, and finds that the crown has brought him all the horrors of that life. Everywhere, in this tragic world, man's thought, translated into act, is transformed into the opposite of itself. His act, the movement of a few ounces of matter in a moment of time, becomes a monstrous flood which spreads over a kingdom. And whatsoever he dreams of doing, he achieves that which he least dreamed of, his own destruction.

All this makes us feel the blindness and helplessness of man. Yet by itself it would hardly suggest the idea of fate, because it shows man as in some degree, however slight, the cause of his own undoing. But other impressions come to aid it. It is aided by everything which makes us feel that a man is, as we say, terribly unlucky; and of this there is, even in

Shakespeare, not a little. Here come in some of the accidents already considered, Juliet's waking from her trance a minute too late, Desdemona's loss of her handkerchief at the only moment when the loss would have mattered, that insignificant delay which cost Cordelia's life. Again, men act, no doubt, in accordance with their characters; but what is it that brings them just the one problem which is fatal to them and would be easy to another, and sometimes brings it to them just when they are least fitted to face it? How is it that Othello comes to be the companion of the one man in the world who is at once able enough, brave enough, and vile enough to ensnare him? By what strange fatality does it happen that Lear has such daughters and Cordelia such sisters? Even character itself contributes to these feelings of fatality. How could men escape, we cry, such vehement propensities as drive Romeo, Antony, Coriolanus, to their doom? And why is it that a man's virtues help to destroy him, and that his weakness or defect is so intertwined with everything that is admirable in him that we can hardly separate them even in imagination?

If we find in Shakespeare's tragedies the source of impressions like these, it is important, on the other hand, to notice what we do *not* find there. We find practically no trace of fatalism in its more primitive, crude and obvious forms. Nothing, again, makes us think of the actions and sufferings of the persons as somewhat arbitrarily fixed beforehand without regard to their feelings, thoughts and resolutions. Nor, I believe, are the facts ever so presented that it seems to us as if the supreme power, whatever it may be, had a special spite against a family or an individual. Neither, lastly, do we receive the impression (which, it must be observed, is not purely fatalistic) that a family, owing to some hideous crime or impiety in early days, is doomed in later days to continue a career of portentous calamities and sins. Shakespeare, indeed, does not appear to have taken much interest in heredity, or to have attached much importance to it.

What, then, is this "fate" which the impressions already considered lead us to describe as the ultimate power in the tragic world? It appears to be a mythological expression for the whole system or order, of which the individual characters form an inconsiderable and feeble part; which seems to determine, far more than they, their native dispositions and their circumstances, and, through these, their action; which is so vast and complex that they can scarcely at all understand

it or control its workings; and which has a nature so definite
and fixed that whatever changes take place in it produce
other changes inevitably and without regard to men's desires
and regrets. And whether this system or order is best called
by the name of fate or no, it can hardly be denied that it
does appear as the ultimate power in the tragic world, and
that it has such characteristics as these. But the name "fate"
may be intended to imply something more—to imply that
this order is a blank necessity, totally regardless alike of
human weal and of the difference between good and evil or
right and wrong. And such an implication many readers
would at once reject. They would maintain, on the contrary,
that this order shows characteristics of quite another kind
from those which made us give it the name of fate, characteristics which certainly should not induce us to forget those
others, but which would lead us to describe it as a moral
order and its necessity as a moral necessity.

v

Let us turn, then, to this idea. It brings into the light those
aspects of the tragic fact which the idea of fate throws into
the shade. And the argument which leads to it in its simplest
form may be stated briefly thus: "Whatever may be said of
accidents, circumstances and the like, human action is, after
all, presented to us as the central fact in tragedy, and also as
the main cause of the catastrophe. That necessity which so
much impresses us is, after all, chiefly the necessary connection of actions and consequences. For these actions we,
without even raising a question on the subject, hold the
agents responsible; and the tragedy would disappear for us if
we did not. The critical action is, in greater or less degree,
wrong or bad. The catastrophe is, in the main, the return of
this action on the head of the agent. It is an example of
justice; and that order which, present alike within the agents
and outside them, infallibly brings it about, is therefore just.
The rigor of its justice is terrible, no doubt, for a tragedy is a
terrible story; but, in spite of fear and pity, we acquiesce,
because our sense of justice is satisfied."

Now, if this view is to hold good, the "justice" of which it
speaks must be at once distinguished from what is called
"poetic justice." "Poetic justice" means that prosperity and
adversity are distributed in proportion to the merits of the
agents. Such "poetic justice" is in flagrant contradiction with

the facts of life, and it is absent from Shakespeare's tragic picture of life; indeed, this very absence is a ground of constant complaint on the part of Dr. Johnson. Δράσαντι παθεῖν, "the doer must suffer"—this we find in Shakespeare. We also find that villainy never remains victorious and prosperous at the last. But an assignment of amounts of happiness and misery, an assignment even of life and death, in proportion to merit, we do not find. No one who thinks of Desdemona and Cordelia; or who remembers that one end awaits Richard III and Brutus, Macbeth and Hamlet; or who asks himself which suffered most, Othello or Iago; will ever accuse Shakespeare of representing the ultimate power as "poetically" just.

And we must go further. I venture to say that it is a mistake to use at all these terms of justice and merit or desert. And this for two reasons. In the first place, essential as it is to recognize the connection between act and consequence, and natural as it may seem in some cases (*e.g.* Macbeth's) to say that the doer only gets what he deserves, yet in very many cases to say this would be quite unnatural. We might not object to the statement that Lear deserved to suffer for his folly, selfishness and tyranny; but to assert that he deserved to suffer what he did suffer is to do violence not merely to language but to any healthy moral sense. It is, moreover, to obscure the tragic fact that the consequences of action cannot be limited to that which would appear to us to follow "justly" from them. And, this being so, when we call the order of the tragic world just, we are either using the word in some vague and unexplained sense, or we are going beyond what is shown us of this order, and are appealing to faith.

But, in the second place, the ideas of justice and desert are, it seems to me, in *all* cases—even those of Richard III and of Macbeth and Lady Macbeth—untrue to our imaginative experience. When we are immersed in a tragedy, we feel towards disposition, actions, and persons such emotions as attraction and repulsion, pity, wonder, fear, horror, perhaps hatred; but we do not *judge*. This is a point of view which emerges only when, in reading a play, we slip, by our own fault or the dramatist's, from the tragic position, or when, in thinking about the play afterwards, we fall back on our everyday legal and moral notions. But tragedy does not belong, any more than religion belongs, to the sphere of these notions; neither does the imaginative attitude in presence of it. While we are in its world we watch what is, seeing that so it happened and must have happened, feeling that it is piteous, dreadful, awful, mysterious, but neither passing sentence on the agents, nor asking whether the behavior of the ultimate power towards them is just. And, therefore, the use of such language in attempts to render our imaginative experience in terms of the understanding is, to say the least, full of danger.

Let us attempt then to restate the idea that the ultimate power in the tragic world is a moral order. Let us put aside the ideas of justice and merit, and speak simply of good and evil. Let us understand by these words, primarily, moral good and evil, but also everything else in human beings which we take to be excellent or the reverse. Let us understand the statement that the ultimate power or order is "moral" to mean that it does not show itself indifferent to good and evil, or equally favorable or unfavorable to both, but shows itself akin to good and alien from evil. And, understanding the statement thus, let us ask what grounds it has in the tragic fact as presented by Shakespeare.

Here, as in dealing with the grounds on which the idea of fate rests, I choose only two or three out of many. And the most important is this. In Shakespearean tragedy the main source of the convulsion which produces suffering and death is never good: good contributes to this convulsion only from its tragic implication with its opposite in one and the same character. The main source, on the contrary, is in every case evil; and, what is more (though this seems to have been little noticed), it is in almost every case evil in the fullest sense, not mere imperfection but plain moral evil. The love of Romeo and Juliet conducts them to death only because of the senseless hatred of their houses. Guilty ambition, seconded by diabolic malice and issuing in murder, opens the action in *Macbeth*. Iago is the main source of the convulsion in *Othello*; Goneril, Regan and Edmund in *King Lear*. Even when this plain moral evil is not the obviously prime source within the play, it lies behind it: the situation with which Hamlet has to deal has been formed by adultery and murder. *Julius Caesar* is the only tragedy in which one is even tempted to find an exception to this rule. And the inference is obvious. If it is chiefly evil that violently disturbs the order of the world, this order cannot be friendly to evil or indifferent between evil and good, any more than a body which is convulsed by poison is friendly to it or indifferent to the distinction between poison and food.

Again, if we confine our attention to the hero, and to those cases where the gross and palpable evil is not in him but elsewhere, we find that the comparatively innocent hero still shows some marked imperfection or defect,—irresolution, precipitancy, pride, credulousness, excessive simplicity, excessive susceptibility to sexual emotions, and the like. These defects or imperfections are certainly, in the wide sense of the word, evil, and they contribute decisively to the conflict and catastrophe. And the inference is again obvious. The ultimate power which shows itself disturbed by this evil and reacts against it, must have a nature alien to it. Indeed its reaction is so vehement and "relentless" that it would seem to be bent on nothing short of good in perfection, and to be ruthless in its demand for it.

To this must be added another fact, or another aspect of the same fact. Evil exhibits itself everywhere as something negative, barren, weakening, destructive, a principle of death. It isolates, disunites, and tends to annihilate not only its opposite but itself. That which keeps the evil man prosperous, makes him succeed, even permits him to exist, is the good in him (I do not mean only the obviously "moral" good). When the evil in him masters the good and has its way, it destroys other people through him, but it also destroys *him*. At the close of the struggle he has vanished, and has left behind him nothing that can stand. What remains is a family, a city, a country, exhausted, pale and feeble, but alive through the principle of good which animates it; and, within it, individuals who, if they have not the brilliance or greatness of the tragic character, still have won our respect and confidence. And the inference would seem clear. If existence in an order depends on good, and if the presence of evil is hostile to such existence, the inner being or soul of this order must be akin to good.

These are aspects of the tragic world at least as clearly marked as those which, taken alone, suggest the idea of fate. And the idea which they in their turn, when taken alone, may suggest, is that of an order which does not indeed award "poetic justice," but which reacts through the necessity of its own "moral" nature both against attacks made upon it and against failure to conform to it. Tragedy, on this view, is the exhibition of that convulsive reaction; and the fact that the spectacle does not leave us rebellious or desperate is due to a

more or less distinct perception that the tragic suffering and
death arise from collision, not with a fate or blank power,
but with a moral power, a power akin to all that we admire
and revere in the characters themselves. This perception
produces something like a feeling of acquiescence in the
catastrophe, though it neither leads us to pass judgment on
the characters nor diminishes the pity, the fear, and the sense
of waste, which their struggle, suffering and fall evoke. And,
finally, this view seems quite able to do justice to those
aspects of the tragic fact which give rise to the idea of fate.
They would appear as various expressions of the fact that the
moral order acts not capriciously or like a human being, but
from the necessity of its nature, or, if we prefer the phrase,
by general laws,—a necessity or law which of course knows
no exception and is as "ruthless" as fate.

It is impossible to deny to this view a large measure of
truth. And yet without some amendment it can hardly satisfy. For it does not include the whole of the facts, and
therefore does not wholly correspond with the impressions
they produce. Let it be granted that the system or order
which shows itself omnipotent against individuals is, in the
sense explained, moral. Still—at any rate for the eye of
sight—the evil against which it asserts itself, and the persons
whom this evil inhabits, are not really something outside
the order, so that they can attack it or fail to conform to it;
they are within it and a part of it. It itself produces them,—
produces Iago as well as Desdemona, Iago's cruelty as well as
Iago's courage. It is not poisoned, it poisons itself. Doubtless
it shows by its violent reaction that the poison *is* poison, and
that its health lies in good. But one significant fact cannot
remove another, and the spectacle we witness scarcely warrants the assertion that the order is responsible for the good
in Desdemona, but Iago for the evil in Iago. If we make this
assertion we make it on grounds other than the facts as
presented in Shakespeare's tragedies.

Nor does the idea of a moral order asserting itself against
attack or want of conformity answer in full to our feelings regarding the tragic character. We do not think of Hamlet
merely as failing to meet its demand, of Antony as merely
sinning against it, or even Macbeth as simply attacking it.
What we feel corresponds quite as much to the idea that they
are *its* parts, expressions, products; that in their defect or evil
it is untrue to its soul of goodness, and falls into conflict and
collision with itself; that, in making them suffer and waste

themselves, *it* suffers and wastes itself; and that when, to save its life and regain peace from this intestinal struggle, it casts them out, it has lost a part of its own substance,—a part more dangerous and unquiet, but far more valuable and nearer to its heart, than that which remains,—a Fortinbras, a Malcolm, an Octavius. There is no tragedy in its expulsion of evil: the tragedy is that this involves the waste of good.

Thus we are left at last with an idea showing two sides or aspects which we can neither separate nor reconcile. The whole or order against which the individual part shows itself powerless seems to be animated by a passion for perfection: we cannot otherwise explain its behavior towards evil. Yet it appears to engender this evil within itself, and in its effort to overcome and expel it is agonized with pain, and driven to mutilate its own substance and to lose not only evil but priceless good. That this idea, though very different from the idea of a blank fate, is no solution of the riddle of life is obvious; but why should we expect it to be such a solution? Shakespeare was not attempting to justify the ways of God to men, or to show the universe as a Divine Comedy. He was writing tragedy, and tragedy would not be tragedy if it were not a painful mystery. Nor can he be said even to point distinctly, like some writers of tragedy, in any direction where a solution might lie. We find a few references to gods or God, to the influence of the stars, to another life: some of them certainly, all of them perhaps, merely dramatic—appropriate to the person from whose lips they fall. A ghost comes from Purgatory to impart a secret out of the reach of its hearer—who presently meditates on the question whether the sleep of death is dreamless. Accidents once or twice remind us strangely of the words, "There's a divinity that shapes our ends." More important are other impressions. Sometimes from the very furnace of affliction a conviction seems borne to us that somehow, if we could see it, this agony counts as nothing against the heroism and love which appear in it and thrill our hearts. Sometimes we are driven to cry out that these mighty or heavenly spirits who perish are too great for the little space in which they move, and that they vanish not into nothingness but into freedom. Sometimes from these sources and from others comes a presentiment, formless but haunting and even profound, that all the fury of conflict, with its waste and woe, is less than half the truth, even an illusion, "such stuff as dreams are made on." But these faint and scattered intimations that the tragic world, being but a fragment of a whole beyond our vision, must needs be a contradiction and no ultimate truth, avail nothing to interpret the mystery. We remain confronted with the inexplicable fact, or the no less inexplicable appearance, of a world travailing for perfection, but bringing to birth, together with glorious good, an evil which it is able to overcome only by self-torture and self-waste. And this fact or appearance is tragedy.

(1904)

PART X

On Interpretation

RIPENESS IS ALL

J. V. Cunningham

I am concerned in these essays with understanding precisely what Shakespeare meant. It is true that "when we read Shakespeare's plays," as one scholar says, "we are always meeting our own experiences and are constantly surprised by some phrase which expresses what we thought to be our own secret or our own discovery." But the danger is that the meaning we find may really be our own secret, our own discovery, rather than Shakespeare's, and the more precious and beguiling for being our own. The danger I have in mind can be illustrated by our attitude toward one of the most famous of Shakespearean phrases, "Ripeness is all." It is a favorite quotation of Mr. Eliot's. "It seems to me," he says in discussing the question of truth and belief in poetry, "to have profound emotional meaning, with, at least, no literal fallacy." He does not specify what this meaning is, but I take it that it is something not strictly denotative though emotionally compelling.

The phrase, indeed, has seemed to many to represent a profound intuition into reality and to sum up the essence of Shakespearean, or even of human, tragedy. It speaks quite nearly to us. What it means to each will perhaps depend on his own experience and his own way of relating the texture of experience to the insights of literature. Yet all would agree that "Ripeness is all" gathers into a phrase something of the ultimate value of this life; it reassures us that maturity of experience is a final good, and that there is a fullness of feeling, an inner and emotional completion in life that is attainable and that will resolve our tragedies. Such at least seems to be the interpretation of a recent critic. "After repeated disaster," he says of Gloucester in *King Lear*:

he can assent, "And that's true too," to Edgar's "Ripeness is all." For man may ripen into fulness of being, which means, among other things, that one part of him does not

335

rule all the rest and that one moment's mood does not close off all the perspectives available to him.

In this way we discover in Shakespeare's phrase the secret morality of our own times. It is a meaning I can enter into quite as deeply as anyone, but it is not what Shakespeare meant.

Shakespeare meant something much more traditional. The phrase occurs in *King Lear*. In an earlier scene Edgar had prevented Gloucester from committing suicide, that act which consummates the sin of despair, and Gloucester had accepted the situation in the true spirit of Christian resignation:

> henceforth I'll bear
> Affliction till it do cry out itself
> 'Enough, enough,' and die.

4. 6. 75-7

But now Gloucester seems to relapse for a moment, saying: "No further, sir; a man may rot even here." And Edgar stiffens his resolution with these words:

> Men must endure
> Their going hence even as their coming hither:
> Ripeness is all.

5. 2. 9-11

The context is the desire for death. The conclusion is that as we were passive to the hour of our birth so we must be passive to the hour of our death. So far, surely, the speech is an affirmation of the spirit of resignation, and it would be reasonable to suppose that the summary clause at the end, "Ripeness is all," is but the final restatement of this attitude. It was certainly an available attitude. The experience of Christian resignation was dense with the history of the Western spirit, and that history was alive and present in Shakespeare's time; it spoke daily from the pulpit and in the private consolations of intimate friends. The theme, furthermore, was a favorite with Shakespeare. It had been fully explored in the Duke's great speech in *Measure for Measure*:

> Be absolute for death. Either death or life
> Will thereby be the sweeter. Reason thus with life:
> If I do lose thee I do lose a thing

> That none but fools would keep. A breath thou art,
> Servile to all the skyey influences
> That do this habitation where thou keep'st
> Hourly afflict. Merely thou art death's fool;
> For him thou labour'st by thy flight to shun,
> And yet runn'st toward him still. . .
>   Yet in this life
> Lie hid moe thousand deaths; yet death we fear
> That makes these odds all even.

3. 1. 5-13, 39-41

But the finest expression, other than in the passage from *Lear,* is Hamlet's speech to Horatio as he goes to the catastrophe:

> . . . we defy augury; there's a special providence in the fall of a sparrow. If it be now, 'tis not to come; if it be not to come, it will be now; if it be not now, yet it will come: the readiness is all.   5. 2. 230-3

This is as much as to say that we must endure our going hence, be it when it may, since the hour of our death is in the care of Providence: *the readiness is all.*

It has been said that this is Stoic, and certainly *augury* hints toward Antiquity. But he who speaks of a special providence in the fall of a sparrow could trust an audience in the age of Elizabeth to think of Christian theology and the New Testament:

> And fear not them which kill the body, but are not able to kill the soul: but rather fear him which is able to destroy both body and soul in hell. Are not two sparrows sold for a farthing? *and one of them shall not fall on the ground without your Father.* But the very hairs of your head are all numbered. Fear ye not therefore, ye are of more value than many sparrows.

> Watch therefore: for ye know not what hour your Lord doth come. But know this, that if the goodman of the house had known in what watch the thief would come, he would have watched, and would not have suffered his house to be broken up. *Therefore be ye also ready*: for in such hour as ye think not the Son of man cometh.

It was not only Seneca and his sons who could urge men to meet death with equanimity. Bishop Latimer, the Protestant

martyr, in a sermon preached before King Edward VI speaks
the thought and almost the words of Hamlet:

> *Unusquisque enim certum tempus habet praedefinitum a*
> *Domino:* "For every man hath a certain time appointed him
> of God, and God hideth that same time from us." For some
> die in young age, some in old age, according as it pleaseth
> him. He hath not manifested to us the time because he would
> have us at all times ready; else if I knew the time, I would
> presume upon it, and so should be worse. But he would have
> us ready at all times, and therefore he hideth the time of
> our death from us. . . . But of that we may be sure, there
> shall not fall one hair from our head without his will; and
> we shall not die before the time that God hath appointed
> unto us: which is a comfortable thing, specially in time of
> sickness or wars. . . . There be some which say, when their
> friends are slain in battle, "Oh, if he had tarried at home, he
> should not have lost his life." These sayings are naught: for
> God hath appointed every man his time. To go to war in
> presumptuousness, without an ordinary calling, such going to
> war I allow not: but when thou art called, go in the name
> of the Lord; and be well assured in thy heart that thou canst
> not shorten thy life with well-doing.

The similarity of the phrase in *Hamlet* to the one in *Lear*
is so close that the first may be taken as the model and
prototype of the other. But in *Lear* the phrase has been
transmuted, and with it the idea and attitude. The deliberate
and developed rhetoric of *Measure for Measure* has served
its purpose to explore the area of experience, and has been put
aside. The riddling logicality of Hamlet's speech has been
simplified to the bare utterance of:

> Men must endure
> Their going hence even as their coming hither

and the concept of the arbitrariness of birth has been introduced to reinforce the arbitrariness of death. Finally, Hamlet's precise and traditional statement, "the readiness is all,"
has been transformed into a metaphor.

What does the metaphor mean? There is no need for
conjecture; it had already by the time of *Lear* become trite
with use, and with use in contexts closely related to this. In
Thomas Wilson's *Art of Rhetoric* (1560) we read:

Among fruit we see some apples are soon ripe and fall from

the tree in the midst of summer; other be still green and tarry till winter, and hereupon are commonly called winter fruit: even so it is with man, some die young, some die old, and some die in their middle age.

Shakespeare has Richard in *Richard II* comment on the death of John of Gaunt:

> The ripest fruit first falls, and so doth he:
> His time is spent . . .

> 2. 1. 153-4

That is, as fruit falls in the order of ripeness, so a man dies when his time is spent, at his due moment in the cosmic process. Again, Touchstone's dry summary of life and time in *As You Like It*:

> And so, from hour to hour, we ripe and ripe,
> And then, from hour to hour, we rot and rot . . .

> 2. 7. 26-7

does not mean that we ripen to maturity and then decline, but that we ripen toward death, and then quite simply and with no metaphors rot.

But death is not incidental to Shakespearean tragedy; it is rather the defining characteristic. Just as a Shakespearean comedy is a play that has a clown or two and ends in marriages, so a tragedy involves characters of high estate and concludes with violent deaths. The principle of its being is death, and when this is achieved the play is ended. In this sense, then "Ripeness is all" is the structural principle of Shakespearean tragedy. Thus in *Richard III* the Cassandra-like chorus, the old Queen Margaret, enters alone as the play draws rapidly on to the final catastrophe and says:

> So now prosperity begins to mellow
> And drop into the rotten mouth of death

> 4. 4. 1-2

And in *Macbeth*, Malcolm says toward the close:

> Macbeth
> Is ripe for shaking, and the pow'rs above
> Put on their instruments.

> 4. 3. 237-9

In this passage the powers above, who are the agents of Providence, are associated with the ripened time. Providence is destiny, and in tragedy destiny is death.

By "Ripeness is all," then, Shakespeare means that the fruit will fall in its time, and man dies when God is ready. The phrase gathers into the simplest of sentences, the most final of linguistic patterns, a whole history of attempted formulations, and by the rhetorical device of a traditional metaphor transposes a state into a process. Furthermore, the metaphor shifts our point of view from a man's attitude toward death, from the "readiness" of Hamlet and the "Men must endure" of the first part of Edgar's speech, to the absoluteness of the external process of Providence on which the attitude depends.

But this is not what the phrase means to the uninstructed modern reader, and this poses a problem. The modern meaning is one that is dear to us and one that is rich and important in itself. It would be natural to ask, Need we give it up? I see no reason why we should give up the meaning: maturity of experience is certainly a good, and the phrase in a modern context is well enough fitted to convey this meaning. But it is our phrase now, and not Shakespeare's, and we should accept the responsibility for it. The difference in meaning is unmistakable: ours looks toward life and his toward death; ours finds its locus in modern psychology and his in Christian theology. If we are secure in our own feelings we will accept our own meanings as ours, and if we have any respect for the great we will penetrate and embrace Shakespeare's meaning as his. For our purpose in the study of literature, and particularly in the historical interpretation of texts, is not in the ordinary sense to further the understanding of ourselves. It is rather to enable us to see how we could think and feel otherwise than as we do. It is to erect a larger context of experience within which we may define and understand our own by attending to the disparity between it and the experience of others.

In fact, the problem that is here raised with respect to literature is really the problem of any human relationship: Shall we understand another on his terms or on ours? It is the problem of affection and truth, of appreciation and scholarship. Shakespeare has always been an object of affection and an object of study. Now, it is common experience that affection begins in misunderstanding. We see our own meanings in what we love and we misconstrue for our own purposes. But life will not leave us there, and not only because of external pressures. What concerns us is naturally an object of study. We sit across the room and trace the lineaments of experience on the face of concern, and we find it is not what we thought it was. We come to see that what Shakespeare is saying is not what we thought he was saying, and we come finally to appreciate it for what it is. Where before we had constructed the fact from our feeling, we now construct our feeling from the fact. The end of affection and concern is accuracy and truth, with an alteration but no diminution of feeling.

—Reprinted from *Woe or Wonder* (Denver, 1951), pp. 9-15.

A PLEA FOR THE LIBERTY OF INTERPRETING 343

A PLEA FOR THE LIBERTY OF INTERPRETING

Lascelles Abercrombie

I need not remind this audience of the several revolutions
that have occurred in the history of Shakespearean criticism;
and I suppose it will be admitted that they have not yet
brought us to anything like stability. The Romantics were
fond of asserting the infinite in Shakespeare: certainly there
seems no end to the criticism of him. But perhaps the
endlessness of Shakespearean criticism is like the endlessness
of Einstein's space—you keep on going round and round.
Lately, as every one knows, the tendency has been to discredit that boundless liberty of interpretation which the Romantics claimed. We mistrust nowadays what one of the most
eminent of our scientific critics has called "mere connoisseur-
ship"; we prefer to rely, for our interpretation of Shakespeare, on patient and exact understanding of his conditions—
the conditions under which he worked, and the conditions
under which his work has been preserved to us. Instead of
soaring into the Empyrean, we attend to the theater and the
printing house. Nevertheless, I have sometimes thought I
could detect signs that the process of Shakespearean criticism
is once more on the turn: we may perhaps have come to the
beginning of another revolution, which will land us once
more where the Romantics stood. Not in their posture; I
suggest no return to romantic adoration of the miraculous
poet and the infinite genius: such conceptions belong to the
nature of romanticism, not to the criticism of Shakespeare.
No: it is not to romanticism, but to the ground on which the
romantic attitude to Shakespeare stood, that I look for the
next revolution to take us. And that, I submit, is safe
ground: safer, I belive, than the ground we stand on now.
For, however romanticism may have rolled its eyes and
rhapsodized, it did at any rate stand on this: that Shake-

The British Academy Shakespeare Lecture for 1930, from
Proceedings of the British Academy XVI, published for the
Academy by the Oxford University Press. Reprinted by per-
mission.

speare is to be regarded, first and foremost, as an artist, and his compositions as works of art. . . . I proceed now to what I have to say on this question of liberty in criticism.

Let me begin with what I do not mean by it. An acute and much-to-be-admired critic once discussed the fourth book of the *Aeneid,* to the effect that the humane and enlightened Vergil had, by drawing the character of Dido, marked a stage in the emancipation of women. This was certainly taking a liberty with Vergil, and to prove it an unwarrantable liberty there is no need to appeal to the unknowable, Vergil's *intentions.* We merely have to appeal to what Vergil did—the *result* to which his art worked. And what he did is this: he compels his readers to feel with the utmost poignancy the terrible dilemma in which Aeneas found himself, by making the woman who had entangled him, and sought to divert him from his noble purpose, not a mere wanton adventuress, but a splendid and adorable creature. But our critic was an enthusiast for female enfranchisement; and he could not encounter a splendid and adorable woman anywhere without thinking, "She ought to have the vote!" For all I know Vergil may have thought so too; what is certain is, that to associate Dido with the emancipation of women is to go clean outside anything Vergil's art has to give us.

Again, another critic interprets *Paradise Lost* as a revelation of the spirit of Calvinism. We need not be so scrupulous here about appealing to the poet's intentions. We may be pretty sure that, had anything remotely like Calvinism occurred to Milton while he was composing *Paradise Lost,* he would not have dictated it to his daughters; he would have spat it out, while "hatefullest disrelish writhed his jaws." But Milton (with very doubtful propriety) is called a Puritan; for some reason Puritanism carried, for this critic, a strong suggestion of Calvinism; and so he interprets *Paradise Lost* not by taking what the poem has to give him, but by allowing this private association of his own to intrude and attach itself in accordance with a habit of mind which has nothing whatever to do with the art of Milton. In short, by liberty of interpretation, I do not mean liberty to read into a play of Shakespeare's whatever feeling or idea a modern reader may loosely and accidentally associate with its subject: associate it, that is, not because he found it in the play, but because some idiosyncrasy of his own suggested it and irresponsibly brought it in from his private world. But I do mean that anything which may be found in that art, even if it is only the modern reader who can find it there, may legitimately be taken as its meaning. *Judge by results*, I say; not by the results of reverie, which the poem merely sets going, and in which attention may ramble anywhere it pleases, for that is not criticism at all; but certainly by any result that may come of living in the art of the play and attending to everything it consists of: and I say that, so long as it keeps within that boundary, there is no proper ground for objection, if this attention seems to be modern in its nature. To put it more precisely, instead of "modern" I might say, a species of attention at once more analytic in its scrutiny of detail and more comprehensive in its synthesis of the play into a unity, than the author ever intended his work to undergo. But note! I have used the word *intended* here; and that should warn us we are on dangerous ground. I said advisedly, that to plead for liberty might be to plead for an attention that *seems* to be modern in this sense; for we cannot *know* that Shakespeare was careless of his detail—for instance, in his time-schemes—or introduced matter without troubling about its function in the play as a whole, because he counted on having only to appeal to some not very exacting kind of attention.

But to come to a concrete instance. When, at the end of *Henry IV,* the Prince, on his way to his coronation, so brutally and yet, all things considered, so justly, rejects Falstaff, we have an incident that most readers find startling, and many shocking: an incident, at any rate, which if the play is to be criticized at all, cries out for comment and, if possible, interpretation. Now its interpretation seems not only possible but inevitable, if we look for it in the right place: not in the mechanics of play construction, namely, but in the character of Henry. The incident, in fact, throws back, over the whole of his character as it has so far been (somewhat enigmatically) presented, a sudden and brilliantly transforming illumination. Some such revelation as this Shakespeare had indeed more than once unobtrusively warned his audience to expect; but scarcely to expect anything like so remarkable and complete a transfiguration. For we now understand what the scapegrace Prince has been all through the two parts of *Henry IV*. He is the kind of person who can touch pitch without being defiled; or rather he is the kind of personality that can no more be smircht by circumstance than white-hot iron by dust. Avid of experience, he is so sure of his own integrity, that he can mix with cheerful scoundrels, and like them enjoy the most reprehensible behaviour, knowing that he will finally emerge untarnished. An admirable but not very lovable psychology: and drawn to perfection when this incident of the rejection of Falstaff concludes and retrospectively illuminates the whole series of previous incidents.

Now this, I submit, is what the play actually does give us: this interpretation is nothing extraneous, it is simply a possible way of understanding what is to be found in Shakespeare's art. However, it will, I am sure, be objected to, that it is too *modern*. It will probably be said, that there is here no psychology at all worth speaking of; all the rejection of Falstaff means is, that Shakespeare had somehow or other to get rid of Falstaff as far as Henry's dramatic future was concerned, and he saw the chance of a striking moment of stage effect in doing so. His Elizabethan audience would never see more in it than that, and he never expected more than that to be seen in it.

This way of reasoning is typical of the mood which realistic criticism opposes to what I call liberty of interpretation; and it may be noticed that, though it professes to explain, it gives up the very notion of interpretation. It is to be met with on any aspect of Shakespeare; but it has perhaps made itself especially noticeable in questions of characterization. Probably not many critics would agree that Cleopatra is to be regarded merely as an uncoordinated series of moments of striking stage effect: Cleopatra was an unfortunate instance to choose for pushing this method to extremes, since nowhere does apparent inconsistency of behavior make a more convincing impression of single personality. No conceivable audience of human beings could watch this series of moments without connecting them; and if Shakespeare had intelligence enough to stage the incidents themselves, one after another, he might easily have had intelligence enough to design a connection which no one can help seeing. But Professor Schücking's way of dealing with Cleopatra merely shows to what lengths the methods of realistic criticism can be taken. It is, however, precisely the same kind as the criticism which warns us not to meddle too nicely with the psychological subtleties and problems which a modern mind may discover in Shylock, say, or in Hamlet. And why not? Because— so the warning goes—Shakespeare is to be judged as what he actually was, not for what we can make of him. That is to say—and these are the two great reasons alleged against liberty of interpreting—he is to be judged as a man writing for the stage (and for a particular kind of stage) and as an Elizabethan poet writing for Elizabethan audiences. To interpret him in terms which would not come off on the stage, or could not be understood by an Elizabethan audience, is, strictly speaking, not to interpret Shakespeare's work at all, but our own superfluity of sophistication.

Well, and is he not an Elizabethan? So much so, that, unless he is regarded rather as an Elizabethan dramatist than as a world poet, the development of his art, and therewith the animating spirit of it, cannot possibly be understood. In studying Elizabethan drama, there is one factor of capital importance which must always be borne in mind. What Elizabethan audiences chiefly delighted to see, and what an Elizabethan dramatist had to give them (and, being himself an Elizabethan, delighted to give them) was a spectacle of the *variety* of life. The more variety that could be crowded into a couple of hours—the greater the range of the possibilities of life—the better the play, in Elizabethan taste. That was the main end Elizabethan drama had to serve; that was why a dramatist would not scruple to jam together into one play (as in *The Changeling*) two utterly unconnected stories; that was why Elizabethan drama became the greatest exhibition of human character the world has ever seen, from the heights to the depths of it, from its most tragic splendour to its most imbecile absurdity; that was why, as swiftly as it grew up, Elizabethan drama decayed, "strangled in its waste fertility." This demand was the governing condition under which Shakespeare worked. It was not good for some poets— Marlowe, for instance; but it exactly suited Shakespeare— nay, it was as much the inspiration as the condition of his work. The whole development of his drama is a continually exploring effort to bring larger and richer and finer variety into the unity of dramatic form. The effort is the secret of his failures as well as of his successes; *Measure for Measure* is a characteristic instance of both. Very generally, his dramatic development may be described as proceeding from the method perfected in *A Midsummer Night's Dream*—the method of bringing together into one action a set of sharply contrasted groups of fixed characters—to the method of which *A Winter's Tale* may be taken as typical—where character itself changes under the changes of fortune which it brings upon itself. This is the prevailing direction in his perpetual endeavour to dramatize the endless variety of life; but of course the two methods overlap, for as early as *The Two Gentlemen of Verona* we find him experimenting with the mutual influence of character and fortune, and even in *The Tempest* the persons are displayed in contrasted groups. But whatever form it takes, the development of his art is a direct response to the taste of his time.

Thus, it is hardly possible to exaggerate the importance of Shakespeare's Elizabethanism, since, as I say, it not only conditions but inspires his work. But it seems to me the queerest misconception of that importance, to make it impose limitations on the interpreting of his poetry. Granted that it fired his genius to work under such conditions: still, it was *his* genius: it was Shakespeare who was inspired. Even if we suppose that his Elizabethanism did, in some way or other, circumscribe his meaning to his contemporaries, why should that limitation be maintained now that the Elizabethan mind is dead and gone? Why not let him mean all he can mean? Why impose on Shakespeare limitations which no one would think of imposing, say, on Homer? And after all, what are the grounds for supposing that what Shakespeare meant to the Elizabethans need be limited at all? Who knows that he did not mean to them what he means to us? Indeed, there are two very serious deficiencies in the argument that Shakespeare ought not to be understood except as an Elizabethan audience would have understood him. In the first place, what is meant by an Elizabethan audience? For presumably there would be in it as many kinds and degrees of intelligence as there are in an audience today. In the next place, what was an Elizabethan audience really like? And that, I venture to think, is not in the power of any one to answer, except in terms so broad as to be here quite useless. Until, however, these two questions are completely answered, this argument against the liberty I plead for can hardly be sustained. Its abstract validity seems extremely questionable; and it fails to make itself intelligible in any concrete form.

But Shakespeare wrote for the theater; and we read him in a book—at least, it is a hundred to one that the Shakespeare we criticize is the Shakespeare we read. Here we certainly have something considerable; for every one knows how the impression a play makes on us when we see it acted may differ from the impression it makes when we read it in cold type. Is it to be argued from this that criticism, to be valid, must keep within the impression made by the play in the theater? To some extent that may be argued. Look, for instance, at those time schemes which some critics have made such a work about. It is entirely to the plays as reading matter that their discrepancies and incoherences and uncertainties belong. In the theater, time schemes simply do not exist; the mere sequence and linkage of the events are enough to employ the sort of attention we exercise there. Shakespeare, writing for the theater, did not worry about keeping to an accurate time scheme, knowing very well that his audience would never notice whether he kept to it or not. Criticism which occupies itself with this matter may well be called irrelevant, since the matter is itself irrelevant to the kind of existence the art was designed to take. But do these time schemes, often so vague and difficult, really trouble us when we read Shakespeare? I think not: not, at any rate if we read a play, straightforwardly and without interruption, in order to take it in as a work of art. It is only when we pull it to pieces that the time scheme may appear questionable. In straightforward reading, just as in the theater, the sequence of events is all that matters. There is nothing so odd in Shakespeare as the time scheme of the *Agamemnon*; yet for generations of readers no one noticed it. Indeed, to criticize time at all in a drama, so long as the action is sufficiently given by the mere sequence of the events, is equally irrelevant whether the play is read or acted. For, in spite of the notable differences between reading a play and seeing it acted, the two impressions are but two versions of the same work of art.

Shakespeare not only wrote for the theater, but for a very peculiar kind of theater. In many ways it seems to have been the finest instrument which dramatic art has ever devised for itself; and Shakespeare's technique is so exactly adapted to this instrument, and shows such complete mastery of it, that one is tempted to call it waste of time to produce him on any stage that does not pretty closely correspond with the stage he wrote for. But this fact is equally important in quite another way. The effective existence of a play in the Elizabethan theater depended almost wholly on the acting; and the actors depended very specially on their words, for their art was rather to capture the imagination of the audience than to produce anything that could be called an illusion. The language of the play had in consequence to be of a highly imaginative kind, for the most part: what is called poetic language, whether in verse or not. And that response to such language could be reckoned on, is one of the things we do know for certain about an Elizabethan audience. But it was very soon found that this highly imaginative language could make its effect independently of the actors; in fact, practically throughout the whole course of Elizabethan drama, plays had a dual existence—on the stage, and in print. Those critics who exhort us never to forget that Shakespeare's work belongs to the theater, are apt to forget that Shakespeare's public had no scruples at all about taking his plays as reading matter; and that Shakespeare himself approved of this dual existence for his own plays cannot, I think, nowadays be doubted. Did he calculate on it? It looks as if some of his contemporaries had the reading public at least at the back of their minds when they wrote their plays; and some (Chapman and Jonson, for instance) seem to have kept more prominently in their consciousness than that, the opportunity of appealing beyond the theater. It is commonly assumed, however, that Shakespeare thought of nothing but the stage. Is not this rather a romantic notion? In the first place, we do not know. In the second place, though obviously the stage came easily first with him, is it humanly possible that he could have been entirely oblivious of the public which might read him? To take two very different instances: unless he had the reading public somewhere in his mind, I do not see how we are to account for *Hamlet* and *Troilus and Cressida*.

But my plea for liberty of interpretation does not depend on hypothesis. Ultimately, it simply demands recognition of the nature of a work of art. A work of art is not a book or a picture, not a medium or an instrument, not even the use of a medium or a performance on an instrument, unless it is taken in and understood. This is obvious enough. When we talk of *Macbeth*, say, as a book or a performance on the stage, what we really mean is the book when we read it, the performance when we witness it. A work of art does not exist until it is experienced by an individual mind. It will always be an individual experience; but at the same time it is an experience given to this individual mind by another mind, and wholly governed by the conditions under which it is given. Thus a play, like any other work of art, consists of a series of three terms: the author, his medium or technique, and the recipient. Of these three terms, the first is the only one that can never change; and the fact that this term is always the same gives us the sense in which it is possible to say, that through all its existences it is always the same play. But the third term, the recipient, changes every time the play comes into existence at all; and it is even possible for changes to occur in the middle term, the technique, provided the change conserves what the author committed in it. Thus a symphony may be transcribed as a pianoforte duet: a remarkable change, but one which, in the case of his own symphonies, Brahms himself carried out. And thus too the medium of *Macbeth* may change from the theater to the printed page: perhaps an even more remarkable change, but one which, it appears, Shakespeare himself approved of, and may even to some extent have had in mind. He might very well approve of it, since the printed page merely gave him another way of making essentially the same appeal to imagination. So that, in spite of whatever differences there may be between them, whether we criticize the *Macbeth* we see in the theater, or the *Macbeth* we read, it is still Shakespeare's *Macbeth* we are criticizing: in that sense, it is in either case the same *Macbeth.*

The existence of a work of art, in fact, is not material at all, but spiritual. It is a continually creative existence, for it exists by continually creating experience. In one sense, this means that it is a continually changing existence; for the experiences it creates must always be individual and therefore unique experiences. Yet in another sense it is always the same; for it always exists in unbroken connection with its author, who *forms* the experience he gives. It will now appear why liberty of interpretation must necessarily be granted if Shakespeare's plays are regarded as works of art. Every reader or spectator is at liberty to say what the play means to him. The reason is a simple one: the play, as a work of art, has no other existence. To limit interpretation to what the play may have meant to Elizabethans is, frankly, to exclude the existence of the play as a work of art; for as a work of art it does not exist in what it may have meant to some one else, but in what it means to me: that is the only way it can exist. In any case, it had as many different existences in an Elizabethan theater as there were heads in the audience. But, when I say a play exists in what it means to any one who will receive it, the implication is plain, that everything is excluded from that existence which is not given by the author's technique. The existence of a work of art is completed by the recipient's *attention* to what the author says to him; whatever may come in through *inattention* to that does not belong to the art at all. It is not liberty of interpreting when a critic sees the emancipation of women in Dido, or James I in Hamlet; it is simply failure to attend to the poet, and thus does not come within the series of the three terms which constitutes a work of art—it has no part in that connection between the mind of the poet and the mind of the recipient which is the essence of a poem. But when there is that connection, when the response of individual imagination is wholly governed by the poet's technique, then poetry comes into existence. And liberty of interpreting necessarily comes too; for that is simply another way of saying, that the response, though goverened by the poet, cannot in the nature of things be anything but individual. The rule tolerates no exceptions. The field of Shakespearean studies is a vast one, and almost every kind of talent can find occupation there. But it all exists because Shakespeare was a poet: all comes from that, and back to that everything goes at last. To regard Shakespeare as an artist is our first and last duty. But so to regard him is to admit what would never be denied in the case of any other poet. Whenever it is his art that is being criticized, liberty of interpretation must be allowed, in the sense in which I have tried to define it.

ALSO OF INTEREST

LOVE IN THE WESTERN WORLD*
Denis de Rougemont   Premier M314   95¢

Beginning with the Tristan legend and proceeding to such figures as Don Juan and the Marquis de Sade, de Rougemont explores the persistence of the urge to illicit love alongside the universal acceptance of marriage as a necessary institution.

SHAKESPEAREAN TRAGEDY*
A. C. Bradley   Premier M263   95¢

The classic interpretation of *Hamlet, Othello, King Lear,* and *Macbeth* by the renowned Shakespearean scholar and critic.

SITUATIONS
Jean-Paul Sartre   Premier M303   95¢

Essays on the role of the artist in society, with special attention to Nathalie Sarraute, André Gide, Albert Camus, Paul Nizan, Merleau-Ponty, and the Renaissance painters, Tintoretto and Giacometti. Includes Sartre's account of his celebrated split and subsequent feud with Camus.

THE WORDS
Jean-Paul Sartre   Premier T400   75¢

The philosopher-writer's autobiography of his childhood explores and evaluates the whole use of books and language in human experience.